Prentice Hall Realidades 1

Leveled Vocabulary and Grammar Workbook
Core Practice

PEARSON

Boston, Massachusetts   Chandler, Arizona   Glenview, Illinois   Upper Saddle River, New Jersey

PEARSON

ISBN-13: 978-0-13-322571-6
ISBN-10:   0-13-322571-2

20   18

Prentice Hall **Realidades** 1

Leveled Vocabulary and Grammar Workbook
Guided Practice

PEARSON

Boston, Massachusetts   Chandler, Arizona   Glenview, Illinois   Upper Saddle River, New Jersey

Table of Contents

Dear Parents and Guardians:

Learning a second language can be both exciting and fun. As your child studies Spanish, he or she will not only learn to communicate with Spanish speakers, but will also learn about their cultures and daily lives. Language learning is a building process that requires considerable time and practice, but it is one of the most rewarding things your child can learn in school.

Language learning calls on all of the senses and on many skills that are not necessarily used in other kinds of learning. Students will find their Spanish class different from other classes in a variety of ways. For instance, lectures generally play only a small role in the language classroom. Because the goal is to learn to communicate, students interact with each other and with their teacher as they learn to express themselves about things they like to do (and things they don't), their personalities, the world around them, foods, celebrations, pastimes, technology, and much more. Rather than primarily listening to the teacher, reading the text, and memorizing information as they might in a social studies class, language learners will share ideas; discuss similarities and differences between cultures; ask and answer questions; and work with others to practice new words, sounds, and sentence structures. Your child will be given a variety of tasks to do in preparation for such an interactive class. He or she will complete written activities, perform listening tasks, watch and listen to videos, and go on the Internet. In addition, to help solidify command of words and structures, time will need to be spent on learning vocabulary and practicing the language until it starts to become second nature. Many students will find that using flash cards and doing written practice will help them become confident using the building blocks of language.

To help you help your child in this endeavor, we offer the following insights into the textbook your child will be using, along with suggestions for ways that you can help build your child's motivation and confidence—and as a result, their success with learning Spanish.

Textbook Organization

Your child will be learning Spanish using *REALIDADES*, which means "realities." The emphasis throughout the text is on learning to use the language in authentic, real ways. Chapters are organized by themes such as school life, food and health, family and celebrations, etc. Each chapter begins with a section called **A primera vista** (*At First Glance*): **Vocabulario en contexto**, which gives an initial presentation of new grammar and vocabulary in the form of pictures, short dialogues, audio recordings, and video. Once students have been exposed to the new language, the **Manos a la obra** (*Let's Get to Work*): **Vocabulario en uso** and **Manos a la obra: Gramática y vocabulario en uso** sections offer lots of practice with the language as well as explanations of how the language works. The third section, **¡Adelante!** (*Moving Ahead!*), provides activities for your child to use the language by understanding readings, giving oral or written presentations, and learning more about the cultural perspectives of Spanish speakers. Finally, all chapters conclude with an at-a-glance review of the chapter material called **Repaso del capítulo** (*Chapter Review*), with summary lists and charts, and practice activities like those on the chapter test. If students have trouble with a given task, the **Repaso del capítulo** tells them where in the chapter they can go to review.

Here are some suggestions that will help your child become a successful language learner.

Routine:
Provide a special, quiet place for study, equipped with a Spanish-English dictionary, pens or pencils, paper, computer, and any other items your child's teacher suggests.

- Encourage your child to study Spanish at a regular time every day. A study routine will greatly facilitate the learning process.

Strategy:

- Remind your child that class participation and memorization are very important in a foreign language course.
- Tell your child that in reading or listening activities, as well as in the classroom, it is not necessary to understand every word. Suggest that they listen or look for key words to get the gist of what's being communicated.
- Encourage your child to ask questions in class if he or she is confused. Remind the child that other students may have the same question. This will minimize frustration and help your child succeed.

Real-life connection:

- Outside of the regular study time, encourage your child to review words in their proper context as they relate to the chapter themes. For example, when studying the chapter about community places, Capítulo 3B, have your child bring flash cards for place names on a trip into town and review words for the places you pass along the way. Similarly, while studying Capítulo 4A vocabulary, bring out family photos and remind your child of the toys he or she used to have and the activities that he or she liked. Ask your child to name the toys and activities in Spanish. If your child can include multiple senses while studying (see the school and say *escuela*, or taste ice cream and say *helado*), it will help reinforce study and will aid in vocabulary retention.
- Motivate your child with praise for small jobs well done, not just for big exams and final grades. A memorized vocabulary list is something to be proud of!

Review:

- Encourage your child to review previously learned material frequently, and not just before a test. Remember, learning a language is a building process, and it is important to keep using what you've already learned.
- To aid vocabulary memorization, suggest that your child try several different methods, such as saying words aloud while looking at a picture of the items, writing the words, acting them out while saying them, and so on.
- Suggest that your child organize new material using charts, graphs, pictures with labels, or other visuals that can be posted in the study area. A daily review of those visuals will help keep the material fresh.
- Help your child drill new vocabulary and grammar by using the charts and lists in the **Manos a la obra: Vocabulario en uso, Manos a la obra: Gramática y vocabulario en uso,** and **Repaso del capítulo** sections.

Resources:

- Offer to help frequently! Your child may have great ideas for how you can facilitate his or her learning experience.
- Ask your child's teacher, or encourage your child to ask, about how to best prepare for and what to expect on tests and quizzes.
- Ask your child's teacher about the availability of audio recordings and videos that support the text. The more your child sees and hears the language, the greater the retention. There are also on-line and CD-ROM based versions of the textbook that may be useful for your child.
- Visit www.realidades.com with your child for more helpful tips and practice opportunities, including downloadable audio files that your child can play at home to practice Spanish. Enter the appropriate Web Code from the list on the next page for

the section of the chapter that the class is working on and you will see a menu that lists the available audio files. They can be listened to on a computer or on a personal audio player.

Capítulo	A primera vista—Vocabulario en contexto	Manos a la obra—Vocabulario en uso and —Gramática y vocabulario en uso	Repaso
Para empezar			jcd-0099
Capítulo 1A	jcd-0187	jcd-0188	jcd-0189
Capítulo 1B	jcd-0197	jcd-0198	jcd-0199
Capítulo 2A	jcd-0287	jcd-0288	jcd-0289
Capítulo 2B	jcd-0297	jcd-0298	jcd-0299
Capítulo 3A	jcd-0387	jcd-0388	jcd-0389
Capítulo 3B	jcd-0397	jcd-0398	jcd-0399
Capítulo 4A	jcd-0487	jcd-0488	jcd-0489
Capítulo 4B	jcd-0497	jcd-0498	jcd-0499
Capítulo 5A	jcd-0587	jcd-0588	jcd-0589
Capítulo 5B	jcd-0597	jcd-0598	jcd-0599
Capítulo 6A	jcd-0687	jcd-0688	jcd-0689
Capítulo 6B	jcd-0697	jcd-0698	jcd-0699
Capítulo 7A	jcd-0787	jcd-0788	jcd-0789
Capítulo 7B	jcd-0797	jcd-0798	jcd-0799
Capítulo 8A	jcd-0887	jcd-0888	jcd-0889
Capítulo 8B	jcd-0897	jcd-0898	jcd-0899
Capítulo 9A	jcd-0987	jcd-0988	jcd-0989
Capítulo 9B	jcd-0997	jcd-0998	jcd-0999

Above all, help your child understand that a language is not acquired overnight. Just as for a first language, there is a gradual process for learning a second one. It takes time and patience, and it is important to know that mistakes are a completely natural part of the process. Remind your child that it took years to become proficient in his or her first language, and that the second one will also take time. Praise your child for even small progress in the ability to communicate in Spanish, and provide opportunities for your child to hear and use the language.

Don't hesitate to ask your child's teacher for ideas. You will find the teacher eager to help you. You may also be able to help the teacher understand special needs that your child may have, and work together with him or her to find the best techniques for helping your child learn.

Learning to speak another language is one of the most gratifying experiences a person can have. We know that your child will benefit from the effort, and will acquire a skill that will serve to enrich his or her life.

Notes

Realidades **1**

Para empezar

Nombre _____

Fecha _____

Hora _____

Vocabulary Flash Cards, Sheet 1

Write the Spanish vocabulary word below each picture. If there is a word or phrase, copy it in the space provided. Be sure to include the article for each noun.

Buenos días.	**Buenas noches.**	**Buenas tardes.**
_____ _____	_____ _____	_____ _____
¡Hola!	**¿Cómo te llamas?**	**Me llamo...**
_____	_____ _____	_____ _____
Encantado, Encantada.	**Igualmente.**	**Mucho gusto.**
_____ , _____	_____	_____ _____

Realidades ❶

Para empezar

Nombre _____

Fecha _____

Hora _____

Vocabulary Flash Cards, Sheet 2

¿Cómo
está
Ud.?

_____

_____

_____

¿Cómo
estás?

_____

_____

¿Qué
pasa?

_____

_____

¿Qué
tal?

_____

_____

¿Y tú?

_____

¿Y
usted (Ud.)?

_____

_____

(muy)
bien

_____

_____

regular

_____

gracias

_____

nada

_____

señor,
Sr.

_____,

_____

señora,
Sra.

_____,

_____

señorita,
Srta.

_____,

_____

¡Adiós!

_____

Hasta
luego.

_____

Hasta
mañana.

_____

¡Nos
vemos!

_____

uno

_____

Realidades 1

Para empezar

Nombre _____

Fecha _____

Hora _____

Vocabulary Flash Cards, Sheet 4

dos	tres	cuatro
_____	_____	_____
cinco	seis	siete
_____	_____	_____
ocho	nueve	diez
_____	_____	_____

Realidades ⬤

Nombre _____

Hora _____

Para empezar

Fecha _____

Vocabulary Flash Cards, Sheet 5

¿Qué hora es?

_____

_____

`1:00`

Es _____

_____.

`2:00`

Son _____

_____.

`3:05`

Son _____

_____

_____.

`4:10`

Son _____

_____

_____.

`5:15`

Son _____

_____

_____.

`6:30`

Son _____

_____

_____.

`8:52`

Son _____

_____

_____.

`6:40`

Son _____

_____

_____.

_____

_____

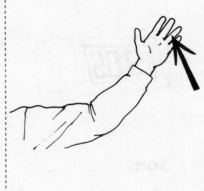

_____

_____

_____

_____

Tear out this page. Write the English words on the lines. Fold the paper along the dotted line to see the correct answers so you can check your work.

En la escuela

Buenos días. _____

Buenas noches. _____

Buenas tardes. _____

¡Hola! _____

¿Cómo te llamas? _____

Me llamo... _____

Encantado, _____
Encantada.

Igualmente. _____

Mucho gusto. _____

señor, Sr. _____

señora, Sra. _____

señorita, Srta. _____

¡Adiós! _____

Hasta luego. _____

Hasta mañana. _____

¡Nos vemos! _____

Fold In →

Realidades ①

Para empezar

Nombre _____

Hora _____

Fecha _____

Vocabulary Check, Sheet 2

Tear out this page. Write the Spanish words on the lines. Fold the paper along the dotted line to see the correct answers so you can check your work.

Good morning. _____

Good evening. _____

Good afternoon. _____

Hello! _____

What is your name? _____

My name is . . . _____

Delighted. _____

_____

Likewise. _____

Pleased to meet you. _____

sir, Mr. _____

madam, Mrs. _____

miss, Miss _____

Good-bye! _____

See you later. _____

See you tomorrow. _____

See you! _____

Fold In →

Realidades ❶

Para empezar

Nombre _____

Fecha _____

Hora _____

Guided Practice Activities P-1

Vowel sounds

• Like English, Spanish has five basic vowels, **a, e, i, o,** and **u**. But unlike English, each Spanish vowel sounds nearly the same in every word, which will help you figure out how to pronounce any Spanish word you see.

A. The letter **a** is pronounced "ah," as in the English word "father." Write three Spanish words related to *body parts* (**el cuerpo**) that contain the letter **a**. Say each word as you write it, paying special attention to the **a**.

_____   _____   _____

B. The letter **e** is pronounced "ay," as in the English word "pay." Write three Spanish *numbers under ten* that contain the letter **e**. Say each word as you write it, paying special attention to the **e**.

_____   _____   _____

C. The letter **i** is pronounced "ee," as in the English word "see." Write two Spanish words used in *greetings* that contain the letter **i**. Say each word as you write it, paying special attention to the **i**.

_____   _____   _____

D. The letter **o** is pronounced "oh," as in the English word "go." Write three Spanish *numbers over ten* that contain the letter **o**. Say each word as you write it, paying special attention to the **o**.

_____   _____   _____

E. The letter **u** is pronounced "oo," as in the English word "zoo." Write three Spanish words that you've learned so far that contain the letter **u**. Say each word as you write it, paying special attention to the **u**.

_____   _____   _____

Realidades 1

Para empezar

Nombre _____

Fecha _____

Hora _____

Guided Practice Activities P-2

The letter *c*

- The letter **c** has two different sounds in Spanish. When it is followed by **a, o, u,** or any consonant other than **h,** it is a "hard **c**" and is pronounced like the **c** in "cat." Say these words with a hard **c**:

  cómo   práctica   encantado

- When the letter **c** is followed by **e** or **i,** it is a "soft **c**" and is pronounced like the **s** in "Sally." Say these words with a soft **c**:

  doce   gracias   silencio

A. Write out the numbers below (which all contain at least one letter **c**) in Spanish on the blanks provided.

1. 4   _____

2. 0   _____

3. 13   _____

4. 100   _____

5. 11   _____

6. 5   _____

7. 16   _____

8. 14   _____

9. 55   _____

10. 48   _____

B. Now, say aloud each of the words you wrote, paying special attention to the letter **c**. Go back to the answers you gave in **part A** and underline each hard **c** (as in **c**at). Circle each soft **c** (as in **S**ally). **Ojo:** Some words contain more than one **c**.

Realidades 1

Para empezar

Nombre _____

Fecha _____

Hora _____

Vocabulary Flash Cards, Sheet 1

Write the Spanish vocabulary word below each picture. If there is a word or phrase, copy it in the space provided. Be sure to include the article for each noun.

_____	_____	_____
_____	_____	_____
_____	_____	_____
_____	_____	_____

Realidades 1

Para empezar

Nombre _____

Hora _____

Fecha _____

Vocabulary Flash Cards, Sheet 2

la sala
de clases

_____ _____

el
año

_____

el
día

_____

el
mes

_____

la
semana

_____

¿Qué día
es hoy?

_____

¿Cuál es
la fecha?

_____

Es el primero de enero.

_____ _____

_____

Es el tres de marzo.

_____ _____

_____

Es el cinco de mayo.

_____ _____

_____

Es el catorce de febrero.

_____ _____

_____

Es el once de septiembre.

_____ _____

_____

Es el veinticinco de diciembre.

_____ _____

_____

mañana

_____

hoy

_____

en

_____

Realidades 1

Para empezar

Nombre _____

Fecha _____

Hora _____

Vocabulary Flash Cards, Sheet 4

¿Cuántos?,
¿Cuántas?

_____,

_____

hay

_____

por
favor

_____

_____

¿Cómo se
dice...?

_____

_____

Se
dice...

_____

_____

¿Cómo se
escribe...?

_____

_____

Se
escribe...

_____

_____

¿Qué
quiere
decir...?

_____

_____

Quiere
decir...

_____

_____

Realidades 1

Para empezar

Nombre _____

Hora _____

Fecha _____

Vocabulary Check, Sheet 1

Tear out this page. Write the English words on the lines. Fold the paper along the dotted line to see the correct answers so you can check your work.

En la clase

el bolígrafo _____

la carpeta _____

el cuaderno _____

el estudiante,
la estudiante _____

la hoja de papel _____

el lápiz _____

el libro _____

el profesor,
la profesora _____

el pupitre _____

la sala de clases _____

el año _____

el día _____

el mes _____

la semana _____

hoy _____

mañana _____

Fold In

Realidades 1

Para empezar

Nombre _____

Hora _____

Fecha _____

Vocabulary Check, Sheet 2

Tear out this page. Write the Spanish words on the lines. Fold the paper along the dotted line to see the correct answers so you can check your work.

pen _____

folder _____

notebook _____

student _____

_____

sheet of paper _____

pencil _____

book _____

teacher _____

_____

(student) desk _____

classroom _____

year _____

day _____

month _____

week _____

today _____

tomorrow _____

Fold In

More *c* sounds

- In **Activity P-2** you learned that the letter **c** has two different sounds in Spanish: "hard **c**" and "soft **c**." The "hard **c**" sound is also created by the letter groups **que** and **qui**. **Que** is always pronounced like the English "kay" and **qui** is always pronounced like the English word "key." Say these words:

    quince   **que**   **quiere**

A. Remember that the hard **c** is sometimes spelled with a **c** and sometimes with a **q**. Underline the words in each group below with a hard **c** ("**c**at") sound. Say each word aloud as you read it.

1. clase / García / doce
2. trece / cien / carpeta
3. equis / cierren / dieciséis
4. gracias / saquen / Cecilia
5. cero / silencio / catorce
6. once / cuaderno / diciembre

B. Circle the words in each group with a soft **c** ("**S**ally") sound. Say each word aloud as you read it.

1. Ricardo / cuarto / atención
2. diciembre / cómo / octubre
3. carpeta / cuaderno / Alicia
4. qué / quiere / decir
5. cien / Cristina / cuántos
6. saquen / cierren / capítulo

Realidades ①

Para empezar

Nombre _____

Hora _____

Fecha _____

Guided Practice Activities P-4

The *h* sound

- In Spanish, some letters have different pronunciations than they do in English. For example, the letter **j** is pronounced like the letter *h* in the English word "hat," but even more strongly and in the back of the throat. The letter **g**, when followed by **e** or **i**, also has the same "h" sound. However, the Spanish letter **h** is always silent! Say these words aloud:

    Jorge   jueves   hay   hasta   hoja

A. Circle all of the words below with a *pronounced* "h" sound. Don't be fooled by the silent letter **h**! Say each word aloud as you read it.

julio	hoy	hasta
~~h~~oja	Jorge	Juan
junio	Guillermo	hora
José	página	hay
juego	¡Hola!	Eugenia

B. Now, go back to the words in **part A** and draw a diagonal line through every silent **h**. The first one has been done for you. Did you notice that **hoja** has both a silent **h** and a **j** that has a *pronounced* "h" sound?

Realidades ❶

Para empezar

Nombre _____

Fecha _____

Hora _____

Vocabulary Flash Cards, Sheet 1

_____

_____

_____

_____

_____

_____

_____

_____

_____

Realidades **1**

Para empezar

Nombre _____

Fecha _____

Hora _____

Vocabulary Flash Cards, Sheet 2

la
estación

_____

_____

¿Qué
tiempo
hace?

_____

_____

_____

_____

_____

_____

_____

_____

_____

_____

_____

_____

_____

Realidades ❶

Para empezar

Nombre _____

Hora _____

Fecha _____

Vocabulary Check, Sheet 1

Tear out this page. Write the English words on the lines. Fold the paper along the dotted line to see the correct answers so you can check your work.

El tiempo

Hace calor. _____

Hace frío. _____

Hace sol. _____

Hace viento. _____

Llueve. _____

Nieva. _____

la estación _____

el invierno _____

el otoño _____

la primavera _____

el verano _____

Fold In

Realidades 1

Para empezar

Nombre _____

Hora _____

Fecha _____

Vocabulary Check, Sheet 2

Tear out this page. Write the Spanish words on the lines. Fold the paper along the dotted line to see the correct answers so you can check your work.

It's hot.   _____

It's cold.   _____

It's sunny.   _____

It's windy.   _____

It's raining.   _____

It's snowing.   _____

season   _____

winter   _____

fall, autumn   _____

spring   _____

summer   _____

To hear a complete list of the vocabulary for this chapter, go to www.realidades.com and type in the Web Code jcd-0099. Then click on **Repaso del capítulo.**

Fold In

Special letters

- When studying the alphabet, you will notice a few letters that you may not have seen before. In addition to the letters we have in English, Spanish also has **ll**, **ñ**, and **rr**.

  a) **ll** is pronounced like a "y" in English, as in the word "**y**ellow."

  b) **ñ** is pronounced like the combination "ny," as in the English word "ca**ny**on."

  c) **rr** is a "rolled" sound in Spanish. It is made by letting your tongue vibrate against the roof of your mouth, and sounds a bit like a cat purring or a child imitating the sound of a helicopter.

Look at the pictures below and fill in the blanks in the words or phrases with either the letter **ll**, **ñ**, or **rr**. Be sure to say each word aloud as you write it, practicing the sounds of the new letters.

1. Es la se_____ora Guité_____ez.

4. _____ueve en la primavera.

2. Me _____amo Gui_____ermo.

5. Hace viento en el oto_____o.

3. Es el libro de espa_____ol.

Realidades ①

Para empezar

Nombre _____

Hora _____

Fecha _____

Guided Practice Activities P-6

The letters *b* and *v*

• In Spanish, the letters **b** and **v** are both pronounced with a "b" sound, like in the English word "**b**oy." This makes pronunciation simple, but can make spelling more challenging! Say the following words:

Buenos días. **¡Nos vemos!** **brazo** **veinte** **bolígrafo** **verano**

The phrases below all contain either **b** or **v**. Pronounce both with a "b" sound, and write the correct letter in the blanks in each conversation.

1. —Hola, profesor.

—_____uenos días, estudiantes.

2. —¿Qué tiempo hace en el otoño?

—Hace _____iento.

3. En fe_____rero hace mucho frío.

—Sí, hace frío en el in_____ierno.

4. —¿Qué tiempo hace en la prima_____era?

—Llue_____e pero hace calor.

5. —¿Qué día es hoy?

—Hoy es el _____einte de no_____iembre.

6. —Le_____ántense, por fa_____or.

—Sí, profesora.

7. —¿Cómo estás?

—_____ien, pero me duele el _____razo.

Write the Spanish vocabulary word below each picture. If there is a word or phrase, copy it in the space provided. Be sure to include the article for each noun.

_____ _____

_____ _____

_____ _____ _____

_____ _____ _____

_____ _____ _____

_____ _____ _____

Realidades 1

Capítulo 1A

Nombre _____

Hora _____

Fecha _____

Vocabulary Flash Cards, Sheet 3

_____

_____   _____

_____

_____

sí

_____

_____

también

y

_____

pues...

ni... ni

o

_____

_____
_____

_____
_____

_____
_____

_____
_____

_____
_____

_____
_____

_____
_____

_____
_____

_____
_____

Tear out this page. Write the English words on the lines. Fold the paper along the dotted line to see the correct answers so you can check your work.

bailar _____

cantar _____

correr _____

dibujar _____

escribir cuentos _____

escuchar música _____

esquiar _____

hablar por
teléfono _____
_____

ir a la escuela _____

jugar
videojuegos _____
_____

leer revistas _____

montar en
bicicleta _____
_____

montar en
monopatín _____

Fold In

Tear out this page. Write the Spanish words on the lines. Fold the paper along the dotted line to see the correct answers so you can check your work.

to dance   _____

to sing   _____

to run   _____

to draw   _____

to write stories   _____

to listen to music   _____

to ski   _____

to talk on
the phone   _____

    _____

to go to school   _____

to play
video games   _____

    _____

to read magazines   _____

to ride a
bicycle   _____

    _____

to skateboard   _____

    _____

Fold In

Tear out this page. Write the English words on the lines. Fold the paper along the dotted line to see the correct answers so you can check your work.

nadar   _____

pasar tiempo   _____
con amigos   _____

patinar   _____

practicar deportes   _____

tocar la guitarra   _____

trabajar   _____

usar la   _____
computadora   _____

ver la tele   _____

_____

Fold In

Tear out this page. Write the Spanish words on the lines. Fold the paper along the dotted line to see the correct answers so you can check your work.

to swim _____

to spend time
with friends _____

_____

to skate _____

to play sports _____

_____

to play the guitar _____

to work _____

to use the
computer _____

_____

to watch
television _____

Fold In

To hear a complete list of the vocabulary for this chapter,
go to www.realidades.com and type in the Web Code jcd-0189.
Then click on **Repaso del capítulo.**

Realidades ①

Capítulo 1A

Nombre _____

Hora _____

Fecha _____

Guided Practice Activities 1A-1

Infinitives (p. 32)

- The most basic form of a verb is an *infinitive*.
- In English, infinitives have the word "to" in front of them such as *to walk* or *to swim*.
- In Spanish, infinitives end in **-ar (nadar)**, **-er (leer)**, or **-ir (escribir)**.

A. Look at each infinitive below and underline its ending. Follow the model.

Modelo   patin<u>ar</u>

1. escribir	**4.** esquiar	**7.** leer
2. nadar	**5.** usar	**8.** jugar
3. correr	**6.** dibujar	**9.** ver

B. Now, write the infinitive in the correct column of the chart. Is it an **-ar** verb, **-er** verb, or **-ir** verb? The first one has been done for you.

-ar verbs	*-er* verbs	*-ir* verbs

C. Complete the sentences with infinitives from **part A** to express what you like and don't like to do.

1. Me gusta _____ y _____.

2. No me gusta _____.

3. Me gusta mucho _____.

Negatives (p. 36)

- To make an English sentence negative, you usually use the word "not": *I do **not** like to sing.*
- To make a Spanish sentence negative, you usually put **no** in front of the verb or expression: *No me gusta cantar.*
- To answer a Spanish question negatively, you often use **no** twice: **¿Te gusta bailar?** *No, no me gusta.*
- To say that you do not like something at all, you add the word **nada**: **No, no me gusta *nada*.**
- To say you don't like either of two choices, use **ni... ni**: **No me gusta *ni* correr *ni* practicar deportes.**

A. Look at the sentences and circle only the *negative* words you see. Some sentences do not have negative words. Follow the model. (*Hint:* There should be eight words circled.)

Modelo   No me gusta cantar.

1. ¿Te gusta bailar?
2. No, no me gusta bailar.
3. ¿Te gusta patinar?
4. No, no me gusta nada.
5. No me gusta ni bailar ni patinar.

B. You circled three different negative words in **part A** above. What are they? Write them on the lines.

_____   _____   _____

C. Use the negative words **no, ni,** and **nada** to complete the following conversation.

ELENA: Enrique, ¿te gusta escuchar música?

ENRIQUE: No, _____ me gusta.

ELENA: ¿Te gusta bailar?

ENRIQUE: _____, no me gusta bailar.

ELENA: No te gusta _____ escuchar música _____ bailar. ¿Qué te gusta hacer?

ENRIQUE: ¡Me gusta ver la tele!

ELENA: ¡Uy, no me gusta _____!

realidades.com

• Web Code: jcd-0104

Negatives *(continued)*

D. Complete the sentences with activities you don't like. You can use the drawings for ideas of activities.

1. No me gusta _____.

2. No me gusta _____.

3. No me gusta ni _____ ni _____.

E. Now answer the questions negatively. Follow the models.

| Modelos | ¿Te gusta esquiar?
No, no me gusta esquiar.

¿Te gusta correr y nadar?
No, no me gusta ni correr ni nadar. |
|---|---|

1. ¿Te gusta dibujar?

_____

2. ¿Te gusta cantar?

_____

3. ¿Te gusta escribir cuentos?

_____

4. ¿Te gusta esquiar y nadar?

_____

5. ¿Te gusta patinar y correr?

Expressing agreement or disagreement (p. 38)

- To agree with what another person <u>likes</u>, use **a mí también**:
    - —Me gusta patinar.
    - —**A mí también.**
- To agree with what another person <u>dislikes</u>, use **a mí tampoco**:
    - —No me gusta cantar.
    - —**A mí tampoco.**

A. The word web shows positive (agreement) words and negative (disagreement) words that you have learned. Look at the sample conversation, paying attention to the words **también** and **tampoco**. One of these two words is positive and one is negative. Write each word in the correct circle of the word web.

JUAN: A mí me gusta correr.

ANA: A mí **también**.

JUAN: No me gusta cantar.

ANA: A mí **tampoco**.

B. Now, complete the following exchanges with either **también** or **tampoco**.

1. JORGE: A mí me gusta mucho dibujar.

   SUSANA: A mí _____.

2. LUIS: No me gusta nada hablar por teléfono.

   MARCOS: A mí _____.

3. OLIVIA: A mí no me gusta ni bailar ni correr.

   ALBERTO: A mí _____.

4. NATALIA: Me gusta esquiar. ¿Y a ti?

   JAVIER: A mí _____.

5. SARA: A mí no me gusta trabajar.

   PABLO: A mí _____.

6. LORENA: Me gusta mucho montar en bicicleta. ¿Y a ti?

   MARTA: A mí _____.

C. Look back at the exchanges in **part B** above. Put a plus (+) next to the exchange if it is positive. Put a minus (–) next to it if it is negative.

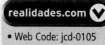

- Web Code: jcd-0105

Realidades ①

Capítulo 1A

Nombre _____

Fecha _____

Hora _____

Guided Practice Activities 1A-5

Lectura: ¿Qué te gusta hacer? (pp. 40–41)

A. The reading in your textbook contains four self-descriptions by students from various parts of the Spanish-speaking world. Read the following selection about Marisol. Then answer the questions that follow.

> *"¿Te gusta practicar deportes y escuchar música? ¡A mí me gusta mucho! También me gusta jugar al básquetbol. ¡Hasta luego!"*

1. Go back to the reading above and circle the sentence where Marisol is asking you a question.

2. Underline the words that tell you that Marisol is talking about things that she likes.

3. Now list the activities that Marisol likes to do in the spaces below:

_____   _____   _____

B. Read the following selection written by Pablo and answer the questions that follow.

> *"Me gusta mucho jugar al vóleibol y al tenis. Me gusta escribir cuentos y también me gusta organizar fiestas con amigos. No me gusta ni jugar videojuegos ni ver la tele. ¡Hasta pronto!"*

1. Underline the words that tell you that Pablo is talking about things that he likes.

2. Circle the things Pablo does not like.

3. Pablo is from «Guinea Ecuatorial». How would you write that in English?

_____

C. Some quotes from the reading are listed below. Identify the speaker of each by writing in their name and country of origin. Follow the model.

Modelo   "Me gusta jugar al básquetbol." _Marisol_   _Puerto Rico_

1. "Me gusta mucho ver la tele."   _____   _____

2. "Me gusta escribir cuentos."   _____   _____

3. "Me gusta hablar por teléfono con amigos."   _____   _____

4. "Me gusta organizar fiestas con amigos."   _____   _____

5. "Me gusta tocar el piano."   _____   _____

Presentación oral (p. 43)

Task: Pretend that you are a new student at school. You have been asked to tell the class a little bit about your likes and dislikes.

A. Fill in each empty space in the diagram with at least two activities that represent you.

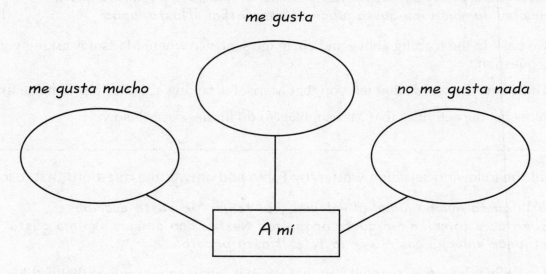

me gusta

me gusta mucho

no me gusta nada

A mí

B. As part of your presentation, you will need to introduce yourself to everyone before you begin talking about your likes and dislikes. Think about how you would introduce yourself in Spanish to someone you don't know. Write one possibility below.

_____

C. Now, add to your greeting by talking about what you like and dislike. Using your information from the diagram in **part A**, write three sentences describing what you like, what you like a lot, and what you do not like.

1. Me gusta _____.

2. Me gusta mucho _____.

3. No me gusta _____.

D. Your teacher will always evaluate your presentations using a rubric, which is like a checklist of elements needed to perform your task. The fewer items completed, the lower the score. Some of the items for this presentation include:

- how much information you communicate
- how easy it is to understand you
- how clearly and neatly your visuals match what you are saying

Realidades ❶

Capítulo 1B

Nombre _____

Fecha _____

Hora _____

Vocabulary Flash Cards, Sheet 1

Write the Spanish vocabulary word below each picture. If there is a word or phrase, copy it in the space provided. Be sure to include the article for each noun.

Realidades **1**

Nombre _____

Hora _____

Capítulo 1B

Fecha _____

Vocabulary Flash Cards, Sheet 2

_____

_____

_____

_____

_____

**bueno,
buena**

_____,

_____

**atrevido,
atrevida**

_____,

_____

paciente

_____

**reservado,
reservada**

_____,

_____

simpático, simpática	talentoso, talentosa	yo
_____, _____	_____, _____	_____
él	ella	la familia
_____	_____	_____ _____
el amigo	la amiga	a veces
_____ _____	_____ _____	_____ _____

muy	**pero**	**según**
_____	_____	_____
según mi familia		
_____		
_____	_____	_____
_____	_____	_____
_____	_____	_____
_____	_____	_____

Realidades 1

Capítulo 1B

Nombre _____

Fecha _____

Hora _____

Vocabulary Check, Sheet 1

Tear out this page. Write the English words on the lines. Fold the paper along the dotted line to see the correct answers so you can check your work.

artístico,
artística   _____

atrevido,
atrevida   _____

bueno, buena   _____

deportista   _____

desordenado,
desordenada   _____

estudioso,
estudiosa   _____

gracioso,
graciosa   _____

impaciente   _____

inteligente   _____

ordenado,
ordenada   _____

paciente   _____

perezoso,
perezosa   _____

Fold In

Realidades ❶

Capítulo 1B

Nombre _____

Fecha _____

Hora _____

Vocabulary Check, Sheet 2

Tear out this page. Write the Spanish words on the lines. Fold the paper along the dotted line to see the correct answers so you can check your work.

artistic _____

_____

daring _____

_____

good _____

sports-minded _____

messy _____

_____

studious _____

_____

funny _____

_____

impatient _____

intelligent _____

neat _____

_____

patient _____

lazy _____

_____

Fold In
↓

Realidades 1

Capítulo 1B

Nombre _____

Hora _____

Fecha _____

Vocabulary Check, Sheet 3

Tear out this page. Write the English words on the lines. Fold the paper along the dotted line to see the correct answers so you can check your work.

reservado, reservada   _____

serio, seria   _____

simpático, simpática   _____

sociable   _____

talentoso, talentosa   _____

trabajador, trabajadora   _____

el chico   _____

la chica   _____

el amigo   _____

la amiga   _____

yo   _____

él   _____

ella   _____

muy   _____

según mi familia   _____

_____

Fold In

Tear out this page. Write the Spanish words on the lines. Fold the paper along the dotted line to see the correct answers so you can check your work.

reserved, shy   _____

_____

serious   _____

nice, friendly   _____

_____

sociable   _____

talented   _____

_____

hardworking   _____

_____

boy   _____

girl   _____

friend (male)   _____

friend (female)   _____

I   _____

he   _____

she   _____

very   _____

according to
my family   _____

To hear a complete list of the vocabulary for this chapter,
go to www.realidades.com and type in the Web Code jcd-0199.
Then click on **Repaso del capítulo**.

Fold In

Adjectives (p. 55)

- Words that describe people and things are called adjectives.
- Most Spanish adjectives have two forms: masculine (ends in -**o** like **simpático**) and feminine (ends in -**a** like **estudiosa**).
- Masculine adjectives are used with masculine nouns: <u>Tomás</u> **es simpátic<u>o</u>**.
- Feminine adjectives are used with feminine nouns: <u>Luisa</u> **es estudios<u>a</u>**.
- Adjectives that end in -**e** and -**ista** may be used with either masculine or feminine nouns:

    <u>Tomás</u> **es inteligent<u>e</u>**. <u>Luisa</u> **es inteligent<u>e</u> también.**

    <u>Marcos</u> **es muy deport<u>ista</u>**. <u>Ana</u> **es muy deport<u>ista</u> también.**

- Adjectives with the masculine form -**dor** have -**dora** as the feminine form:

    <u>Juan</u> **es trabaja<u>dor</u>**. <u>Susana</u> **es trabaja<u>dora</u> también.**

A. Look at the adjectives below. Circle the ending of the adjective: -**o**, -**a**, -**or**, -**ora**, -**e**, or -**ista**.

1. trabajador	**4.** ordenada	**7.** trabajadora
2. deportista	**5.** inteligente	**8.** sociable
3. paciente	**6.** simpática	**9.** estudioso

B. Now, organize the adjectives from **part A** by writing them in the chart under the correct column heading. One has been done for you.

Masculine endings		Feminine endings		Masculine or feminine	
-o	-or	-a	-ora	-e	-ista
	trabajador				

C. Now look at the following sentences. Write **M** next to the sentences where the adjective is masculine. Write **F** next to the sentences where the adjective is feminine. Write **E** next to the sentences where the adjective could be *either* masculine or feminine.

_____ **1.** Yo soy muy simpática.   _____ **6.** Tú eres muy trabajador.

_____ **2.** Tú eres muy estudioso.   _____ **7.** Yo soy muy paciente.

_____ **3.** Tú eres muy ordenado.   _____ **8.** Yo soy muy deportista.

_____ **4.** Yo soy muy trabajadora.   _____ **9.** Tú eres muy reservada.

_____ **5.** Yo soy muy inteligente.   _____ **10.** Tú eres muy impaciente.

Adjectives (continued)

D. Choose the correct adjective to complete each sentence and write it in the blank.

1.

Raúl es (**estudioso** / **estudiosa**) _____.

2.

Rebeca es (**artístico** / **artística**) _____.

3.

Pedro es muy (**ordenado** / **ordenada**) _____.

4.

Paulina es muy (**atrevido** / **atrevida**) _____.

5.

Javier es (**trabajador** / **trabajadora**) _____.

6.

Elena es (**perezoso** / **perezosa**) _____.

E. Now, choose the correct adjective in each sentence to describe yourself. Write the adjective in the blank.

1. Yo soy (**paciente** / **impaciente**) _____.

2. Soy (**simpático** / **simpática**) _____.

3. También soy (**trabajador** / **trabajadora**) _____.

4. No soy (**serio** / **seria**) _____.

• Web Code: jcd-0114

Definite and indefinite articles (p. 60)

- **El** and **la** are the Spanish *definite articles*. They mean the same as "the" in English.
- You use **el** with masculine nouns: **el libro**. You use **la** with feminine nouns: **la carpeta**.
- **Un** and **una** are the Spanish *indefinite articles*. They mean the same as "a" and "an" in English.
- You use **un** with masculine nouns: **un libro**. You use **una** with feminine nouns: **una carpeta**.

A. Look at the ending of each noun in this group. Decide if the noun is masculine or feminine. Write **M** next to the masculine words and **F** next to the feminine words. Follow the model.

Modelo ___F___ computadora

1. _____ año   3. _____ libro   5. _____ carpeta
2. _____ semana   4. _____ hoja   6. _____ profesor

B. Now, look at the words from **part A** again and circle the definite article **el** for the masculine words and the definite article **la** for the feminine words.

1. (**el** / **la**) año   3. (**el** / **la**) libro   5. (**el** / **la**) carpeta
2. (**el** / **la**) semana   4. (**el** / **la**) hoja   6. (**el** / **la**) profesor

C. Look at the ending of each noun below. Decide if the word is masculine or feminine. Write **M** next to the masculine words and **F** next to the feminine words.

1. _____ cuaderno   3. _____ revista   5. _____ bicicleta
2. _____ amigo   4. _____ familia   6. _____ cuento

D. Now, look at the words from **part C** again and circle the indefinite article **un** for the masculine words and the indefinite article **una** for the feminine words.

1. (**un** / **una**) cuaderno   3. (**un** / **una**) revista   5. (**un** / **una**) bicicleta
2. (**un** / **una**) amigo   4. (**un** / **una**) familia   6. (**un** / **una**) cuento

E. Circle the correct definite or indefinite article to complete each sentence.

1. (**El** / **La**) estudiante es estudiosa.   5. (**El** / **La**) profesor es trabajador.
2. (**El** / **La**) profesora es buena.   6. (**Un** / **Una**) estudiante es artístico.
3. (**Un** / **Una**) amigo es simpático.   7. (**El** / **La**) amiga es inteligente.
4. (**Un** / **Una**) estudiante es atrevida.   8. (**Un** / **Una**) estudiante es reservada.

Realidades ①

Capítulo 1B

Nombre _____

Fecha _____

Hora _____

Guided Practice Activities 1B-4

Word order: Placement of adjectives (p. 62)

- English adjectives usually come *before* the noun they describe.
- Spanish adjectives usually come *after* the noun they describe:

  Olga es una <u>chica talentosa</u>.

- Many Spanish sentences follow this pattern:

  <u>subject noun</u> + <u>verb</u> + <u>indefinite article and noun</u> + <u>adjective</u>
      1   2   3   4

  <u>Roberto</u> <u>es</u> <u>un estudiante</u> <u>bueno</u>.   **<u>Serena</u> <u>es</u> <u>una chica</u> <u>inteligente</u>.**
    1   2   3   4   1   2   3   4

A. Look at the following groups of words. Write a number from **1** to **4** below each word according to what kind of word it is. Follow the model and use the examples above.

- Write **1** for subject nouns.
- Write **2** for verbs.
- Write **3** for indefinite articles and nouns.
- Write **4** for adjectives.

Modelo   es / Diego / talentoso / un estudiante
           2   1   4   3

1. seria / Olga / una estudiante / es

2. un amigo / es / bueno / Guillermo

3. Javier / un estudiante / es / trabajador

4. es / Concha / simpática / una chica

5. es / una estudiante / Ana / inteligente

6. Manuel / es / atrevido / un chico

B. Now, write the complete sentence for each example from **part A** by putting the words in order by the numbers you added, going from 1 to 4. Follow the model.

Modelo   *Diego es un estudiante talentoso.*

1. _____

2. _____

3. _____

4. _____

5. _____

6. _____

realidades.com
- Web Code: jcd-0115

Lectura: Un *self-quiz* (p. 64–65)

A. You have seen many cognates used in your textbook. Cognates are related words in different languages; for example, the word **profesor** in Spanish is a *professor* or *teacher* in English. Cognates occur in your vocabulary lists and in readings. Look at the cognates below and write the English word for each on the line provided. Follow the model.

> **Modelo**   bicicleta   <u>*bicycle*</u>

1. computadora _____
2. básquetbol _____
3. la tele _____
4. los colores _____

5. verbo _____
6. usar _____
7. organizar _____
8. estudiar _____

B. Now, read the following section from your textbook. You will find even more cognates in this reading. Find the Spanish word that corresponds to each English word below. Write the Spanish word on the lines provided.

> *¡Los colores revelan tu personalidad!*
> *¿Eres una chica? ¿Te gusta el verde? Eres una chica natural.*
> *¿Eres una chica? ¿Te gusta el azul? Eres muy talentosa.*
> *¿Eres una chica? ¿Te gusta el violeta? Eres muy independiente.*

- personality _____
- natural _____
- talented _____
- independent _____
- violet _____

C. The reading in your textbook is a self-quiz that tells you information about your personality based on the colors you like and whether you are a boy or a girl. Based on the information given below and what you learned from the reading, circle if you are a boy or a girl. Then, write what color you like. Follow the model.

> **Modelo**   Eres romántico. Eres (**un chico** / **una chica**). Te gusta ____<u>*el violeta*</u>____ .

1. Eres atrevido. Eres (**un chico** / **una chica**). Te gusta _____ .
2. Eres muy talentosa. Eres (**un chico** / **una chica**). Te gusta _____ .
3. Eres artística. Eres (**un chico** / **una chica**). Te gusta _____ .

Presentación escrita (p. 67)

Task: Write an e-mail in which you introduce yourself to a prospective pen pal.

❶ **Prewrite.** In order to introduce yourself to a new friend, you need to first organize what you are going to include. Fill in the form below with your personal information.

Me llamo _____.

Soy (*use adjectives to describe yourself*) _____

_____ .

Me gusta _____ .

No me gusta _____ .

❷ **Draft.** Read the following e-mail that another student has written. You should use this to guide you in drafting your own e-mail.

> ¡Hola! Me llamo Pilar. Soy una chica artística y muy independiente. Me gusta mucho dibujar y usar la computadora, pero me gusta más bailar. Me gusta la música salsa. No me gusta nada practicar deportes. ¿Cómo eres tú? Escríbeme pronto.

Now, create an e-mail similar to the one above writing in your information from **part 1**.

¡Hola! Me llamo _____. Soy (**un chico** / **una chica**) _____

_____ y _____. Me gusta mucho _____

_____, pero me gusta más _____ .

Me gusta _____. No me gusta _____.

¿Cómo eres tú? Escríbeme pronto.

❸ **Revise.** Exchange papers with another student in your class. Use the following checklist to review your partner's e-mail and also when you rewrite yours. If you need help figuring out what is correct, use the model from the **Prewrite** section above.

_____ Is there enough information provided for each question in the prewrite stage?
- stated his/her name
- described himself/herself
- said what he/she likes to do
- said what he/she doesn't like to do

_____ Is the spelling correct? (Use a dictionary if you are not sure.)

_____ Are the adjectives in the correct form? (Think, is the student male or female?)

_____ Is there an opening and a closing?

❹ **Publish.** Write your revised e-mail on a separate sheet of paper. Your teacher may ask you to type the e-mail and send it to a prospective pen pal.

Realidades ①

Capítulo 2A

Nombre _____

Hora _____

Fecha _____

Vocabulary Flash Cards, Sheet 1

Write the Spanish vocabulary word below each picture. If there is a word or phrase, copy it in the space provided. Be sure to include the article for each noun.

Horario	
Hora	Clase
Primera hora	inglés
Segunda hora	matemáticas
Tercera hora	arte
Cuarta hora	ciencias sociales
Quinta hora	el almuerzo
Sexta hora	tecnología
Séptima hora	español
Octava hora	educación física
Novena hora	ciencas naturales

_____

_____

_____

_____

_____

_____

_____

_____

_____

Nombre _____

Hora _____

Fecha _____

Vocabulary Flash Cards, Sheet 2

_____

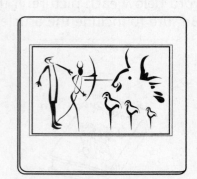

_____

_____

_____

_____

_____

la clase

_____

hablar

_____

necesito

_____

en la ... hora	**primero, primera**	**segundo, segunda**
_____ _____ _____	_____, _____	_____, _____
tercero, tercera	**cuarto, cuarta**	**quinto, quinta**
_____, _____	_____, _____	_____, _____
sexto, sexta	**séptimo, séptima**	**octavo, octava**
_____, _____	_____, _____	_____, _____

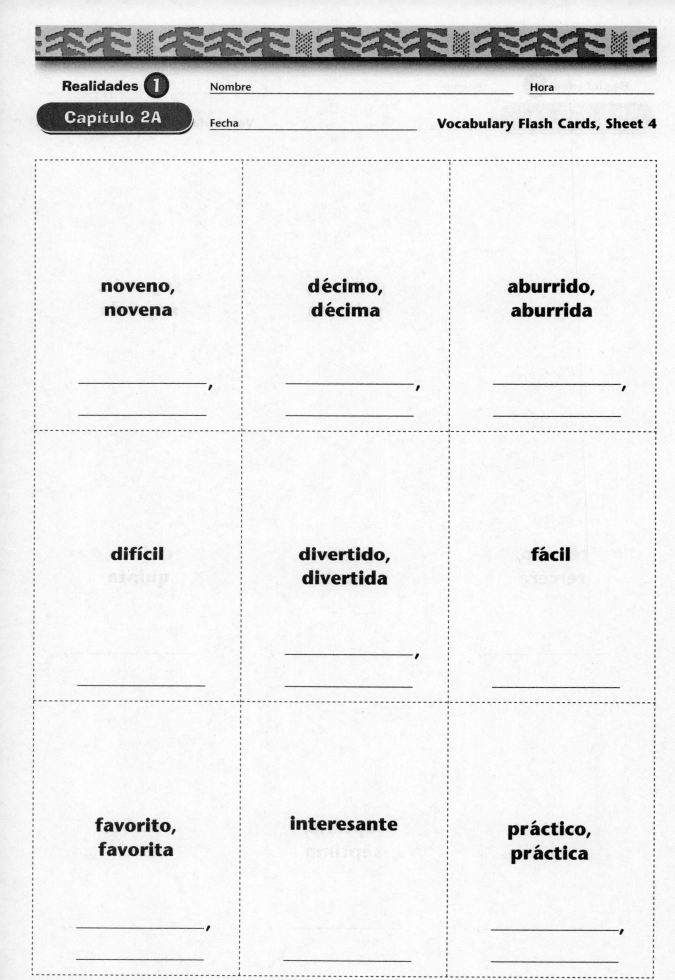

**noveno,
novena**

_____,

_____

**décimo,
décima**

_____,

_____

**aburrido,
aburrida**

_____,

_____

difícil

_____

**divertido,
divertida**

_____,

_____

fácil

_____

**favorito,
favorita**

_____,

_____

interesante

_____

**práctico,
práctica**

_____,

_____

Realidades 1

Capítulo 2A

Nombre

Fecha

Hora

Vocabulary Flash Cards, Sheet 5

más... que	**a ver...**	**¿Quién?**
para	**mucho**	**la tarea**
la clase de...	**necesitas**	**(yo) tengo**

**(tú)
tienes**

_____

_____

_____

_____

_____

_____

_____

_____

_____

_____

_____

_____

_____

_____

_____

_____

_____

_____

Tear out this page. Write the English words on the lines. Fold the paper along the dotted line to see the correct answers so you can check your work.

el almuerzo   _____

la clase   _____

arte   _____

español   _____

ciencias naturales   _____

ciencias sociales   _____

educación física   _____

inglés   _____

matemáticas   _____

tecnología   _____

el horario   _____

la tarea   _____

enseñar   _____

estudiar   _____

hablar   _____

primero, primera   _____

segundo, segunda   _____

Fold In

Realidades ❶

Capítulo 2A

Nombre _____

Fecha _____

Hora _____

Vocabulary Check, Sheet 2

Tear out this page. Write the Spanish words on the lines. Fold the paper along the dotted line to see the correct answers so you can check your work.

lunch _____

class _____

art _____

Spanish _____

science _____

social studies _____

physical education _____

English _____

mathematics _____

technology/ _____
computers

schedule _____

homework _____

to teach _____

to study _____

to talk _____

first _____

second _____

Fold In

Realidades ❶

Capítulo 2A

Nombre _____

Fecha _____

Hora _____

Vocabulary Check, Sheet 3

Tear out this page. Write the English words on the lines. Fold the paper along the dotted line to see the correct answers so you can check your work.

tercero, tercera   _____

cuarto, cuarta   _____

quinto, quinta   _____

sexto, sexta   _____

séptimo, séptima   _____

octavo, octava   _____

noveno, novena   _____

décimo, décima   _____

la calculadora   _____

la carpeta de   _____
argollas   _____

el diccionario   _____

aburrido, aburrida   _____

difícil   _____

fácil   _____

Fold In

Tear out this page. Write the Spanish words on the lines. Fold the paper along the dotted line to see the correct answers so you can check your work.

third _____

fourth _____

fifth _____

sixth _____

seventh _____

eighth _____

ninth _____

tenth _____

calculator _____

three-ring
binder _____
  _____

dictionary _____

boring _____

difficult _____

easy _____

Fold In

To hear a complete list of the vocabulary for this chapter,
go to www.realidades.com and type in the Web Code jcd-0289.
Then click on **Repaso del capítulo.**

Subject pronouns (p. 82)

- The subject of the sentence tells who is doing the action. It is often a name:
  <u>Ana</u> canta.
- Subject pronouns replace people's names to say who is doing an action:
  <u>Ella</u> canta. <u>Tú</u> bailas.
- Here are the Spanish subject pronouns:

Singular	Plural
yo (I)	**nosotros** (we, *masculine or mixed*)
tú (you, *familiar*)	**nosotras** (we, *feminine*)
usted (you, *formal*)	**vosotros** (you, *familiar plural, masculine or mixed*)
él (he)	**vosotras** (you, *familiar plural, feminine*)
ella (she)	**ustedes** (you, *formal plural*)
	ellos (they, *masculine or mixed*)
	ellas (they, *feminine*)

- **Vosotros** and **vosotras** are primarily used in Spain.
- **Usted** and **ustedes** are formal forms that are used with people you address with a title, such as **señor** and **doctor**.
- In Latin America, **ustedes** is also used when addressing two or more people you call **tú** individually.

A. Write the twelve subject pronouns listed above in the correct category of the chart. Follow the model.

Singular			Plural		
Masculine only	**Feminine only**	**Masculine or feminine**	**Masculine or mixed**	**Feminine only**	**Masculine or feminine**
él					

B. Look at the English subject pronouns below. Use the list above to help you circle the Spanish subject pronoun that corresponds to the English pronoun.

1. *I* (**él** / **yo**)
2. *we* (**nosotros** / **vosotros**)
3. *you* (**ella** / **usted**)
4. *they* (**ellos** / **ustedes**)
5. *he* (**tú** / **él**)
6. *we* (**usted** / **nosotras**)
7. *you* (**nosotras** / **tú**)
8. *you* (**ellas** / **ustedes**)
9. *she* (**él** / **ella**)
10. *they* (**nosotras** / **ellas**)

realidades.com ⊙
• Web Code: jcd-0203

Realidades **1**

Capítulo 2A

Nombre _____

Hora _____

Fecha _____

Guided Practice Activities 2A-2

Subject pronouns (*continued*)

C. Circle the subject pronoun that is best associated with each group of names.

1. Susana, Luisa, Marta: (**ellos** / **ellas**)

2. Pablo: (**él** / **ella**)

3. el señor Rivas: (**tú** / **usted**)

4. la señora Rivas: (**tú** / **usted**)

5. Alberto y tú: (**ustedes** / **nosotros**)

6. Sandra y ella: (**ellos** / **ellas**)

7. Marcos y María: (**ellos** / **ellas**)

8. el señor Rodríguez y la señora Rodríguez: (**ustedes** / **vosotros**)

9. Teresa: (**él** / **ella**)

10. Martín y Roberto: (**ellos** / **ellas**)

D. Look at the following drawings and answer the questions using subject pronouns. Follow the model.

Modelo
¿Quién es?

Es _____*él*_____ .

1.
¿Quién es?

Es _____ .

4.
¿Quién soy?

Soy _____ .

2.
¿Quiénes son?

Son _____ .

5.
¿Quiénes son?

Somos _____ .

3.
¿Quién es?

Es _____ .

realidades.com
• Web Code: jcd-0203

Realidades ①

Capítulo 2A

Nombre _____

Fecha _____

Hora _____

Guided Practice Activities 2A-3

Present tense of -ar verbs (p. 84)

- An infinitive is the most basic form of a verb. In English, infinitives have the word "to" in front of them (to talk). In Spanish, infinitives end in -ar, -er, or -ir.
- The largest number of Spanish infinitives end in -ar: **hablar, cantar**, etc.
- To create the present tense of most of these verbs, drop the -ar from the stem: **habl-, cant-**, etc.
- Add the verb endings:

yo: add **-o: hablo**	nosotros/nosotras: add **-amos:** hablamos
tú: add **-as: hablas**	vosotros/vosotras: add **-áis:** habláis
usted/él/ella: add **-a: habla**	ustedes/ellos/ellas: add **-an:** hablan

A. Look at each verb form. Circle the ending. Follow the model.

Modelo   estudi(a)

1. hablas
2. nado
3. canta
4. tocamos
5. trabajas

6. patinamos
7. dibujan
8. bailo
9. pasan
10. escucha

B. Now, look at the same list of verb forms from **part A** and circle the subject pronoun that matches each verb.

1. (**usted** / **tú**) hablas
2. (**yo** / **ella**) nado
3. (**usted** / **yo**) canta
4. (**nosotros** / **vosotros**) tocamos
5. (**tú** / **usted**) trabajas

6. (**ellos** / **nosotras**) patinamos
7. (**ustedes** / **nosotros**) dibujan
8. (**yo** / **él**) bailo
9. (**ellas** / **usted**) pasan
10. (**ella** / **ustedes**) escucha

Present tense of -ar verbs (continued)

C. Complete each sentence by writing the correct **-ar** verb ending on the line provided. Follow the model.

Modelo   Ellas mont*an* en bicicleta.

1. Marta trabaj_____ .

2. Yo cant_____ .

3. Tú esquí_____ .

4. Ellos patin_____ .

5. Nosotros bail_____ .

D. Now, complete each sentence with the correct verb form of the infinitive in parentheses. Follow the model.

Modelo   Tú (nadar) _*nadas*_ .

1. Yo (bailar) _____ .

2. Ella (cantar) _____ .

3. Nosotros (trabajar) _____ .

4. Ustedes (patinar) _____ .

5. Ellos (esquiar) _____ .

6. Tú (nadar) _____ .

7. Él (dibujar) _____ .

8. Ellas (usar) _____ la computadora.

E. Create complete sentences using the subject pronoun provided. Follow the model.

Modelo   tú / 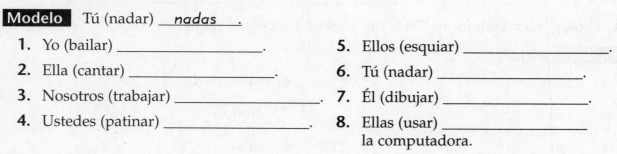 _*Tú dibujas.*_

1. él /

_____

2. nosotros /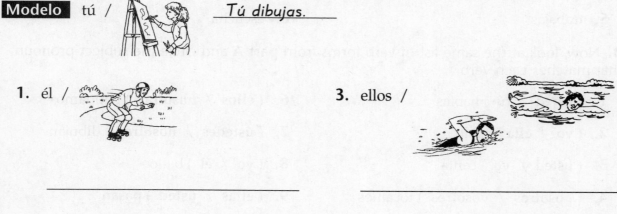

_____

3. ellos /

_____

4. yo /

_____

realidades.com
• Web Code: jcd-0204

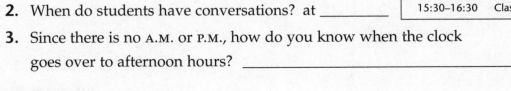

Lectura: La Escuela Español Vivo (pp. 90–91)

A. The reading in your textbook is a brochure for a school called **Español Vivo**. The following is an excerpt from that reading. Read and answer the questions that follow.

> ‖ *Es verano, el mes de junio. Eres estudiante en Santa Ana, un pueblo en las montañas de Costa Rica.* ‖

1. Underline the season and month in the paragraph above.

2. Circle the town and country where the school is located.

3. What does the word **montañas** mean? _____

B. Here is another excerpt from that same reading. Read and answer the questions below.

> ‖ *Hay cinco estudiantes en tu clase. Uds. escuchan, hablan y practican el español todo el día. También usan la computadora.* ‖

1. How many students are in the class? _____

2. Circle the four activities from the reading that students do in class (just circle the verbs).

3. How many of the verbs that you circled in number 2 go with the word **el español**? _____ Which ones? _____

C. Look at the reading on the top of the second page in your textbook.

1. Circle the one activity listed below that is NOT something you can do on the weekends in Costa Rica.

    a. visitar un volcán   **c.** nadar en el mar Mediterráneo

    b. visitar un parque nacional   **d.** nadar en el océano Pacífico

2. There are many cognates in the four examples above. Write the Spanish word or words, choosing from examples **a** through **d**, that go with the English words below.

    • visit _____   • Mediterranean _____

    • volcano _____   • Pacific Ocean _____

    • national park _____

D. Look at the schedule for the school day in the **Español Vivo** school. Answer the questions that follow.

Hora	lunes a viernes
08:00–10:30	Clases de español
10:30–11:00	Recreo
11:00–13:00	Clases de español
13:00–14:00	Almuerzo
14:00–15:30	Conversaciones
15:30–16:30	Clase de música y baile

1. At what times do the students go to classes?

    at _____, _____, and _____

2. When do students have conversations? at _____

3. Since there is no A.M. or P.M., how do you know when the clock goes over to afternoon hours? _____

Presentación oral (p. 93)

Task: Imagine that a student from Costa Rica has just arrived at your school. Tell the student about some of your classes.

A. Fill in the chart below with information on three of your classes. Follow the model.

Hora	Clase	Comentarios	Profesor(a)
primera	la clase de arte	me gusta dibujar	el Sr. Gómez

B. Before writing up your own presentation, read the following sample. Read it out loud the second time through to get an idea of how long it will take you to do your presentation.

> En la primera hora tengo la clase de arte. Me gusta dibujar. La clase es mi favorita. El Sr. Gómez es el profesor.

When speaking, remember to do the following:

_____ speak clearly

_____ use complete sentences

_____ read all information

C. Now, fill in the paragraph below with information about one of your classes.

En la _____ hora tengo la clase de _____.

Me gusta _____. La clase es _____.

_____ es el (la) profesor(a).

D. When the teacher asks you to present your work, you will describe the one class as you see it in **part C.** Your teacher will be grading you on:

• how complete your preparation is
• how much information you communicate
• how easy it is to understand you.

Write the Spanish vocabulary word below each picture. If there is a word or phrase, copy it in the space provided. Be sure to include the article for each noun.

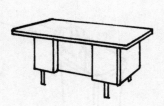

_____

_____

_____

_____

¿Dónde?

_____

_____

_____

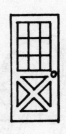

_____

_____

de

_____

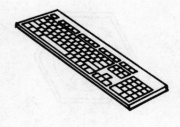

_____

_____

_____

_____

Hay

_____

al lado de

_____ _____

_____

detrás de

_____

_____

allí

_____

debajo de

_____

_____

encima de

_____

aquí

_____

delante de

_____

en

_____

unos,
unas

_____

mi

_____

tu

_____

Es un(a)...

_____

_____

¿Qué es esto?

_____

_____

los,
las

_____

_____

_____

_____

_____

_____

_____

_____

_____

_____

_____

Tear out this page. Write the English words on the lines. Fold the paper along the dotted line to see the correct answers so you can check your work.

la bandera _____

el cartel _____

la computadora _____

la mochila _____

_____

la pantalla _____

la papelera _____

_____

el ratón _____

el reloj _____

el sacapuntas _____

_____

el teclado _____

el escritorio _____

la mesa _____

la silla _____

la puerta _____

Fold In ←

Tear out this page. Write the Spanish words on the lines. Fold the paper along the dotted line to see the correct answers so you can check your work.

flag   _____

poster   _____

computer   _____

bookbag,   _____
backpack

(computer) screen   _____

wastepaper   _____
basket

(computer) mouse   _____

clock   _____

pencil   _____
sharpener

(computer) keyboard _____

desk   _____

table   _____

chair   _____

door   _____

Fold In →

Nombre _____

Hora _____

Fecha _____

Tear out this page. Write the English words on the lines. Fold the paper along the dotted line to see the correct answers so you can check your work.

la ventana _____

al lado de _____

allí _____

aquí _____

debajo de _____

delante de _____

detrás de _____

¿Dónde? _____

en _____

encima de _____

Hay _____

Fold In →

Tear out this page. Write the Spanish words on the lines. Fold the paper along the dotted line to see the correct answers so you can check your work.

window   _____

next to   _____

there   _____

here   _____

underneath   _____

in front of   _____

behind   _____

Where?   _____

in, on   _____

on top of   _____

There is, There are   _____

To hear a complete list of the vocabulary for this chapter, go to www.realidades.com and type in the Web Code jcd-0299. Then click on **Repaso del capítulo.**

Fold In

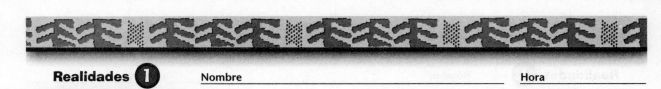

The verb *estar* (p. 107)

- Irregular verbs do not follow the same pattern as regular verbs.
- **Estar** (*to be*) is irregular. Its **yo** form (**estoy**) is different from the regular **-ar yo** form. Its **tú**, **usted/él/ella**, and **ustedes/ellos/ellas** forms are different because they have an accent on the **a**: **estás, está, están**.
- Here are the forms of **estar**:

yo	**estoy**	nosotros/nosotras	**estamos**
tú	**estás**	vosotros/vosotras	**estáis**
usted/él/ella	**está**	ustedes/ellos/ellas	**están**

- **Estar** is used to tell how someone feels or to give a location.

A. Circle the ending of each form of **estar**.

1. yo estoy
2. tú estás
3. Ud. está

4. nosotras estamos
5. ellos están

B. Now, complete each sentence by writing in the correct ending for the correct form of **estar**.

1. Tú est_____ en la clase de arte.
2. Ellos est_____ en la clase de ciencias.
3. Nosotros est_____ en la clase de español.
4. Yo est_____ en la clase de matemáticas.
5. Él est_____ en la clase de literatura.
6. Usted est_____ en la oficina.
7. Ustedes est_____ en la sala de clase.
8. Nosotras est_____ en la clase de tecnología.

C. Complete each sentence with the correct form of **estar**.

1. Yo _____ bien.
2. Tú _____ muy bien.
3. Ella _____ regular.
4. Nosotras _____ bien.

5. Usted _____ regular.
6. Ellos _____ bien.
7. Él _____ regular.
8. Ustedes _____ bien.

The verb *estar (continued)*

D. Complete the conversation with correct forms of **estar.**

LUISA: ¡Buenos días! ¿Cómo _____ ustedes?

ANA E INÉS: Nosotras _____ bien. ¿Y tú? ¿Cómo _____?

LUISA: Yo _____ muy bien. ¿Dónde _____ Marcos y Marta?

ANA: Marcos _____ en la clase de español. Marta _____ en la clase de matemáticas.

E. Create complete sentences with **estar.** Follow the model.

Modelo usted / estar / en la clase de matemáticas

   Usted está en la clase de matemáticas _____.

1. tú / estar / en la clase de español

   _____.

2. ellas / estar / en la clase de arte

   _____.

3. nosotros / estar / en la clase de inglés

   _____.

4. usted / estar / en la clase de matemáticas

   _____.

5. yo / estar / en la clase de tecnología

   _____.

6. él / estar / en la clase de ciencias sociales

   _____.

Realidades ❶

Capítulo 2B

Nombre _____

Fecha _____

Hora _____

Guided Practice Activities 2B-3

The plurals of nouns and articles (p. 110)

Plural of nouns		Plural definite articles		Plural indefinite articles	
Ends in vowel	Ends in consonant	Masculine	Feminine	Masculine	Feminine
add -s: libros, sillas	add -es: relojes, carteles	**los** (*the*) los libros	**las** (*the*) las sillas	**unos** (*some, a few*) unos libros	**unas** (*some, a few*) unas sillas

● Nouns that end in **-z** change the **z** to **c** in the plural: **lápiz → lápices.**

A. Circle the ending of each noun. Is it a vowel or a consonant? Write **V** for vowel or **C** for consonant next to each word.

1. _____ cartel
2. _____ teclado
3. _____ mochila
4. _____ mes

5. _____ bandera
6. _____ reloj
7. _____ estudiante
8. _____ profesor

B. Now, look at the same words from **part A** and add the endings to make them plural.

1. cartel_____
2. teclado_____
3. mochila_____
4. mes_____

5. bandera_____
6. reloj_____
7. estudiante_____
8. profesor_____

C. Now, write the *complete* plural form of each word from **part B.**

1. cartel _____
2. teclado _____
3. mochila _____
4. mes _____
5. bandera _____
6. reloj _____
7. estudiante _____
8. profesor _____

Realidades ①

Capítulo 2B

Nombre _____

Hora _____

Fecha _____

Guided Practice Activities 2B-4

The plurals of nouns and articles (*continued*)

D. Identify whether each of the words from **part C** are masculine or feminine. Write **M** for masculine or **F** for feminine next to each word.

1. _____ cartel
2. _____ teclado
3. _____ mochila
4. _____ mes

5. _____ bandera
6. _____ reloj
7. _____ pupitre
8. _____ profesor

E. Now, look at the words from **part D** in the plural. Circle the correct definite article, masculine or feminine.

1. (**los** / **las**) carteles
2. (**los** / **las**) teclados
3. (**los** / **las**) mochilas
4. (**los** / **las**) meses

5. (**los** / **las**) banderas
6. (**los** / **las**) relojes
7. (**los** / **las**) pupitres
8. (**los** / **las**) profesores

F. Look at each noun below and write **los** or **las**, depending on whether the word is masculine or feminine.

1. _____ puertas
2. _____ ventanas
3. _____ horarios

4. _____ lápices
5. _____ ratones
6. _____ pantallas

G. Look at the words from **part E** again. This time, circle the correct indefinite article, masculine or feminine.

1. (**unos** / **unas**) carteles
2. (**unos** / **unas**) teclados
3. (**unos** / **unas**) mochilas
4. (**unos** / **unas**) meses

5. (**unos** / **unas**) banderas
6. (**unos** / **unas**) relojes
7. (**unos** / **unas**) pupitres
8. (**unos** / **unas**) profesores

H. Look at the nouns from **part F** again. Now, write **unos** or **unas**, depending on whether the word is masculine or feminine.

1. _____ puertas
2. _____ ventanas
3. _____ horarios

4. _____ lápices
5. _____ ratones
6. _____ pantallas

realidades.com ▼
• Web Code: jcd-0213

Lectura: El UNICEF y una convención para los niños (pp. 114–115)

A. The reading in your textbook talks about the organization UNICEF (United Nations International Children's Emergency Fund). You will see many cognates in the reading. Look through the reading and find the Spanish words that most closely resemble the ones below. Write the words in the spaces provided.

1. convention   _____
2. dignity   _____
3. nations   _____
4. protection   _____
5. special   _____

6. diet   _____
7. opinions   _____
8. community _____
9. violence   _____
10. privilege   _____

B. Look at the first paragraph from the reading in your textbook. Write down three things that are said to be privileges for children.

1. _____
2. _____
3. _____

C. Read the following excerpt from your textbook and answer the questions that follow.

|| *UNICEF...tiene siete oficinas regionales en diversas naciones y un Centro de Investigaciones en Italia.* ||

1. Where does UNICEF have seven regional offices?

_____

2. Where is there a Center of Investigation for UNICEF?

_____

D. Look again at the bulleted list in your textbook and list five things in the spaces below that the convention said that all children need.

1. _____
2. _____
3. _____
4. _____
5. _____

Presentación escrita (p. 117)

Task: Pretend you have a pen pal from Mexico who is coming to visit your school next semester. Write your pen pal a note describing your Spanish classroom.

❶ Prewrite.

A. On a separate sheet of paper draw a sketch of your Spanish classroom. You will use this as a reference when writing your note. Try to include four or five different items.

B. Label the items in your sketch using words from your vocabulary.

❷ Draft.

A. Read the sample note written by another student. Use this to guide your own writing.

> En mi sala de clases hay cinco ventanas. Mi pupitre está al lado del escritorio del profesor. La puerta está detrás de mi pupitre. Hay una bandera encima de la mesa de computadoras.

B. Look at the sample note again and list, in the spaces below, all of the classroom objects mentioned.

_____   _____   _____

_____   _____   _____

C. Compare the list of words in **part B** with the words you labeled in your sketch. This will help you get an idea of how similar your draft will be to the model. Create three sentences below filling in what items are in your classroom and where they are located.

1. Hay _____ .

2. _____ está _____ .

3. _____ está _____ .

❸ Revise.

Revise. Read through your draft to see if it makes sense to you. Share your work with a partner who should check the following:

_____ Are the sentences easy to understand?

_____ Did you leave out anything from your drawing?

_____ Are there any spelling or grammar errors?

_____ If there are any problems with your draft, make a revised draft.

Realidades 1

Capítulo 3A

Nombre _____

Fecha _____

Hora _____

Vocabulary Flash Cards, Sheet 1

Write the Spanish vocabulary word below each picture. If there is a word or phrase, copy it in the space provided. Be sure to include the article for each noun.

Realidades ❶

Capítulo 3A

Nombre _____

Fecha _____

Hora _____

Vocabulary Flash Cards, Sheet 2

_____ _____

_____ _____

_____ _____

_____ _____

_____ _____

_____ _____

_____ _____

_____ _____

_____ _____

_____

_____

_____

_____

_____

_____

_____

_____

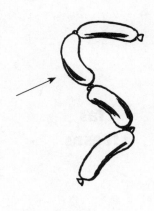

_____

_____

_____

_____

_____

_____

_____

_____

la manzana _____ _____	la ensalada _____ _____	en el almuerzo _____ _____ _____
la naranja _____ _____	las fresas _____ _____	en el desayuno _____ _____ _____
el pan tostado _____ _____ _____	el desayuno _____ _____	la comida _____ _____

Realidades ①

Capítulo 3A

Nombre

Hora

Fecha

Vocabulary Flash Cards, Sheet 5

beber

comer

compartir

nunca

siempre

todos
los días

por
supuesto

¡Qué
asco!

¿Verdad?

Realidades ①

Capítulo 3A

Nombre _____

Hora _____

Fecha _____

Vocabulary Flash Cards, Sheet 6

comprender _____	con _____	¿Cuál? _____
más o menos _____ _____ _____	sin _____	Me encanta(n). . . _____ _____
Te encanta(n). . . _____ _____	Me gusta(n). . . _____ _____	Te gusta(n). . . _____ _____

Tear out this page. Write the English words on the lines. Fold the paper along the dotted line to see the correct answers so you can check your work.

en el desayuno   _____

los huevos   _____

el pan   _____

el pan tostado   _____

el plátano   _____

la salchicha   _____

el tocino   _____

el yogur   _____

en el almuerzo   _____

la ensalada
de frutas   _____

las fresas   _____

la galleta   _____

la hamburguesa   _____

el jamón   _____

las papas fritas   _____

el perrito caliente   _____

la pizza   _____

Fold In

Realidades ①

Capítulo 3A

Nombre

Hora

Fecha

Vocabulary Check, Sheet 2

Tear out this page. Write the Spanish words on the lines. Fold the paper along the dotted line to see the correct answers so you can check your work.

for breakfast _____

eggs _____

bread _____

toast _____

banana _____

sausage _____

bacon _____

yogurt _____

for lunch _____

fruit salad _____

_____

strawberries _____

cookie _____

hamburger _____

ham _____

French fries _____

hot dog _____

pizza _____

Fold In →

Tear out this page. Write the English words on the lines. Fold the paper along the dotted line to see the correct answers so you can check your work.

el sándwich de jamón y queso   _____

la sopa de verduras   _____

el agua   _____

el café   _____

el jugo de manzana   _____

el jugo de naranja   _____

la leche   _____

la limonada   _____

el refresco   _____

el té helado   _____

beber   _____

comer   _____

la comida   _____

compartir   _____

nunca   _____

siempre   _____

todos los días   _____

Fold In

Tear out this page. Write the Spanish words on the lines. Fold the paper along the dotted line to see the correct answers so you can check your work.

ham and cheese   _____
sandwich   _____

vegetable soup   _____

_____

water   _____

coffee   _____

apple juice   _____

orange juice   _____

milk   _____

lemonade   _____

soft drink   _____

iced tea   _____

to drink   _____

to eat   _____

food, meal   _____

to share   _____

never   _____

always   _____

every day   _____

Fold In

To hear a complete list of the vocabulary for this chapter,
go to www.realidades.com and type in the Web Code jcd-0389.
Then click on **Repaso del capítulo**.

Present tense of -*er* and -*ir* verbs (p. 132)

- Like the -**ar** verbs you learned previously, regular -**er** and -**ir** verbs follow a similar pattern in the present tense.
- For -**er** and -**ir** verbs, drop the -**er** or -**ir** from the infinitive (**comer, escribir,** etc.) and add the appropriate endings. The endings are the same for -**er** and -**ir** verbs except for in the **nosotros** and **vosotros** forms.

Present tense of -*er* verbs: *comer*	
yo: add -**o**: **como**	nosotros/nosotras: add -**emos**: **comemos**
tú: add -**es**: **comes**	vosotros/vosotras: add -**éis**: **coméis**
usted/él/ella: add -**e**: **come**	ustedes/ellos/ellas: add -**en**: **comen**

Present tense of -*ir* verbs: *escribir*	
yo: add -**o**: **escribo**	nosotros/nosotras: add -**imos**: **escribimos**
tú: add -**es**: **escribes**	vosotros/vosotras: add -**ís**: **escribís**
usted/él/ella: add -**e**: **escribe**	ustedes/ellos/ellas: add -**en**: **escriben**

A. Circle the ending in each verb form below.

1. escribimos
2. comparten
3. bebes
4. corre
5. ven

6. leo
7. escribes
8. comprendemos
9. comparto
10. ve

B. Now, look at the list of verbs in **part A**. Circle the correct subject pronoun for each verb.

1. (**ustedes** / **nosotros**) escribimos
2. (**ustedes** / **ella**) comparten
3. (**nosotros** / **tú**) bebes
4. (**yo** / **ella**) corre
5. (**ellos** / **nosotros**) ven

6. (**yo** / **él**) leo
7. (**usted** / **tú**) escribes
8. (**nosotras** / **ellos**) comprendemos
9. (**usted** / **yo**) comparto
10. (**usted** / **ustedes**) ve

Realidades 1

Capítulo 3A

Nombre _____

Hora _____

Fecha _____

Guided Practice Activities 3A-2

Present tense of -er and -ir verbs (continued)

C. Complete each sentence by writing the correct **-er** verb ending for each word.

1. Yo beb_____ agua.

2. Nosotras corr_____.

3. Ella comprend_____ todo.

4. Tú le_____ una revista.

5. Ustedes com_____.

6. Nosotros le_____ unos libros.

D. Now, complete each sentence by writing the correct **-ir** verb ending.

1. Tú escrib_____ una carta.

2. Él compart_____ la comida.

3. Ellas escrib_____ cuentos.

4. Nosotros escrib_____ poemas.

5. Yo compart_____.

6. Nosotras compart_____.

E. Complete each sentence with the correct verb form of the infinitive in parentheses. Follow the models.

> **Modelo** Tú (escribir) _____escribes_____.
>
> Ella (comer)_____come_____.

1. Yo (leer) _____.

2. Ella (escribir) _____.

3. Nosotros (ver) _____.

4. Tú (compartir) _____.

5. Nosotros (escribir) _____.

6. Ellos (beber) _____.

7. Usted (compartir) _____.

8. Ellas (leer) _____.

F. Now, write complete sentences using the words provided. Follow the model.

> **Modelo** tú / ver / la / tele
>
> _Tú ves la tele._

1. yo / leer / una / revista

   _____.

2. tú / compartir / el / cuarto

   _____.

3. ellos / beber / té / helado

   _____.

4. nosotros / comer / papas fritas

   _____.

5. ella / escribir / una / carta

   _____.

6. nosotros / compartir / la / comida

   _____.

7. usted / correr / 10 kilómetros

   _____.

8. ustedes / escribir / cuentos

   _____.

realidades.com

• Web Code: jcd-0303

Me gustan, me encantan (p. 135)

- To say you like one thing, use **me gusta** (*I like*) or **me encanta** (*I love*).

- To say you like more than one thing, use **me gustan** or **me encantan**.

- Put **no** in front of **me gusta** or **me gustan** to say you don't like one or more things:
  No me gusta el café. No me gustan los huevos.

One thing (singular)	More than one thing (plural)
Me **gusta la leche.**	Me **gustan las manzanas.**
Me **encanta el té.**	Me **encantan los jugos.**

A. Look at each noun. Write **S** if the noun is singular. Write **P** if it is plural.

1. _____ el cereal   **5.** _____ las salchichas

2. _____ el tocino   **6.** _____ las papas

3. _____ los huevos   **7.** _____ el pan

4. _____ las manzanas   **8.** _____ la pizza

B. Now, look at sentences using the same nouns from **part A**. Complete the verbs by writing **a** for the singular nouns and **an** for the plural nouns. Follow the models.

Modelos   Me encant _*a*___ el café.

          Me encant _*an*___ las fresas.

1. Me gust_____ el cereal.   **5.** Me encant_____ las salchichas.

2. Me gust_____ el tocino.   **6.** Me gust_____ las papas.

3. Me encant_____ los huevos.   **7.** Me encant_____ el pan.

4. Me gust_____ las manzanas.   **8.** Me gust_____ la pizza.

C. Complete the following exchanges by circling the correct word in parenthesis.

1. ELENA: ¿Te (**gusta** / **gustan**) el helado?

     ENRIQUE: ¡Sí! Me (**encanta** / **encantan**) el helado.

2. BERTA: No me (**gusta** / **gustan**) las fresas.

     ANA: ¿No? ¡Me (**encanta** / **encantan**) las fresas!

3. JOSÉ: Me (**encanta** / **encantan**) la pizza.

     LUIS: ¿Sí? A mí no. ¡Pero me (**encanta** / **encantan**) las hamburguesas!

Realidades ①

Capítulo 3A

Nombre _____

Hora _____

Fecha _____

Guided Practice Activities 3A-4

Me gustan, me encantan (continued)

D. Complete the following sentences by writing **encanta** or **encantan**.

1. Me _____ el queso.

2. Me _____ los plátanos.

3. Me _____ los jugos.

4. Me _____ el pan.

5. Me _____ el yogur.

6. Me _____ las galletas.

E. Complete the following sentences by writing **gusta** or **gustan**.

1. ¿Te _____ las sopas?

2. No me _____ el queso.

3. No me _____ la leche.

4. No me _____ el tocino.

5. ¿Te _____ las naranjas?

6. ¿Te _____ las papas fritas?

F. Choose words from the list to complete each sentence about what you like or don't like.

el cereal	el desayuno	los huevos	las salchichas	el yogur
las hamburguesas	el jamón	el queso	el café	el té
los perritos calientes	la sopa de verduras	la pizza	las galletas	el jamón

1. Me gusta _____.

2. No me gusta _____.

3. Me gustan _____.

4. No me gustan _____.

5. ¡Me encanta _____!

6. ¡Me encantan _____!

G. Look at each drawing. Then write a sentence to say whether you like it or not. Follow the models.

Modelos   *Me gustan los huevos* .   OR   *No me gustan los huevos* .

Me gusta la pizza .   OR   *No me gusta la pizza* .

1. _____

2. _____

3. _____

4. _____

realidades.com

• Web Code: jcd-0304

Lectura: Frutas y verduras de las Américas (pp. 138–139)

A. As you can see by its title, the reading in your textbook is about fruits and vegetables. Think about some fruits and vegetables that you eat. Write the names (in English) of three fruits and three vegetables in the spaces below.

FRUITS	VEGETABLES
_____	_____
_____	_____
_____	_____

B. Below are some Spanish words from the reading, categorized by whether they are a fruit or a vegetable. Choose the English word from the bank that you think is the best meaning for each example and write it in the blank.

potato   beans   corn   pineapple   avocado   papaya

Frutas:

1. papaya _____

2. piña _____

3. aguacate _____

Verduras:

4. papa _____

5. frijoles _____

6. maíz _____

C. On the first page of the reading you see pictures of an avocado, a mango, and a papaya. Read the information below about each fruit and answer the questions that follow.

Aguacate:
- La pulpa es fuente de energía y proteínas.
- Tiene vitaminas A y B.

Mango:
- Es originalmente de Asia.
- Tiene calcio y vitaminas A y C.

Papaya:
- Contiene mucha agua.
- Tiene más vitamina C que la naranja.

1. Which fruits have vitamin A? _____

2. Which fruits have vitamin C? _____ _____

3. Which fruit is not originally from the Americas? _____

D. Look at the recipe for a **Licuado de plátano** on the second page of the reading in your textbook. If the following statements are true, circle **C** for **cierto** (*true*); if they are false, circle **F** for **falso** (*false*).

1. **C F** The **licuado** is a hot beverage.

2. **C F** A **plátano** is a banana.

3. **C F** Milk is used in the recipe.

4. **C F** The blender is called a **licuadora**.

5. **C F** You should blend the ingredients for 2 minutes.

Presentación oral (p. 141)

Task: You and a partner will role-play a telephone conversation in Spanish between an American exchange student and a host student in Uruguay. You will each take one of the two roles and gather information about the other person.

A. You will role-play this conversation with a partner. Your role will be that of the host student. Here's how to prepare:

On a separate sheet of paper, make a list of two questions in Spanish that you might ask the exchange student. Find out:

(a) what his or her favorite activities are
(b) what he or she likes to eat and drink for breakfast (or lunch)

B. Revise your work.

1. Work with your partner to coordinate answers and to come up with a greeting and a farewell for your conversation. Here is a way to begin:

HOST STUDENT: ¡Hola, Pablo! Soy Rosa.

EXCHANGE STUDENT: ¡Hola, Rosa! ¿Cómo estás?

HOST STUDENT: Bien, gracias.

2. Now, work on completing the conversation. Use filler words that you have learned and the information you have collected from **part A**. See below for a model.

HOST STUDENT: Pues Pablo, ¿te gusta ir a la escuela?

EXCHANGE STUDENT: Sí, me gusta mucho. Me gusta dibujar y escribir cuentos. ¿Y tú? ¿Qué te gusta hacer en la escuela?

HOST STUDENT: A mí también me gusta ir a la escuela. Me gusta mucho correr y practicar deportes, pero no me gusta estudiar mucho. Me gusta más la hora de almuerzo. ¿Qué te gusta comer en el almuerzo?

EXCHANGE STUDENT: Yo como un sándwich de jamón y queso o una hamburguesa. ¿Y tú?

HOST STUDENT: A mí me encantan las ensaladas. No me gusta nada la carne. ¿Qué te gusta beber?

EXCHANGE STUDENT: Yo bebo los refrescos todos los días. ¿Qué bebes tú?

HOST STUDENT: A mí me gustan los jugos de frutas o bebo agua.

3. Finally, work on your ending. Look again at the **Para empezar** chapter in your textbook to get ideas for how to say good-bye. Below is a sample of how to end the conversation modeled above.

EXCHANGE STUDENT: Bien, pues, ¡Hasta luego!

HOST STUDENT: ¡Nos vemos!

C. You will be asked to present your conversation with your partner. The host student will go first. Listen to what your partner says and continue the conversation appropriately.

Nombre _____

Hora _____

Fecha _____

Vocabulary Practice, Sheet 1

Write the Spanish vocabulary word below each picture. If there is a word or phrase, copy it in the space provided. Be sure to include the article for each noun.

la carne

las grasas

_____

_____

_____

_____

_____

_____

_____

_____

_____

_____

_____

_____

_____

_____

_____

_____

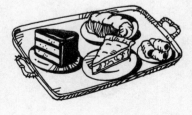

_____

_____

Realidades 1

Capítulo 3B

Nombre _____

Fecha _____

Hora _____

Vocabulary Practice, Sheet 3

_____

_____

_____

_____

**levantar
pesas**

_____

_____

_____

_____

**Tengo
hambre.**

_____

_____

**hacer
ejercicio**

_____

_____

_____

_____

caminar

_____

_____

**para
la salud**

_____

_____

para mantener la salud _____ _____ _____ _____	**Creo que...** _____	**Estoy de acuerdo.** _____ _____
prefiero _____	**Creo que sí.** _____ _____	**No estoy de acuerdo.** _____ _____
deber _____	**Creo que no.** _____	**cada día** _____

Realidades 1

Capítulo 3B

Nombre _____

Hora _____

Fecha _____

Vocabulary Practice, Sheet 5

¿Por qué?

_____

_____

**muchos,
muchas**

_____,

_____

**malo,
mala**

_____,

_____

porque

_____

**todos,
todas**

_____,

_____

**sabroso,
sabrosa**

_____,

_____

algo

_____

horrible

_____

prefieres

_____

Realidades 1

Capítulo 3B

Nombre _____

Fecha _____

Hora _____

Vocabulary Practice, Sheet 6

hago

_____

creer

_____

ser

_____

haces

_____

cada día

_____

_____

_____

_____

_____

_____

Tear out this page. Write the English words on the lines. Fold the paper along the dotted line to see the correct answers so you can check your work.

la cena   _____

el bistec   _____

la carne   _____

el pescado   _____

el pollo   _____

la cebolla   _____

los guisantes   _____

las judías verdes   _____

la lechuga   _____

las papas   _____

los tomates   _____

las uvas   _____

las zanahorias   _____

el arroz   _____

los cereales   _____

los espaguetis   _____

las grasas   _____

la mantequilla   _____

el helado   _____

Fold In

Realidades 1

Capítulo 3B

Nombre _____

Hora _____

Fecha _____

Vocabulary Check, Sheet 2

Tear out this page. Write the Spanish words on the lines. Fold the paper along the dotted line to see the correct answers so you can check your work.

dinner   _____

beefsteak   _____

meat   _____

fish   _____

chicken   _____

onion   _____

peas   _____

green beans   _____

lettuce   _____

potatoes   _____

tomatoes   _____

grapes   _____

carrots   _____

rice   _____

grains   _____

spaghetti   _____

fats   _____

butter   _____

ice cream   _____

Fold In →

Realidades ①

Capítulo 3B

Nombre _____

Hora _____

Fecha _____

Vocabulary Check, Sheet 3

Tear out this page. Write the English words on the lines. Fold the paper along the dotted line to see the correct answers so you can check your work.

los pasteles   _____

las bebidas   _____

caminar   _____

hacer ejercicio   _____

levantar pesas   _____

para mantener
la salud   _____
                    _____

algo   _____

muchos,   _____
muchas

malo, mala   _____

sabroso,   _____
sabrosa   _____

todos,   _____
todas

Fold In

Realidades 1

Capítulo 3B

Nombre _____

Hora _____

Fecha _____

Vocabulary Check, Sheet 4

Tear out this page. Write the Spanish words on the lines. Fold the paper along the dotted line to see the correct answers so you can check your work.

pastries _____

beverages _____

to walk _____

to exercise _____

to lift weights _____

to maintain
one's health _____

something _____

many _____

bad _____

tasty,
flavorful _____

all _____

To hear a complete list of the vocabulary for this chapter,
go to www.realidades.com and type in the Web Code jcd-0399.
Then click on **Repaso del capítulo.**

Fold In

The plurals of adjectives (p. 156)

- Adjectives, just like definite articles, must match the noun they accompany. Singular adjectives go with singular nouns, and plural adjectives go with plural nouns.

- Adjectives that end in **-o** or **-a** must also match the noun. Masculine (**-o**) adjectives go with masculine nouns and feminine (**-a**) adjectives go with feminine nouns.

- Adjectives that end in **-e** do not change to match masculine or feminine nouns. They still change to match singular and plural nouns: **el libro interesante, las clases interesantes**.

	Definite article	**Noun**	**Adjective**
masculine singular	**el**	pan	sabros**o**
feminine singular	**la**	sopa	sabros**a**
masculine plural	**los**	jamones	sabros**os**
feminine plural	**las**	galletas	sabros**as**

A. Look at each noun. Write **M** if it is masculine or **F** if it is feminine.

1. _____ pan
2. _____ sopas
3. _____ yogur
4. _____ salchichas
5. _____ pizza

6. _____ jamón
7. _____ huevos
8. _____ quesos
9. _____ galletas
10. _____ hamburguesa

B. Now, go back to **part A**. Next to the **M** or **F** you wrote next to each noun, write **S** if the noun is singular and **P** if it is plural.

C. Here are the nouns from **part A**. Now there are adjectives with them. Circle the correct adjective form for each noun.

1. pan (**sabroso** / **sabrosos**)
2. sopas (**sabrosos** / **sabrosas**)
3. yogur (**sabrosos** / **sabroso**)
4. salchichas (**sabrosas** / **sabrosa**)
5. pizza (**sabrosos** / **sabrosa**)

6. jamón (**sabroso** / **sabrosa**)
7. huevos (**sabrosa** / **sabrosos**)
8. quesos (**sabrosos** / **sabrosas**)
9. galletas (**sabrosa** / **sabrosas**)
10. hamburguesas (**sabrosos** / **sabrosas**)

Realidades 1

Nombre _____

Hora _____

Capítulo 3B

Fecha _____

Guided Practice Activities 3B-2

The plurals of adjectives (*continued*)

D. Fill in the missing singular or plural form of each masculine adjective in the chart.

Masculine	
singular	**plural**
divertido	
simpático	
	atrevidos
	serios
artístico	

E. Now, fill in the missing singular or plural form of each feminine adjective in the chart.

Feminine	
singular	**plural**
	divertidas
simpática	
	atrevidas
seria	
	artísticas

F. Choose an adjective from the group of words. Write its correct form in the space provided.

serio	seria	serios	serias
atrevido	atrevida	atrevidos	atrevidas
artístico	artística	artísticos	artísticas

1. Laura y Elena estudian mucho. Son _____.

2. Sandra monta en monopatín. Es _____.

3. Mario dibuja. Es _____.

4. Tomás y Beatriz trabajan mucho. Son _____.

5. Lorenzo y Fernando esquían. Son _____.

realidades.com

• Web Code: jcd-0313

The verb *ser* (p. 158)

- You have already learned and used some forms of the verb **ser**, which means *to be*:
   Yo soy serio. Tú eres simpática. Ella es artística.
- **Ser** is an irregular verb. You will need to memorize its forms.

yo	**soy**	nosotros/nosotras	**somos**
tú	**eres**	vosotros/vosotras	**sois**
usted/él/ella	**es**	ustedes/ellos/ellas	**son**

A. Choose the correct subject pronoun for each form of **ser** and circle it.

1. (yo / él) es

2. (ustedes / ella) son

3. (tú / ella) eres

4. (ella / yo) es

5. (usted / tú) es

6. (nosotros / ellas) son

7. (ellos / nosotros) somos

8. (yo / él) soy

B. Now, write the correct form of **ser** next to each subject pronoun.

1. tú _____

2. usted _____

3. ellos _____

4. él _____

5. ellas _____

6. nosotras _____

7. yo _____

8. ustedes _____

C. Complete the exchanges by writing in the correct form of **ser**.

1. VERA: Yo _____ estudiante. ¿Y tú?

   GONZALO: Yo _____ estudiante también.

2. PABLO: Tú _____ muy deportista, ¿no?

   ENRIQUE: Sí, pero yo también _____ muy estudioso.

3. INÉS: Susana y Olivia _____ muy divertidas.

   MARCOS: Sí. Olivia _____ muy simpática también.

4. PACO Y LUIS: Nosotros _____ perezosos. No estudiamos mucho.

   ANA: Bueno, yo _____ muy trabajadora. Me gusta estudiar.

The verb *ser* (*continued*)

D. Look at each drawing. Complete the question with a form of **ser**. Follow the model.

Modelo

¿Cómo _____es_____ él?

1.   ¿Cómo _____ él?

2.   ¿Cómo _____ tú?

3.   ¿Cómo _____ ellas?

4.   ¿Cómo _____ nosotras?

5.   ¿Cómo _____ yo?

E. Now, complete each sentence with the correct form of **ser** and the correct adjective ending. Refer back to the art in **part D**. Follow the model.

Modelo   Él ____*es*____ simpático____.

1. Él _____ artístic_____.

2. Tú _____ perezos_____.

3. Ellas _____ estudios_____.

4. Nosotras _____ inteligente_____.

5. Yo _____ atrevid_____.

realidades.com
• Web Code: jcd-0314

Realidades 1

Capítulo 3B

Nombre _____

Hora _____

Fecha _____

Guided Practice Activities 3B-5

Lectura: La comida de los atletas (pp. 162–163)

> Skimming is a useful technique to help you get through a reading. You think of general information that you are looking for. Then you quickly read the words to find it.

A. List three things you would expect to find in an article about an athlete's eating habits.

1. _____
2. _____
3. _____

B. Skim the article and check off the things in your list from **part A** that you find.

C. Note that the pie chart in your textbook shows how much of an athlete's diet can be divided into three categories. Next to each category below, write the English translation of the word. Then fill in the percentage number according to the pie chart.

	English	Number
1. carbohidratos	_____	_____ %
2. proteínas	_____	_____ %
3. grasas	_____	_____ %

D. The reading in your textbook gives a picture and a short description of what foods are good for each big meal of the day. Next to each food given below circle whether the reading says it is best for **D (desayuno)**, **A (almuerzo)**, or **C (cena)**.

1. **D A C** pan con mantequilla
2. **D A C** pasta
3. **D A C** yogur
4. **D A C** papas
5. **D A C** jalea

E. Read the selection below and answer the questions that follow.

> *La noche antes del partido, el jugador bebe un litro de jugo de naranja, y durante el partido bebe hasta dos litros de agua y bebidas deportivas.*

1. Circle the three kinds of drinks mentioned in the reading.
2. What is a *litro* in English? _____
3. When does the player drink a *litro* of orange juice? _____

Presentación escrita (p. 165)

Task: You will make a poster in Spanish with three suggestions for better health. You will need to research what are proven good eating and exercise habits.

❶ **Prewrite.** Talk to classmates, teachers, the school nurse, or your parents about good eating and exercise habits, especially for teens. Then list their ideas under the following headings to help you organize your information:

- Debes comer _____.
- No debes comer mucho(a) _____.
- Debes beber _____.
- No debes beber mucho(a) _____.
- Debes _____ para mantener la salud.

❷ **Draft.** Create your first draft on a separate sheet of paper. (You do not need to use posterboard for this draft.) List your ideas from the prewrite stage. Organize them in a neat or artistic way. Sketch out the visuals you want to include on the poster.

❸ **Revise.**

A. Someone else will check your work for the following:

_____ Have you communicated the three suggestions well?

_____ Do the visuals help with the meaning?

_____ Will the visuals make the poster attractive?

_____ Are all words spelled correctly?

_____ Are grammar and vocabulary used correctly?

B. Rewrite your poster using the person's suggestions.

❹ **Publish.** Your final draft will be on some sort of posterboard. You will want to carefully add any illustrations and designs you had sketched out in an earlier stage.

❺ **Evaluate.** Your teacher will tell you how your poster will be graded. Your teacher will check:

- your completion of the task
- the accuracy of your vocabulary and grammar
- your effective use of visuals

Realidades 1

Capítulo 4A

Nombre _____

Hora _____

Fecha _____

Vocabulary Flash Cards, Sheet 1

Write the Spanish vocabulary word below each picture. If there is a word or phrase, copy it in the space provided. Be sure to include the article for each noun.

Realidades

Capítulo 4A

Nombre

Fecha

Hora

Vocabulary Flash Cards, Sheet 2

_____ _____

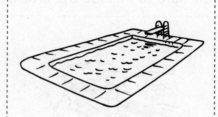

_____ _____

**la
mezquita**

_____ _____

_____ _____

_____ _____

**la
sinagoga**

_____ _____

_____ _____

_____ _____

**el
templo**

_____ _____

Realidades ①

Capítulo 4A

Nombre _____

Fecha _____

Hora _____

Vocabulary Flash Cards, Sheet 3

la casa

_____

_____

Me quedo en casa.

_____ _____

_____

¿Adónde?

_____

_____

en casa

_____

_____

a

_____

_____

a casa

_____

_____

el restaurante

_____

_____

a la, al

_____,

_____

¿Con quién?

_____

_____

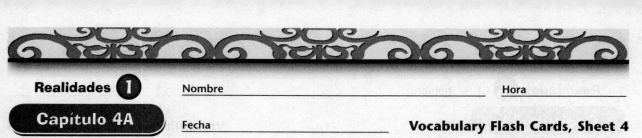

con mis amigos

_____ _____

_____

¿Cuándo?

_____

los fines de semana

_____ _____

_____ _____

con mis/tus amigos

_____ _____

_____

después

_____

los lunes, los martes...

_____

_____

solo, sola

_____,

_____

después de

_____

_____

tiempo libre

_____

_____

Realidades 1

Capítulo 4A

Nombre _____

Hora _____

Fecha _____

Vocabulary Flash Cards, Sheet 5

de

_____

¡No me digas!

_____ _____

_____

_____

¿De dónde eres?

_____

_____

para

_____

_____

generalmente

_____

_____

_____

Realidades ❶

Capítulo 4A

Nombre

Fecha

Hora

Vocabulary Flash Cards, Sheet 6

Realidades 1

Capítulo 4A

Nombre _____

Hora _____

Fecha _____

Vocabulary Check, Sheet 1

Tear out this page. Write the English words on the lines. Fold the paper along the dotted line to see the correct answers so you can check your work.

ir de compras _____

ver una película _____

la lección de piano _____

la biblioteca _____

el café _____

el campo _____

en casa _____

el centro comercial _____

el cine _____

el gimnasio _____

la iglesia _____

la mezquita _____

las montañas _____

el parque _____

la piscina _____

la playa _____

el restaurante _____

Fold In

Tear out this page. Write the Spanish words on the lines. Fold the paper along the dotted line to see the correct answers so you can check your work.

to go shopping   _____

to see a movie   _____

_____

piano lesson (class)   _____

_____

library   _____

café   _____

countryside   _____

at home   _____

mall   _____

_____

movie theater   _____

gym   _____

church   _____

mosque   _____

mountains   _____

park   _____

swimming pool   _____

beach   _____

restaurant   _____

Fold In ←

Realidades 1

Capítulo 4A

Nombre _____

Fecha _____

Hora _____

Vocabulary Check, Sheet 3

Tear out this page. Write the English words on the lines. Fold the paper along the dotted line to see the correct answers so you can check your work.

la sinagoga   _____

el templo   _____

                       _____

el trabajo   _____

solo, sola   _____

¿Cuándo?   _____

después   _____

después (de)   _____

los fines de   _____
semana

los lunes, los   _____
martes...   _____

tiempo libre   _____

Fold In

Tear out this page. Write the Spanish words on the lines. Fold the paper along the dotted line to see the correct answers so you can check your work.

synagogue   _____

temple,   _____
Protestant church

work, job   _____

alone   _____

When?   _____

afterwards   _____

after   _____

on weekends   _____
    _____

on Mondays,   _____
on Tuesdays . . .   _____

free time   _____

Fold In

To hear a complete list of the vocabulary for this chapter,
go to www.realidades.com and type in the Web Code jcd-0489.
Then click on **Repaso del capítulo**.

Realidades **1**

Capítulo 4A

Nombre _____

Fecha _____

Hora _____

Guided Practice Activities 4A-1

The verb *ir* (p. 180)

- The verb **ir** means "to go." It is irregular. Here are its forms.

yo	**voy**	nosotros/nosotras	**vamos**
tú	**vas**	vosotros/vosotras	**vais**
usted/él/ella	**va**	ustedes/ellos/ellas	**van**

- **¡Vamos!** means "Let's go!"

A. Choose the correct subject pronoun for each form of **ir** and circle it.

1. (**tú / él**) va
2. (**yo / usted**) voy
3. (**ellas / nosotras**) vamos
4. (**usted / ustedes**) va

5. (**ustedes / él**) van
6. (**tú / yo**) vas
7. (**ellos / ella**) van
8. (**yo / ella**) va

B. Now, write the correct form of **ir** next to each subject pronoun.

1. ella _____
2. ustedes _____
3. yo _____
4. nosotros _____
5. tú _____
6. él _____
7. ellos _____
8. usted _____

C. Complete each sentence by writing in the correct form of **ir**.

1. Yo _____ al cine para ver una película.
2. Ellas _____ al parque para correr.
3. Nosotros _____ al gimnasio para levantar pesas.
4. Tú _____ al restaurante para comer.
5. Ella _____ a la piscina para nadar.

The verb *ir* (*continued*)

- When **ir** + **a** is followed by the definite article **el**, **a** + **el** combines to form **al**:

  (vamos a) + (el parque) = **Vamos al parque.**

D. Complete each sentence by writing a form of **ir** + **al** or **a la**. Remember to use **al** when the noun after the write-on line is masculine. Use **a la** when the noun is feminine. Follow the models.

Modelos   Ellos _____*van al*_____ parque.

            Ellos _____*van a la*_____ oficina.

1. Silvia _____ casa.

2. Cristina y María _____ café.

3. Tú _____ playa.

4. Nosotros _____ parque.

5. Usted _____ campo.

6. Yo _____ piscina.

- To ask where someone is going, use **¿Adónde?** as in: **¿Adónde vas?**
- To answer, use forms of **ir** + **a** as in: **Voy a la oficina.**

E. Complete the following exchanges by finishing the second sentence with a form of **ir** and the place indicated. Follow the model.

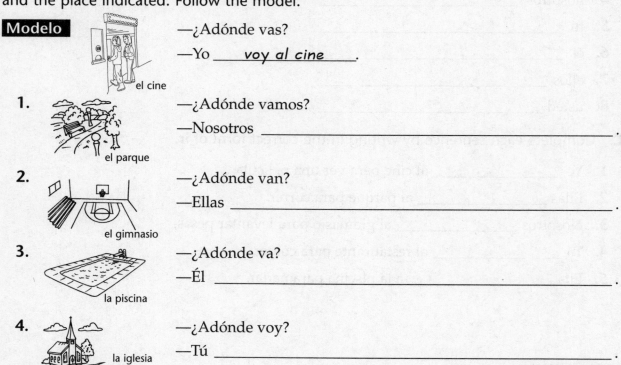

Modelo   el cine   —¿Adónde vas?

                     —Yo _____*voy al cine*_____ .

1.   el parque   —¿Adónde vamos?

                     —Nosotros _____ .

2.   el gimnasio   —¿Adónde van?

                     —Ellas _____ .

3.   la piscina   —¿Adónde va?

                     —Él _____ .

4.   la iglesia   —¿Adónde voy?

                     —Tú _____ .

Asking questions (p. 184)

- Interrogatives are words that you use to ask questions. Here are some Spanish interrogatives.

Categories	Interrogatives		
People	¿Quién?	¿Con quién?	
Location	¿Dónde?	¿Adónde?	¿De dónde?
Things or actions	¿Qué?	¿Cuál?	¿Cuántos? / ¿Cuántas?
Reason	¿Por qué?		
Time	¿Cuándo?		
Description (how)	¿Cómo?		

- You can change a statement into a question by raising your voice at the end:

  ¿Margarita va a la biblioteca? In this case, you do not use an interrogative.

- These kinds of questions expect the answer will be *yes* or *no*. You can add **¿verdad?** (*right?*) to the end to emphasize this: **Margarita va a la biblioteca, ¿verdad?**

A. Each drawing or group of drawings represents a question category in the chart above. Write the interrogatives that go with each group. Follow the model.

Modelo

8:52 — ¿ ___Cuándo___ ?

1. _____
_____
_____

2. _____
_____
_____

3. _____
_____
_____

Asking questions (*continued*)

- In Spanish questions with interrogatives, the verb comes before the subject:
  ¿Adónde va Margarita?

B. Look at the following groups of exchanges. Write in the correct interrogative to complete each exchange. Use the interrogatives listed for each group.

Location: ¿Dónde? ¿Adónde?

1. —¿_____ van Natalia y Roberto?
   —Van a la biblioteca para estudiar.

2. —¿_____ levantas pesas?
   — Levanto pesas en el gimnasio.

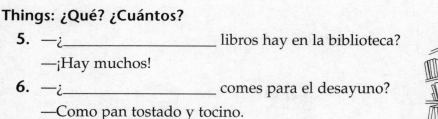

People: ¿Quién? ¿Con quién?

3. —¿_____ hablas mucho por teléfono?
   —Hablo mucho con mi amiga Tina. Ella es muy divertida.

4. —¿_____ es su profesor de español?
   — Es la señora Oliveros. Es muy inteligente.

Things: ¿Qué? ¿Cuántos?

5. —¿_____ libros hay en la biblioteca?
   —¡Hay muchos!

6. —¿_____ comes para el desayuno?
   —Como pan tostado y tocino.

Reason and Description: ¿Por qué? ¿Cómo?

7. —¿_____ estudias tanto?
   — Soy muy trabajadora y me gusta leer.

8. —¿_____ es la clase de matemáticas?
   — Es interesante, pero difícil.

- Web Code: jcd-004

Realidades ❶

Capítulo 4A

Nombre _____

Hora _____

Fecha _____

Guided Practice Activities 4A-5

Asking questions (*continued*)

C. Look at each group of phrases. Put them in order to form a question by numbering each group 1, 2, or 3. Then write them in order on the write-on line below. Follow the model. You can also look at the questions in **part B** for examples.

Modelo	Paulina / adónde / va
	3 1 2

¿ ___*Adónde va Paulina*___ ?

1. es / el profesor de español / quién

_____

2. sillas / hay / cuántas

_____

3. Luisa / adónde / va

_____

4. cómo / ella / es

_____

5. corren / dónde / ellos

_____

6. con quién / habla / Margarita

_____

Lectura: Al centro comercial (pp. 188–189)

A. List four events that you think would take place at a special-event week in a shopping center near you.

    1. _____   3. _____

    2. _____   4. _____

B. According to the reading in your book, what are the dates for the event week at the Plaza del Sol? Write the answers in English below, next to the days of the week you are given.

Monday, _____   Friday, _____

Tuesday, _____   Saturday, _____

Wednesday, _____   Sunday, _____

Thursday, _____

C. Look at the word bank below. Choose which expression in English best matches with the words you are given and write it in the spaces provided.

Andean music	**Yoga class**	**Evening of jazz**
Evening of tango	**Photography show**	**Yoga performance**

    1. Música andina   _____

    2. Clase de yoga   _____

    3. Noche de jazz   _____

    4. Exposición de fotografía   _____

    5. Exhibición de yoga   _____

    6. Noche de tango   _____

D. Read the description of Andean music and answer the questions that follow.

‖ *El grupo Sol Andino toca música andina fusionada con bossa nova y jazz el lunes a las 8.00 P.M. Abierto al público.* ‖

    1. Circle the name of the group in the paragraph above.

    2. What does this group fuse with its brand of Andean music?

    _____ and _____

    3. Can the public attend this show? _____

Realidades ①

Capítulo 4A

Nombre _____

Fecha _____

Hora _____

Guided Practice Activities 4A-7

Lectura: Al centro comercial (*continued*)

E. Read the description of the yoga class and answer the questions that follow.

> *La práctica de yoga es todos los martes desde las 7.00 hasta las 9.00 P.M. La instructora Lucía Gómez Paloma enseña los secretos de esta disciplina. Inscríbase al teléfono 224-24-16. Vacantes limitadas.*

1. How long does the yoga class last? _____

2. What does the sequence of numbers 224-24-16 stand for? _____

3. Can anyone attend this class? _____

   Why or why not? _____

F. After looking through the readings in your textbook, you know that four events are

Música andina   Clase de yoga   Sábado flamenco   Clase de repostería

explained in detail. These events are listed below. You must choose which event goes with the descriptions you are given. Write the name of the event in the space provided.

1. _____ instructora Lucía Gómez Paloma

2. _____ guitarrista Ernesto Hermoza

3. _____ grupo Sol Andino

4. _____ la Repostería Ideal

5. _____ maestro Rudolfo Torres

6. _____ es el sábado a las 8.00 P.M.

Realidades 1

Capítulo 4A

Nombre _____

Fecha _____

Hora _____

Guided Practice Activities 4A-8

Presentación oral (p. 191)

Task: You and a partner will play the roles of a new student and a student who has been at school for awhile. This student must find out about the new student.

A. You will need to prepare the role of the student who has been at the school for awhile. On a separate sheet of paper, make a list of four questions you have for the new student. Then, think of a greeting to introduce yourself.

First question: Find out where the new student is from.

Second question: Find out what activities the new student likes to do.

Third question: Find out on what days of the week the student likes to do things.

Fourth question: Find out with whom the new student does these activities.

B. You will need to practice your conversation.

1. First, work on the greeting. See below for a model.
   EXPERIENCED STUDENT: ¡Hola, amigo! Soy Ana María. ¿Cómo te llamas?
   NEW STUDENT: Me llamo Miguel Ángel.

2. Now, you will need to put together your questions and answers in a conversation. Use the following as a model:
   EXPERIENCED STUDENT: ¿De dónde eres, Miguel Ángel?
   NEW STUDENT: Soy de Barranquilla, Colombia.
   EXPERIENCED STUDENT: Bien. ¿Qué te gusta hacer en tu tiempo libre?
   NEW STUDENT: Me gusta ir al campo, nadar en el mar y caminar en las montañas.
   EXPERIENCED STUDENT: A mí también me gusta ir al campo. ¿Cuándo vas tú al campo?
   NEW STUDENT: Voy al campo los fines de semana. Me gusta caminar cuando estoy de vacaciones.
   EXPERIENCED STUDENT: ¿Y con quién vas al campo o a las montañas?
   NEW STUDENT: Voy con mi familia.

3. Now work on a closing. Use the following as a model:
   EXPERIENCED STUDENT: ¡Bueno, hasta luego Miguel Ángel!
   NEW STUDENT: ¡Nos vemos, Ana María!

C. You will need to present your conversation. Make sure you do the following in your presentation:

_____ provide and obtain all the necessary information

_____ have no breaks in the conversation

_____ speak clearly

Write the Spanish vocabulary word below each picture. If there is a word or phrase, copy it in the space provided. Be sure to include the article for each noun.

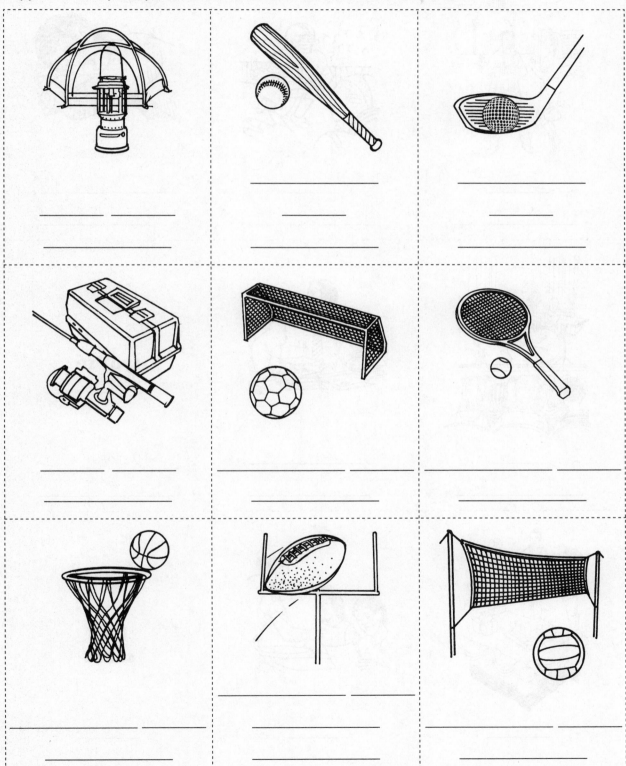

Realidades 1

Capítulo 4B

Nombre _____

Fecha _____

Hora _____

Vocabulary Practice, Sheet 2

_____

_____

_____,

_____
_____,

_____,

(yo) sé

_____ _____

_____
_____

_____

**(tú)
sabes**

_____

Realidades ❶

Capítulo 4B

Nombre _____

Hora _____

Fecha _____

Vocabulary Practice, Sheet 3

**contento,
contenta**

_____,

_____

**¿A qué
hora?**

_____ _____

_____

**de la
mañana**

_____ _____

_____

**enfermo,
enferma**

_____,

_____

**a la
una**

_____ _____

_____

**de la
noche**

_____ _____

_____

mal

_____

**a las
ocho**

_____ _____

_____

**de la
tarde**

_____ _____

_____

Realidades

Capítulo 4B

Nombre _____

Hora _____

Fecha _____

Vocabulary Practice, Sheet 4

este fin de semana _____ _____ _____ _____	**conmigo** _____	**¡Ay! ¡Qué pena!** _____ _____ _____
esta noche _____	**contigo** _____	**¡Genial!** _____
esta tarde _____ _____	**(yo) puedo** _____	**¡Qué buena idea!** _____ _____

Realidades 1

Capítulo 4B

Nombre _____

Hora _____

Fecha _____

Vocabulary Practice, Sheet 5

¡Oye! ___ _____	¿Te gustaría? ___ _____	demasiado _____
lo siento ___ _____	me gustaría ___ _____	entonces _____
(yo) quiero ___ _____	Tengo que... ___ _____	un poco (de) ___ ___ _____

**(tú)
puedes**

_____

_____

**(tú)
quieres**

_____

_____

**ir a +
*infinitive***

_____

_____

_____

_____

_____

_____

_____

_____

_____

_____

_____

_____

_____

_____

_____

_____

Tear out this page. Write the English words on the lines. Fold the paper along the dotted line to see the correct answers so you can check your work.

el baile   _____

el concierto   _____

la fiesta   _____

el partido   _____

ir de cámping   _____

ir de pesca   _____

jugar al
básquetbol   _____
                            _____

jugar al béisbol   _____

jugar al fútbol   _____

jugar al fútbol   _____
americano

jugar al golf   _____

jugar al tenis   _____

jugar al
vóleibol   _____
                            _____

cansado,   _____
cansada

contento,   _____
contenta

Fold In

Tear out this page. Write the Spanish words on the lines. Fold the paper along the dotted line to see the correct answers so you can check your work.

dance   _____

concert   _____

party   _____

game, match   _____

to go camping   _____

to go fishing   _____

to play   _____
basketball
                         _____

to play baseball   _____

to play soccer   _____

to play football   _____

                         _____

to play golf   _____

to play tennis   _____

to play   _____
volleyball
                         _____

tired   _____

                         _____

happy   _____

                         _____

Fold In →

Realidades ❶

Capítulo 4B

Nombre _____

Fecha _____

Hora _____

Vocabulary Check, Sheet 3

Tear out this page. Write the English words on the lines. Fold the paper along the dotted line to see the correct answers so you can check your work.

enfermo,
enferma _____

ocupado,
ocupada _____

triste _____

a la una _____

de la mañana _____

de la noche _____

_____

de la tarde _____

este fin de
semana _____

esta noche _____

esta tarde _____

¡Ay! ¡Qué pena! _____

¡Genial! _____

lo siento _____

¡Qué buena idea! _____

Fold In

Tear out this page. Write the Spanish words on the lines. Fold the paper along the dotted line to see the correct answers so you can check your work.

sick _____

_____

busy _____

_____

sad _____

at one (o'clock) _____

in the morning _____

in the evening, _____
at night

in the afternoon _____

this weekend _____

_____

this evening _____

this afternoon _____

Oh! What a shame! _____

Great! _____

I'm sorry _____

What a good idea! _____

Fold In

To hear a complete list of the vocabulary for this chapter, go to www.realidades.com and type in the Web Code jcd-0499. Then click on **Repaso del capítulo**.

Ir + a + infinitive (p. 206)

- You have already learned to use the verb **ir** (*to go*). To review, here are its forms, which are irregular.

yo	**voy**	nosotros/nosotras	**vamos**
tú	**vas**	vosotros/vosotras	**vais**
usted/él/ella	**va**	ustedes/ellos/ellas	**van**

- As you have learned, the infinitive is the basic form of the verb (**hablar, comer, leer,** etc.). It is equivalent to "to . . ." in English: *to talk, to eat, to read.*
- When you use **ir + a** with an infinitive, it means you or others are *going to do something* in the future. It is the same as "I am going to . . ." in English: **Voy a leer el libro. Vamos a ver la película.**

A. Review by writing the correct form of **ir** next to each subject pronoun.

1. tú _____
2. ellos _____
3. él _____
4. usted _____
5. ella _____
6. yo _____
7. ustedes _____
8. nosotras _____

B. Now complete each sentence with the correct form of **ir**.

1. Marta y Rosa _____ a estudiar esta tarde.
2. Yo _____ a jugar al tenis esta tarde.
3. Tú _____ a montar en monopatín mañana.
4. Nosotras _____ a bailar mañana.
5. Ustedes _____ a correr esta tarde.
6. Serena _____ a ir de cámping mañana.

C. Complete the exchanges with the correct form of **ir**.

1. LAURA: ¿Qué _____ a hacer este fin de semana?

   CARLOS: Yo _____ a jugar al golf.

2. ANA: ¿Qué _____ a hacer ustedes mañana?

   TOMÁS: Nosotros _____ a trabajar.

3. ERNESTO: ¿Qué _____ a hacer Susana hoy?

   RICARDO: Ella y yo _____ a ir al cine.

Ir + a + infinitive (continued)

D. Write questions with **ir + a + hacer**. Follow the models.

Modelos (tú) / hacer hoy

¿Qué _____ *vas a hacer hoy* _____ ?

(ellos) / hacer este fin de semana

¿Qué _____ *van a hacer este fin de semana* _____ ?

1. yo / hacer esta tarde

¿Qué _____ ?

2. nosotros / hacer mañana

¿Qué _____ ?

3. ustedes / hacer hoy

¿Qué _____ ?

4. tú / hacer este fin de semana

¿Qué _____ ?

5. ella / hacer esta mañana

¿Qué _____ ?

E. Write sentences to say what the people shown are going to do tomorrow. Follow the model.

Modelo   Roberto

Roberto va a jugar al béisbol.

1.   Ana

_____

2. Juan y José

_____

3. tú

_____

4. yo

_____

Realidades **1**

Capítulo 4B

Nombre _____

Fecha _____

Hora _____

Guided Practice Activities 4B-3

The verb *jugar* (p. 208)

- **Jugar** (*to play a sport or game*) uses the regular **-ar** present tense endings.
- However, **jugar** does not use the same stem in all its forms. **Jugar** is a *stem-changing verb*. In most forms, it uses **jueg-** + the **-ar** endings. But in the **nosotros/nosotras, vosotros/vosotras** forms, it uses **jug-** + the **-ar** endings.
- Here are the forms of **jugar**:

yo	**juego**	nosotros/nosotras	**jugamos**
tú	**juegas**	vosotros/vosotras	**jugáis**
usted/él/ella	**juega**	ustedes/ellos/ellas	**juegan**

A. Circle the forms of **jugar** in each sentence. Underline the stem in each form of **jugar**.

1. Yo juego al tenis este fin de semana.

2. Ellos juegan al básquetbol esta noche.

3. Nosotros jugamos videojuegos mañana.

4. Ustedes juegan al golf este fin de semana.

5. Tú y yo jugamos al béisbol esta tarde.

6. Tú juegas al fútbol americano este fin de semana.

7. Ella juega al fútbol esta tarde.

8. Nosotras jugamos al vóleibol hoy.

B. Now, write the forms of **jugar** you circled in **part A**. Put them in the corresponding rows of the table. The first one has been done for you.

Subject pronoun	Form of *jugar*
1. yo	*juego*
2. ellos	
3. nosotros	
4. ustedes	
5. tú y yo	
6. tú	
7. ella	
8. nosotras	

Realidades ①

Capítulo 4B

Nombre _____

Fecha _____

Hora _____

Guided Practice Activities 4B-4

The verb *jugar* (*continued*)

C. Write questions with **jugar.** Follow the model.

Modelo	usted

¿A qué juega?

1. tú

_____

2. nosotros

_____

3. yo

_____

4. ella

_____

5. tú y yo

_____

6. ustedes

_____

D. Now write sentences to say what people are playing. Follow the model.

Modelo	Eduardo

Eduardo juega al fútbol.

1. Rosa y Ana

_____

2. nosotros

_____

3. yo

_____

4. tú

_____

5. ustedes

_____

realidades.com

• Web Code: jcd-0414

Realidades **1**

Capítulo 4B

Nombre _____

Fecha _____

Hora _____

Guided Practice Activities 4B-5

Lectura: Sergio y Paola: Dos deportistas dotados (pp. 212–213)

A. A list of personal information is given about each athlete in your textbook reading. Below are several of the categories for each piece of information. Write what you think is the English word for each category below.

1. Nombre _____
2. Fecha de nacimiento _____
3. Lugar de nacimiento _____
4. Su objetivo _____
5. Profesional _____

B. Look at the list of **aficiones** (*interests*) for each athlete below. Then, answer the questions that follow.

SERGIO: Real Madrid, tenis, fútbol, videojuegos

PAOLA: Nadar, practicar gimnasia, viajar, pasar tiempo con su familia

1. Do Sergio and Paola share any interests? _____
2. What interest does Sergio have that is not a sport? _____
3. What interests does Paola have that are not a sport? _____

C. Look at the following sentences from the reading. Circle **S** if they are about Sergio and **P** if they are about Paola.

1. **S P**   Juega para el Club de Campo del Mediterráneo en Borriol.
2. **S P**   Es la mejor clavadista de México.
3. **S P**   Su padre Víctor es golfista profesional.
4. **S P**   Practica su deporte desde la edad de tres años.
5. **S P**   Quiere ser la clavadista número uno del mundo.
6. **S P**   A la edad de 17 años gana su primer torneo de profesionales.

D. Now, answer the questions about the two athletes from the reading. Write in either **Paola, Sergio**, or **both** depending on the best answer.

1. Who was born in 1980? _____
2. Who is from Spain? _____
3. Who likes soccer? _____
4. Who also practices gymnastics? _____
5. Who won an Olympic medal? _____
6. Who wants to be the best athlete in their sport in the world? _____

realidades.com
• Web Code: jcd-0415

Realidades 1

Capítulo 4B

Nombre _____

Hora _____

Fecha _____

Guided Practice Activities 4B-6

Presentación escrita (p. 215)

Task: Pretend you want to invite a friend to an upcoming special event on your calendar. You will need to write one invitation to that friend and anyone else you want to invite.

❶ Prewrite. Think about what event you want to attend. Fill in the information below about the event.

Name of event: _____

When (day and time): _____

Where: _____

Who is going: _____

❷ Draft. Use the information from **step 1** to write a first draft of your invitation on a separate sheet of paper. See below for a model.

> ¡Hola amigos!
>   Quiero invitarlos a una noche de baile caribeño en la sala de reuniones de la iglesia. La fiesta va a ser de las siete de la tarde hasta las once de la noche, el viernes, el cinco de mayo.
>   Quiero verlos a todos ustedes allí.
> Su amiga,
> Melisa

❸ Revise.

A. Read your note and check for the following:

_____ Is the spelling correct? (Consult a dictionary if you are not sure.)

_____ Did you use verbs correctly?

_____ Is all the necessary information included?

_____ Is there anything you should add or change?

B. Rewrite your invitation if there were any problems.

❹ Publish. Write a final copy of your invitation, making any necessary changes. Be sure to write or type neatly, as others will need to read your writing. You may also add a border decoration.

Realidades **1**

Capítulo 5A

Nombre _____

Hora _____

Fecha _____

Vocabulary Flash Cards, Sheet 1

Write the Spanish vocabulary word below each picture. If there is a word or phrase, copy it in the space provided. Be sure to include the article for each noun.

_____
_____

_____
_____

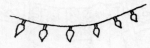

_____
_____

_____
_____

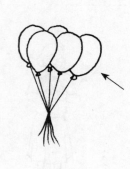

_____
_____

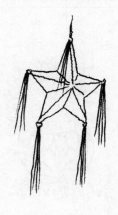

_____
_____

_____
_____

_____
_____

_____
_____

Realidades ①

Capítulo 5A

Nombre _____

Fecha _____

Hora _____

Vocabulary Flash Cards, Sheet 3

el cumpleaños

el esposo

la esposa

_____

_____

_____

_____

_____

_____

_____

_____

_____

_____

_____

_____

_____

_____

_____

_____

_____

_____

el hermanastro

_____

_____

la hermanastra

_____

_____

los hijos

_____

_____

el hijo

_____

_____

la hija

_____

_____

el padrastro

_____

_____

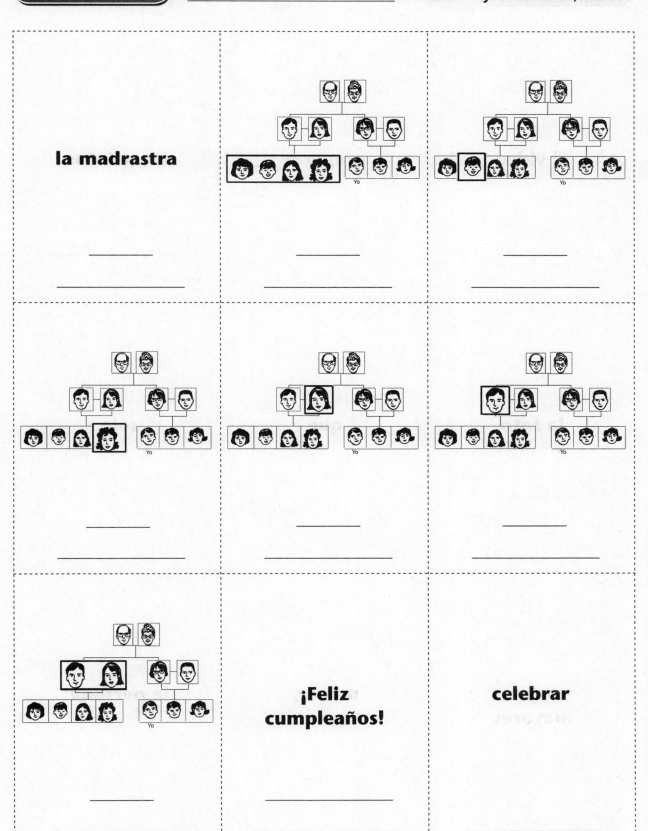

la madrastra

_____

_____

_____

_____

_____

_____

_____

_____

_____

_____

¡Feliz cumpleaños!

_____

_____

celebrar

_____

_____

Realidades ❶

Capítulo 5A

Nombre

Hora

Fecha

Vocabulary Flash Cards, Sheet 6

el video

preparar

sacar fotos

la foto

que

sólo

mayor, mayores

menor, menores

la persona

Tear out this page. Write the English words on the lines. Fold the paper along the dotted line to see the correct answers so you can check your work.

el abuelo   _____

la abuela   _____

el hermano   _____

la hermana   _____

el hijo   _____

la hija   _____

el padre (papá)   _____

la madre (mamá)   _____

el primo   _____

la prima   _____

el tío   _____

la tía   _____

la persona   _____

el gato   _____

el perro   _____

Fold In

Realidades 1

Capítulo 5A

Nombre _____

Fecha _____

Hora _____

Vocabulary Check, Sheet 2

Tear out this page. Write the Spanish words on the lines. Fold the paper along the dotted line to see the correct answers so you can check your work.

grandfather _____

grandmother _____

brother _____

sister _____

son _____

daughter _____

father _____

mother _____

cousin (*male*) _____

cousin (*female*) _____

uncle _____

aunt _____

person _____

cat _____

dog _____

Fold In

Nombre _____   Hora _____

Fecha _____   **Vocabulary Check, Sheet 3**

Tear out this page. Write the English words on the lines. Fold the paper along the dotted line to see the correct answers so you can check your work.

abrir _____

celebrar _____

decorar _____

hacer un video _____

romper _____

sacar fotos _____

la cámara _____

¡Feliz cumpleaños! _____

_____

los dulces _____

la flor, *pl.* las flores _____

el globo _____

la luz, *pl.* las luces _____

el papel picado _____

_____

el pastel _____

el regalo _____

Fold In

Tear out this page. Write the Spanish words on the lines. Fold the paper along the dotted line to see the correct answers so you can check your work.

to open _____

to celebrate _____

to decorate _____

to videotape _____

to break _____

to take pictures _____

camera _____

Happy birthday! _____

_____

candy _____

flower _____

balloon _____

light _____

cut-paper
decorations _____

cake _____

gift, present _____

To hear a complete list of the vocabulary for this chapter,
go to www.realidades.com and type in the Web Code jcd-0589.
Then click on **Repaso del capítulo**.

Fold In

The verb *tener* (p. 228)

- You have already learned some forms of the verb **tener** (*to have*): **tengo, tienes**.
- **Tener** is an irregular verb. Here are its forms.

yo	**tengo**	nosotros/nosotras	**tenemos**
tú	**tienes**	vosotros/vosotras	**tenéis**
usted/él/ella	**tiene**	ustedes/ellos/ellas	**tienen**

A. Write the correct form of **tener** next to each subject pronoun.

1. él _____
2. usted _____
3. ellos _____

4. nosotras _____
5. yo _____
6. tú _____

- **Tener** is used to show relationship or possession.
Tengo dos hermanas.	*I have two sisters.*
Tienes una bicicleta.	*You have a bicycle.*

- **Tener** is also used to express age, hunger, and thirst.
Tengo catorce años.	*I am fourteen years old.*
Tengo hambre.	*I am hungry.*
Tengo sed.	*I am thirsty.*

B. Read each numbered sentence with **tener**. Then write the number of that sentence in the correct column in the chart, depending on whether **tener** is used to express possession, age, thirst/hunger, or relationship. Follow the model.

possession	age	thirst/hunger	relationship
	#		

1. ¿Cuántos años tiene tu tío?
2. Nosotras tenemos diez primos.
3. ¿Tiene sed tu padre?

4. Mi hermana tiene tres años.
5. Yo tengo un regalo para mi abuela.
6. Mis primos tienen mucha hambre.

C. Now look at the following sentences and write in the missing forms of **tener**.

1. Mi prima Ana _____ once años.

2. Yo _____ un regalo para mi tía.

3. Mis hermanos _____ mucha hambre.

4. Nosotros _____ tres gatos.

5. ¿Cuántos años _____ tu padre?

6. ¿ _____ sed tu hermano?

D. Look at the family tree. Write forms of **tener** to complete each sentence below it.

Capitán   León   Alfonso   Alicia

Ramón   Sara   Anita   Eduardo

(16 años)   (10 años)   (19 años)   (22 años)   (12 años)   (15 años)   (9 años)

Patricia   Luis   Mariluisa   Carmen   Roberto   Carlos   Margarita

1. Patricia _____ tres primos.

2. Alfonso y Alicia _____ siete nietos.

3. Carlos _____ un tío.

4. Mariluisa, tú _____ tres hermanos.

5. Roberto y Carlos _____ una hermana.

6. Nosotros _____ un perro y un gato.

E. Now, answer the following questions in complete sentences.

   1. ¿Cuántos años tienes?

      Yo _____.

   2. ¿Cuántos hermanos tienes?

      Yo _____.

   3. ¿Tienes sed?

      Sí / No, _____.

   4. ¿Tienes hambre?

      Sí / No, _____.

Realidades 1

Capítulo 5A

Nombre _____

Hora _____

Fecha _____

Guided Practice Activities 5A-3

Possessive adjectives (p. 232)

- Possessive adjectives are used to indicate who owns what and to show relationships.
- In English, *my, your, his, her, our,* and *their* are possessive adjectives.

yo	**mi/mis**	nosotros nosotras	**nuestro/nuestros** **nuestra/nuestras**
tú	**tu/tus**	vosotros vosotras	**vuestro/vuestros** **vuestra/vuestras**
usted/él/ella	**su/sus**	ustedes/ellos/ellas	**su/sus**

- Spanish possessive adjectives, just like other adjectives, change their endings to reflect number. The **nosotros** and **nosotras** forms (**nuestro, nuestra, nuestros, nuestras**) also change to reflect gender.

mi herman**o** / **mis** herman**os**   BUT:
mi hij**a** / **mis** hij**as**   nuestr**o** tío / nuestr**os** tíos
tu flor / **tus** flores   nuestr**a** tía / nuestr**as** tías

A. Look at each noun. Write **S** if the noun is singular and **P** if it is plural.

1. _____ primo
2. _____ regalos
3. _____ hijas
4. _____ flor

5. _____ pastel
6. _____ tío
7. _____ globos
8. _____ familias

B. Now, circle the correct possessive adjective for each of the nouns from **part A**.

1. (**mi** / **mis**) primo
2. (**su** / **sus**) regalos
3. (**tu** / **tus**) hijas
4. (**mi** / **mis**) flor

5. (**tu** / **tus**) pastel
6. (**mi** / **mis**) tío
7. (**su** / **sus**) globos
8. (**tu** / **tus**) familias

C. Write **mi** in front of each singular noun and **mis** in front of each plural noun.

1. _____ piñata
2. _____ hermanos
3. _____ regalos
4. _____ flores

Realidades

Capítulo 5A

Nombre _____

Hora _____

Fecha _____

Guided Practice Activities 5A-4

Possessive adjectives (continued)

D. Look at each noun. Circle **S** if it is singular and **P** if it is plural. Circle **M** if it is masculine and **F** if it is feminine. Follow the model.

| Modelo | pasteles | (S /(P)) and ((M)/ F) |

1. decoraciones (S / P) and (M / F)   4. flores (S / P) and (M / F)
2. hijos (S / P) and (M / F)   5. luz (S / P) and (M / F)
3. gato (S / P) and (M / F)   6. globos (S / P) and (M / F)

E. Below are the nouns from **part D**. Write **nuestro**, **nuestra**, **nuestros**, or **nuestras** in front of each one. Follow the model.

| Modelo | _nuestros_ pasteles |

1. _____ decoraciones   4. _____ flores
2. _____ hijos   5. _____ luz
3. _____ gato   6. _____ globos

F. Circle the correct word to complete each sentence.

1. Tenemos (**nuestros / nuestras**) decoraciones en el coche.
2. Voy a la fiesta con (**mi / mis**) abuelos.
3. Aquí tienes (**tu / tus**) regalo.
4. Alicia va a hacer una piñata con (**su / sus**) hermano.
5. (**Nuestro / Nuestra**) familia saca muchas fotos en las fiestas.
6. Ella va a la fiesta con (**su / sus**) perro.

G. Write the correct form of the possessive adjective indicated to complete each sentence. Follow the models.

| Modelos | nuestro: | Ella es _nuestra_ tía. |
| | mi: | Roberto y Luis son _mis_ primos. |

1. tu: Elena y Margarita son _____ hermanas.
2. mi: León es _____ perro.
3. nuestro: Ellos son _____ primos.
4. su: Adela es _____ abuela.
5. su: Adela y Hernando son _____ abuelos.
6. nuestro: Roberto es _____ hijo.
7. nuestro: Lidia y Susana son _____ tías.

Realidades

Capítulo 5A

Nombre _____

Hora _____

Fecha _____

Guided Practice Activities 5A-5

Lectura: Mis padres te invitan a mi fiesta de quince años (pp. 238–239)

A. Part of the reading in your textbook is an invitation to a special birthday celebration. Before skimming the reading, write four pieces of information you would expect to find on an invitation to such a party.

1. _____
2. _____
3. _____
4. _____

> *Felipe Rivera López*
> *y Guadalupe Treviño Ibarra*
> *esperan el honor de su asistencia*
> *el sábado, 15 de mayo de 2004*
> *para celebrar los quince años de su hija*
> *María Teresa Rivera Treviño.*

B. Read through the text of the first part of the invitation (top right). Complete the following.

1. Circle the day of the week in the paragraph above.

2. Underline the date of the party.

3. What is the daughter's full name? _____

   _____

> *Misa*
> *a las cuatro de la tarde*
> *Iglesia Nuestra Señora de Guadalupe*
> *2374 Avenida Linda Vista, San Diego, California*
> *Recepción y cena-baile a las seis de la tarde*
> *Restaurante Luna*
> *7373 Calle Florida, San Diego, California*

C. Now, read the second part of the invitation and answer the questions below.

1. Write the times that each of the following takes place:

   (a) the Mass _____   **(b)** the reception _____

2. What will people be doing at the reception? _____

3. At what kind of place will the reception be held? _____

D. Now look back at **part A**. Did you find all of the information you were looking for in the reading? Fill in the simple facts of the reception below.

For whom: _____

Time: _____

Date: _____

Location: _____

Presentación oral (p. 241)

Task: Pretend you are living with a host family in Chile. They want to know about your family back home. Show them photographs of two family members and talk about the people shown.

A. You will need to have brought in two family photos or "created" photos from an imaginary family by using pictures from a magazine. Use the chart below to organize what you want to say about each person. Follow the model and write similar information about your family members.

Nombre	Es mi...	Edad	Actividad favorita
Isabel	hermana menor	9 años	le gusta cantar

B. Since you will be presenting the information above orally, you will need to put everything into complete sentences. Read the model below to get you started. Be sure to practice speaking clearly when you read the model.

> *Se llama Isabel. Ella es mi hermana menor. Tiene nueve años. A Isabel le gusta cantar. Es muy artística.*

C. Fill in the spaces below with the information you gathered from **part A**. Make sure you provide all the information you listed about each person.

Person 1: Se llama _____. (**Él / Ella**) es mi _____.

Tiene _____ años. A _____ le gusta _____.

Es _____.

Person 2: Se llama _____. (**Él / Ella**) es mi _____.

Tiene _____ años. A _____ le gusta _____.

Es _____.

D. Practice your presentation with the photos.
Remember to:

_____ provide all the information on each family member.
_____ use complete sentences.
_____ speak clearly.

Write the Spanish vocabulary word below each picture. If there is a word or phrase, copy it in the space provided. Be sure to include the article for each noun.

Realidades **1**

Capítulo 5B

Nombre _____

Hora _____

Fecha _____

Vocabulary Flash Cards, Sheet 2

_____

_____

_____

_____

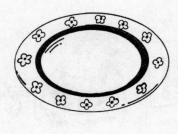

_____

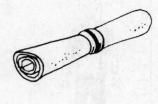

_____

_____

_____

_____

Realidades 1

Capítulo 5B

Nombre _____

Hora _____

Fecha _____

Vocabulary Flash Cards, Sheet 3

traer

el plato principal

Realidades ❶

Capítulo 5B

Nombre _____

Fecha _____

Hora _____

Vocabulary Flash Cards, Sheet 4

corto, corta _____ , _____	**guapo, guapa** _____ , _____	**el joven** _____ _____
la joven _____ _____	**el pelo** _____ _____	**canoso** _____ _____
castaño _____	**negro** _____	**rubio** _____

**pelirrojo,
pelirroja**

_____,

_____

**delicioso,
deliciosa**

_____,

_____

desear

_____

pedir

_____

**rico,
rica**

_____,

_____

Me falta(n)...

_____

Quisiera...

_____

ahora

_____

**¿Algo
más?**

_____

Realidades **1**

Capítulo 5B

Nombre

Fecha

Hora

Vocabulary Flash Cards, Sheet 6

De nada.

_____

_____

otro,
otra

_____,

_____

¿Me trae...?

_____

_____

Le traigo...

_____

_____

¡Qué...!

_____

_____

largo,
larga

_____

_____

yo
traigo

_____

_____

el joven

_____ _____

de postre

_____

_____

Tear out this page. Write the English words on the lines. Fold the paper along the dotted line to see the correct answers so you can check your work.

el hombre _____

la mujer _____

corto, corta _____

joven _____

largo, larga _____

viejo, vieja _____

el pelo _____

canoso _____

castaño _____

negro _____

rubio _____

pelirrojo,
pelirroja _____

desear _____

pedir _____

el plato
principal _____

Fold In

Tear out this page. Write the Spanish words on the lines. Fold the paper along the dotted line to see the correct answers so you can check your work.

man   _____

woman   _____

short (length)   _____

young   _____

long   _____

old   _____

hair   _____

gray   _____

brown (chestnut)   _____

black   _____

blond   _____

red-haired   _____

_____

to want   _____

to order   _____

main dish   _____

_____

Fold In

¿Cómo te llamas?

It is the first day of school in Madrid, and students are getting to know each other. Complete the dialogues by circling the appropriate words and phrases.

1. **A:** ¡Hola! (Hasta luego. / ¿Cómo te llamas?)

   B: Me llamo Rubén. ¿Y tú?

   A: Me llamo Antonio.

   B: (Mucho gusto. / Bien, gracias.)

   A: Igualmente, Rubén.

2. It is 9:00 in the morning.

   A: (¡Buenas tardes! / ¡Buenos días!) ¿Cómo te llamas?

   B: Buenos días. Me llamo Rosalía. ¿Cómo te llamas tú?

   A: Me llamo Enrique. (¿Cómo estás, Rosalía? / Gracias, Rosalía.)

   B: Muy bien, gracias. ¿Y tú?

   A: (Encantado. / Bien.)

   B: Adiós, Enrique.

   A: (¡Sí! / ¡Nos vemos!)

3. It is now 2:00 P.M.

   A: ¡Buenas tardes, Sr. Gómez!

   B: (¡Buenas noches! / ¡Buenas tardes!) ¿Cómo te llamas?

   A: Me llamo Margarita.

   B: Mucho gusto, Margarita.

   A: (Buenos días. / Encantada.) ¡Adiós, Sr. Gómez!

   B: (¡Hasta luego! / ¡Bien!)

Realidades 1

Para empezar

En la escuela

Nombre _____

Fecha _____

Hora _____

Core Practice **P–2**

¿Eres formal o informal?

A. Circle the phrases below that can be used to talk to teachers. Underline the phrases that can be used to talk to other students. Some phrases may be both circled and underlined.

¡Hola!	¿Cómo está Ud.?	Mucho gusto.	¿Qué tal?
Buenos días.	¿Cómo estás?	¿Y usted?	¡Hasta luego!
¡Nos vemos!	Buenos días, señor.	Estoy bien.	¿Y tú?

B. Circle **Ud.** or **tú** to indicate how you would address the person being spoken to.

1. "Hola, Sr. Gómez."   **Ud.**   **Tú**

2. "¿Qué tal, Luis?"   **Ud.**   **Tú**

3. "¿Cómo estás, Paco?"   **Ud.**   **Tú**

4. "¡Buenos días, profesor!"   **Ud.**   **Tú**

5. "Adiós, señora."   **Ud.**   **Tú**

C. Number the following phrases from 1–5 to create a logical conversation. Number 1 should indicate the first thing that was said, and 5 should indicate the last thing that was said.

_____ Bien, gracias, ¿y Ud.?

_____ ¡Hasta luego!

_____ Buenas tardes.

_____ ¡Buenas tardes! ¿Cómo está Ud.?

_____ Muy bien. ¡Adiós!

Realidades ①

Para empezar

En la escuela

Nombre _____

Fecha _____

Hora _____

Core Practice **P–3**

Por favor

Your Spanish teacher has asked you to learn some basic classroom commands. Write the letter of the appropriate phrase next to the picture it corresponds to.

1. _____

2. _____

3. _____

4. _____

5. _____

A. Saquen una hoja de papel.

B. Siéntense, por favor.

C. Repitan, por favor.

D. ¡Silencio, por favor!

E. Levántense, por favor.

Realidades ❶

Para empezar

En la escuela

Nombre _____

Fecha _____

Hora _____

Core Practice **P–4**

Los números

A. Here are some simple math problems. First, fill in each blank with the correct number. Then, find the Spanish word for that number in the word search to the right.

1. $7 \times 8 =$ _____

2. $50, 40,$ _____ $, 20, 10 \ldots$

3. $75 + 7 =$ _____

4. $55, 60, 65,$ _____ $, 75, 80 \ldots$

5. $97, 98, 99,$ _____ $\ldots$

6. $24 \div 2 =$ _____

7. $72, 60,$ _____ $, 36, 24 \ldots$

```
O C H E N T A Y D O S L C T
M O J X U E Y S W H U S S R
O G X L E G I L E C E H M E
G U N V C T B C R T U C G I
O H C O Y A T N E R A U C N
T T C C V A T N W L Y F W T
M B K W C E T U Y O N L O A
E F Q F Q A N B Y F K R L V
H C E E A Y R T D M W D A W
C I N C U E N T A Y S E I S
R E C O J I W C J Y G Q U Q
U L J D I U D G V X D D K G
```

B. As exchange students, you and your classmates are finding it hard to get used to the time difference. Below are some statements about time differences in various U.S and Spanish-speaking cities. Write in the times that correspond to each. Follow the model.

Modelo | `10:30` `10:30` | Cuando son las diez y media en Chicago, son las diez y media en Panamá.

1. | `:` `:` | Cuando es la una y media en Washington, D.C., son las dos y media en Buenos Aires.

2. | `:` `:` | Cuando son las doce y cuarto en la Ciudad de México, es la una y cuarto en San Juan.

3. | `:` `:` | Cuando son las diez en Nueva York, son las diez en La Habana.

4. | `:` `:` | Cuando son las seis y cuarto en San Francisco, son las ocho y cuarto en Lima.

5. | `:` `:` | Cuando son las dos de la mañana (*A.M.*) en Madrid, son las siete de la tarde (*P.M.*) en Bogotá.

realidades.com ✓

• Web Code: jcd-0002

Realidades 1

Para empezar

En la escuela

Nombre _____

Fecha _____

Hora _____

Core Practice **P-5**

El cuerpo

A. You are watching your neighbor's toddler Anita for a few hours after school. She is playing with her **muñequita** (*doll*) Chula and is practicing words to identify body parts. Help her by drawing lines to connect her doll's body parts with their correct names.

el ojo   la boca

el dedo   el estómago

la nariz

la mano

el pie

la cabeza   la pierna

B. Now write three sentences using the phrase **me duele** and body parts.

1. _____

2. _____

3. _____

Realidades ❶

Para empezar

En la clase

Nombre _____

Fecha _____

Hora _____

Core Practice **P–6**

Combinaciones

A. Write the correct article (**el** or **la**, or both) before each of the items below.

1. _____ bolígrafo

2. _____ lápiz

3. _____ sala de clases

4. _____ profesora

5. _____ cuaderno

6. _____ carpeta

7. _____ profesor

8. _____ estudiante

9. _____ pupitre

10. _____ hoja de papel

B. To make sure that there are enough school supplies for everyone, your teacher has asked you to help take inventory. Complete each sentence by writing the name and number of each item pictured. Follow the model.

Modelo   veinticinco   No hay un _*libro*_ . Hay _25_ _____ .

1. sesenta y siete   No hay un _____ . Hay _____ .

2. cien   No hay una _____ . Hay _____ .

3. veintiuno   No hay un _____ . Hay _____ .

4. diecinueve   No hay un _____ . Hay _____ .

5.  treinta y seis   No hay un _____ . Hay _____ .

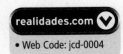

realidades.com
• Web Code: jcd-0004

Realidades 1

Para empezar

En la clase

Nombre _____

Fecha _____

Hora _____

Core Practice **P–7**

El calendario

February has just ended on a leap year. Because of this, Pepe is completely lost in planning out March. Help him get his days straight by using the calendar. Follow the model.

lunes	martes	miércoles	jueves	viernes	sábado	domingo
				1	2	3
4	5	6	7	8	9	10
11	12	13	14	15	16	17
18	19	20	21	22	23	24
25	26	27	28	29	30	31

Modelo   TÚ: Hoy es el cinco de marzo.

PEPE: ¿Es jueves?

TÚ: No, es martes.

1. TÚ: Hoy es el treinta de marzo.

PEPE: ¿Es lunes?

TÚ: _____

2. TÚ: Hoy es el trece de marzo.

PEPE: ¿Es domingo?

TÚ: _____

3. TÚ: Hoy es el veintiuno de marzo.

PEPE: ¿Es domingo?

TÚ: _____

4. TÚ: Hoy es el once de marzo.

PEPE: ¿Es miércoles?

TÚ: _____

5. TÚ: Hoy es el primero de marzo.

PEPE: ¿Es martes?

TÚ: _____

6. TÚ: Hoy es el doce de marzo.

PEPE: ¿Es sábado?

TÚ: _____

7. TÚ: Hoy es el veinticuatro de marzo.

PEPE: ¿Es viernes?

TÚ: _____

8. TÚ: Hoy es el diecisiete de marzo.

PEPE: ¿Es lunes?

TÚ: _____

Realidades ①

Para empezar

En la clase

Nombre _____

Fecha _____

Hora _____

Core Practice **P-8**

La fecha

A. Write out the following dates in Spanish. The first one is done for you.

Día/Mes

2/12 *el dos de diciembre* _____

9/3 _____

5/7 _____

4/9 _____

8/11 _____

1/1 _____

> **¿Recuerdas?**
>
> Remember that when writing the date in Spanish, the day precedes the month.
>
> • 19/12 = el 19 de diciembre = December 19
> • 27/3 = el 27 de marzo = March 27

B. Now, answer the following questions about dates in complete sentences.

1. ¿Cuál es la fecha de hoy?

_____

2. ¿El Día de San Valentín es el trece de enero?

_____

3. ¿Cuál es la fecha del Año Nuevo?

_____

4. ¿La Navidad (*Christmas*) es el 25 de noviembre?

_____

5. ¿Cuál es la fecha del Día de San Patricio?

_____

6. ¿Cuál es la fecha del Día de la Independencia?

_____

7. ¿Cuál es la fecha de mañana?

_____

Realidades 1

Para empezar

El tiempo

Nombre _____

Fecha _____

Hora _____

Core Practice **P-9**

¿Qué tiempo hace?

You and several Spanish-speaking exchange students are discussing the weather of your home countries.

A. Fill in the chart with the missing information for the area in which you live.

Meses	Estación	Tiempo
diciembre enero _____	_____	_____
marzo _____ _____	_____	_____
junio _____ _____	el verano	_____
_____ _____ noviembre	_____	hace viento, hace sol

B. Complete the dialogues below with information from the chart.

1. PROFESORA: ¿Qué tiempo hace en julio?

   ESTUDIANTE: _____

2. PROFESORA: ¿En enero hace calor?

   ESTUDIANTE: _____

3. PROFESORA: ¿En qué meses hace frío?

   ESTUDIANTE: _____

4. PROFESORA: ¿Qué tiempo hace en el verano?

   ESTUDIANTE: _____

5. PROFESORA: ¿Nieva en agosto?

   ESTUDIANTE: _____

Realidades ❶

Para empezar

Nombre _____

Fecha _____

Hora _____

Core Practice **P–10**

Repaso

Fill in the crossword puzzle with the Spanish translation of the English words given below.

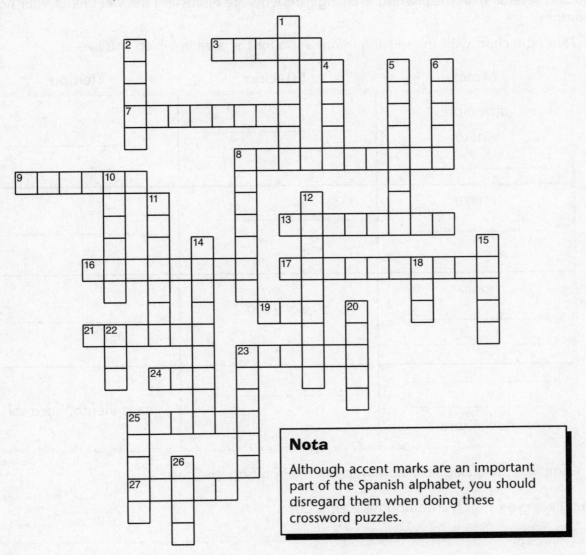

Nota

Although accent marks are an important part of the Spanish alphabet, you should disregard them when doing these crossword puzzles.

Across

3. pencil
7. season
8. See you later!
9. it is raining
13. it is cold
16. winter
17. September
19. day
21. head
23. madam, Mrs.
24. foot
25. week
27. fall

Down

1. Friday
2. Monday
4. it is snowing
5. male teacher
6. January
8. it is sunny
10. summer
11. desk
12. it is hot
14. spring
15. the date
18. month
20. arm
22. year
23. Saturday
25. sir, Mr.
26. Hello

Realidades 1

Para empezar

Nombre _____

Fecha _____

Hora _____

Core Practice **P–11**

Organizer

I. Vocabulary

Greetings and good-byes

_____

_____

_____

_____

Classroom objects

_____

_____

_____

_____

Body parts

_____

_____

_____

_____

_____

_____

Words to talk about time

_____

_____

_____

_____

Phrases to talk about names

_____

_____

Forms of address (Formal)

_____

_____

_____

Forms of address (Informal)

_____

Phrases to ask and tell how you feel

_____

_____

_____

• Web Code: jcd-0007

Realidades 1

Para empezar

Nombre _____

Fecha _____

Hora _____

Core Practice **P–12**

Days of the week	Months of the year
_____	_____
_____	_____
_____	_____
_____	_____
_____	_____
_____	_____
_____	_____

Seasons

_____

_____

_____

_____

Weather expressions

_____

_____

_____

II. Grammar

1. The word *the* is a definite article in English. The singular definite articles in Spanish are _____ and _____ , as in _____ **libro** and _____ **carpeta**.

2. Most nouns ending with _____ are masculine. Most nouns ending with _____ are feminine.

realidades.com

• Web Code: jcd-0007

Realidades ①

Capítulo 1A

Nombre _____

Fecha _____

Hora _____

Core Practice **1A–1**

La pregunta perfecta

Complete each sentence using the word or phrase that best describes the picture.

1. ¿Te gusta _____?

2. A mí me gusta _____.

3. ¿Te gusta _____?

4. No me gusta _____. ¿Y a ti?

5. Pues, me gusta mucho _____.

6. Sí, me gusta mucho _____.

7. ¿Te gusta mucho _____?

8. Me gusta _____.

9. ¡Me gusta mucho _____!

10. No, ¡no me gusta nada _____!

Realidades ①

Capítulo 1A

Nombre _____

Fecha _____

Hora _____

Core Practice **1A–2**

¿A ti también?

Several friends are talking at the bus stop about what they like and do not like to do. Based on the pictures, write the activity that the first person likes or does not like to do. Then, complete the second person's response. Make sure to use **también** or **tampoco** when expressing agreement and disagreement.

ENRIQUE: A mí me gusta mucho _____.
¿A ti te gusta?

1. DOLORES: Sí, _____.

PABLO: Me gusta _____.
¿A ti te gusta?

2. MARTA: No, _____.

JAIME: No me gusta _____.
¿A ti te gusta?

3. JULIO: No, _____.

MARÍA: Me gusta _____.
¿A ti te gusta?

4. JULIA: No _____.

CARMEN: No me gusta nada _____.
¿A ti te gusta?

5. JOSEFINA: Sí, _____.

ROBERTO: Me gusta _____.
¿A ti te gusta?

6. PEDRO: Sí, _____.

14 *A primera vista* ━ *Vocabulario en contexto*

Realidades ❶

Capítulo 1A

Nombre _____

Fecha _____

Hora _____

Core Practice **1A–3**

¿Te gusta o no te gusta?

You are talking to some new students about the things that they like to do. Using the drawings and the model below, complete the following mini-conversations.

Modelo

☺

— ¿Te gusta *hablar por teléfono?*

— *Sí, me gusta mucho.*

☹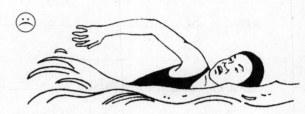

— ¿Te gusta *nadar?*

— *No, no me gusta nada.*

☹

1. — ¿Te gusta _____?

— _____.

☺

2. — ¿Te gusta _____?

— _____.

☺

3. — ¿Te gusta _____?

— _____.

☹

4. — ¿Te gusta _____?

— _____.

☺

5. — ¿Te gusta _____?

— _____.

☺

6. — ¿Te gusta _____?

— _____.

Realidades 1

Capítulo 1A

Nombre _____

Fecha _____

Hora _____

Core Practice **1A–4**

¿Qué te gusta hacer?

Complete the dialogues below to find out what activities these friends like and dislike.

1. MIGUEL: ¿Te gusta ir a la escuela?

   RITA: Sí. _____ mucho ir a la escuela.

   ¿Y _____?

   MIGUEL: Sí, a mí me gusta _____ también. No me gusta

   _____ ver la tele _____ jugar videojuegos.

   RITA: _____ tampoco.

2. JUAN: No _____ patinar.

   PAULA: _____ tampoco. Me gusta leer revistas.

   JUAN: ¿_____ más, trabajar o _____

   _____?

   PAULA: _____ hablar por teléfono.

   JUAN: Sí. A mí _____.

3. AMELIA: A mí _____ pasar tiempo con mis amigos.

   CARLOS: A mí me gusta _____ también.

   AMELIA: ¿Te gusta trabajar?

   CARLOS: No, _____.

   AMELIA: _____ tampoco.

realidades.com
• Web Code: jcd-0102

Realidades **1**

Capítulo 1A

Nombre

Fecha

Hora

Core Practice **1A–5**

El infinitivo

Decide what infinitive each picture represents. Then, based on its ending, write the verb in the appropriate column. Use the model as a guide.

	-ar	-er	-ir
Modelo	patinar		
1.	_____	_____	_____
2.	_____	_____	_____
3.	_____	_____	_____
4.	_____	_____	_____
5.	_____	_____	_____
6.	_____	_____	_____
7.	_____	_____	_____
8.	_____	_____	_____

• Web Code: jcd-0103

Realidades 1

Capítulo 1A

Nombre _____

Fecha _____

Hora _____

Core Practice **1A–6**

Las actividades en común

Cristina is feeling very negative. Using the pictures to help you, write Cristina's negative responses to Lola's questions. Use the model to help you.

Modelo

LOLA: *¿Te gusta patinar?* _____

CRISTINA: *No, no me gusta nada patinar.* _____

1.

LOLA: _____

CRISTINA: _____

2.

LOLA: _____

CRISTINA: _____

3.

LOLA: _____

CRISTINA: _____

4.

LOLA: _____

CRISTINA: _____

5.

LOLA: _____

CRISTINA: _____

realidades.com

• Web Code: jcd-0104

Realidades **1**

Capítulo 1A

Nombre _____

Fecha _____

Hora _____

Core Practice **1A–7**

La conversación completa

At lunch, you overhear a conversation between Sara and Graciela, who are trying to decide what they would like to do after school today. Since it is noisy in the cafeteria, you miss some of what they say. Read the conversation through to get the gist, then fill in the missing lines with what the friends probably said.

GRACIELA: ¿Qué te gusta hacer?

SARA: _____.

GRACIELA: ¿Nadar? Pero es el invierno. ¡Hace frío!

SARA: Sí. Pues, también _____.

GRACIELA: Pero hoy es martes y no hay programas buenos en la tele.

SARA: Pues, ¿qué _____ hacer a ti?

GRACIELA: _____.

SARA: ¡Uf! Hay un problema. No me gusta ni jugar videojuegos ni usar la computadora.

GRACIELA: Hmm . . . ¿_____?

SARA: No, _____ nada patinar.

GRACIELA: ¿Te gusta bailar o cantar?

SARA: No, _____.

GRACIELA: Pues, ¿qué _____, Sara?

SARA: _____ hablar por teléfono.

GRACIELA: ¡A mí también! ¿Cuál es tu número de teléfono?

Realidades

Capítulo 1A

Nombre _____

Fecha _____

Hora _____

Core Practice **1A–8**

Repaso

Fill in the crossword puzzle below with the actions indicated by the pictures.

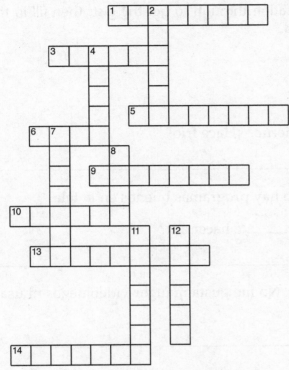

Down

2.

4.

7.

8.

11.

12.

Across

1.

3.

5.

6.

9.

10.

13.

14.

Realidades **1**

Capítulo 1A

Nombre _____

Fecha _____

Hora _____

Core Practice **1A–9**

Organizer

I. Vocabulary

Activities I like to do

_____

_____

_____

_____

_____

Activities I may not like to do

_____

_____

_____

_____

_____

Words to say what I like to do

_____

_____

_____

Words to say what I don't like to do

_____

_____

_____

Words to ask what others like to do

_____

_____

_____

_____

II. Grammar

1. The infinitive in English is expressed by writing the word _____ before a
   verb. In Spanish the infinitive is expressed by the verb endings _____ ,
   _____ , and _____ .

2. In order to say that something doesn't happen in Spanish, use the word
   _____ before the verb.

3. Use the word _____ to agree with someone who likes
   something. Use the word _____ to agree with someone
   who dislikes something.

4. If you do not like either of two choices, use the word _____ .

• Web Code: jcd-0107

Realidades ①

Capítulo 1B

Nombre _____

Fecha _____

Hora _____

Core Practice **1B–1**

¿Cómo es?

At school you see many different types of people. Describe each person you see in the picture by writing the appropriate adjective on the corresponding blank.

1. _____

2. _____

3. _____

4. _____

5. _____

6. _____

7. _____

8. _____

realidades.com
• Web Code: jcd-0111

Realidades 1

Nombre _____

Hora _____

Capítulo 1B

Fecha _____

Core Practice **1B–2**

Un juego de descripción

Each picture below represents a personality trait. Unscramble the word to identify each trait. Write down the trait, and then circle the picture that corresponds to the unscrambled word.

1. ísiattcar _____

2. rvoidate _____

3. ddonaesdreo _____

4. jadartobaar _____

5. iacoarsg _____

6. zeerosap _____

7. vesrdoaer _____

8. utoiesdas _____

Realidades ①

Capítulo 1B

Nombre _____

Fecha _____

Hora _____

Core Practice **1B–3**

¿Cómo eres?

Tito is interviewing Jorge and Ana, two new students from Costa Rica. Tito's questions are written below, but most of Jorge's and Ana's answers are missing. Complete their answers, using the model to help you.

Modelo   TITO: Ana, ¿eres perezosa?

ANA: No, _no soy perezosa_____.

1. TITO: Jorge, ¿eres talentoso?

    JORGE: Sí, _____.

2. TITO: Ana, ¿eres estudiosa?

    ANA: Sí, _____.

3. TITO: Jorge, ¿eres desordenado?

    JORGE: No, _____.

4. TITO: Ana, ¿eres deportista?

    ANA: No, _____.

5. TITO: Jorge, ¿eres sociable?

    JORGE: Sí, _____.

6. TITO: Ana, ¿eres paciente?

    ANA: No, _____.

7. TITO: Jorge, ¿eres inteligente?

    JORGE: Sí, _____.

8. TITO: Ana, ¿eres artística?

    ANA: No, _____.

realidades.com
• Web Code: jcd-0112

Realidades ①

Capítulo 1B

Nombre _____

Hora _____

Fecha _____

Core Practice **1B–4**

¿Qué les gusta?

Based on what each person likes to do, write a description of him or her. Follow the model.

Modelo   A Roberto le gusta esquiar.

Roberto es atrevido.

1. A Esteban le gusta tocar la guitarra.

_____

2. A Pedro le gusta hablar por teléfono.

_____

3. A Claudia le gusta practicar deportes.

_____

4. A Teresa le gusta estudiar.

_____

5. A Luz no le gusta trabajar.

_____

6. A Manuela le gusta ir a la escuela.

_____

7. A Carmen le gusta pasar tiempo con amigos.

_____

8. A Lucía le gusta dibujar.

_____

realidades.com ✔
• Web Code: jcd-0112

Realidades ①

Capítulo 1B

Nombre _____

Fecha _____

Hora _____

Core Practice **1B–5**

Me gusta . . .

Some new exchange students at your school are introducing themselves. Using the model as a guide, fill in the blanks in their statements with the actions and adjectives suggested by the pictures. Do not forget to use the correct (masculine or feminine) form of the adjective.

Modelo

A mí _me gusta leer_ _____ .

Yo _soy inteligente_ _____ .

1.

A mí _____ .

Yo _____ .

2.

A mí _____ .

Yo _____ .

3.

A mí _____ .

Yo _____ .

4.

A mí _____ .

Yo _____ .

5.

A mí _____ .

Yo _____ .

6.

A mí _____ .

Yo _____ .

realidades.com

• Web Code: jcd-0114

Realidades 1

Nombre _____

Hora _____

Capítulo 1B

Fecha _____

Core Practice **1B–6**

¿Un o una?

A. Look at the drawings below and decide if they represent masculine or feminine words. Then, label the item in the space provided. Don't forget to use the appropriate indefinite article (**un** or **una**).

Modelo   _un profesor_

1. _____

2. _____

3. _____

4. _____

5. _____

6. _____

B. Now, look at the drawings below and describe each person. Make sure to use all the words from the word bank. Don't forget to use the correct definite article (**el** or **la**) and to make the adjectives agree with the nouns.

| estudiante | familia | chico | chica | profesor | profesora |

Modelo   _La estudiante_
             es trabajadora.

1. _____

2. _____

3. _____

4. _____

5. _____

6. _____

realidades.com
• Web Code: jcd-0113

Manos a la obra ▬ *Gramática y vocabulario en uso* **27**

Oraciones completas

Choose sentence parts from each of the word banks below, then put them in the correct order to form complete sentences. Follow the model.

Subjects:		**Verbs:**	
Marta	Yo	es soy eres	
El Sr. Brown	Rolando		
La Srta. Moloy	Tú		

Indefinite articles + nouns:		**Adjectives:**	
un estudiante	una estudiante	reservado(a)	deportista
un chico	un profesor	inteligente	estudioso(a)
una chica	una profesora	perezoso(a)	bueno(a)

Modelo   *Yo soy un chico estudioso.* _____

1. _____

2. _____

3. _____

4. _____

5. _____

6. _____

7. _____

8. _____

9. _____

10. _____

realidades.com ✓
• Web Code: jcd-0115

Realidades ❶

Capítulo 1B

Nombre _____

Fecha _____

Hora _____

Core Practice **1B-8**

Repaso

Down ───────────

1. según mi ____
2. no paciente
3. no ordenado
5. Un chico/una chica que practica deportes es ____.
6. *I like:* "Me ____."

8.

11. No es trabajador. Es ____.

13.

15.

16. Le gusta pasar tiempo con amigos. Es ____.

18. —¿Cómo ____?
    —Soy sociable.

Across ───────────

4.
7. *nice, friendly*
9. no es malo, es ____
10. ¿ ____ se llama?

12.

14.

17.

19.

20.

Repaso del capítulo ━ *Crucigrama* **29**

Organizer

I. Vocabulary

Words that describe me

_____

_____

_____

_____

_____

Words that may describe others

_____

_____

_____

_____

_____

Words to ask what someone is like

_____

_____

_____

Words to tell what I am like

_____

_____

_____

II. Grammar

1. Most feminine adjectives end with the letter _____. Most masculine adjectives end with the letter _____.

2. Adjectives that can be either masculine or feminine may end with the letters _____ (as in the word _____) or the letter _____ (as in the word _____).

3. The two singular definite articles are _____ and _____. The two singular indefinite articles are _____ and _____.

4. In Spanish, adjectives come (before/after) the nouns they describe.

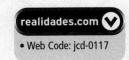

realidades.com

• Web Code: jcd-0117

Realidades **1**

Capítulo 2A

Nombre _____

Hora _____

Fecha _____

Core Practice **2A–1**

Las clases

A. Write the name of the item, and the school subject for which you might use it, in the appropriate column below.

¿Qué es?   ¿Para qué clase?

1. _____   1. _____

2. _____   2. _____

3. _____   3. _____

4. _____   4. _____

5. _____   5. _____

6. _____   6. _____

B. Now, unscramble the letters in each word below to find out what classes you have today and what you need to bring to school.

1. éilsgn: la clase de _____

2. trea: la clase de _____

3. ncoridcoiia: el _____

4. zlpiá: el _____

5. aduclcralao: la _____

6. ngtíalceoo: la clase de _____

7. birol: el _____

8. lpsñoea: la clase de _____

9. cámtmeistaa: la clase de _____

10. rteaa: la _____

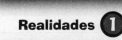

Realidades 1

Capítulo 2A

Nombre _____

Fecha _____

Hora _____

Core Practice **2A–2**

El horario

You have just received your class schedule. Using the model as a guide, write sentences to describe which classes you have and when you have them.

Horario

Hora	Clase
1	inglés
2	matemáticas
3	arte
4	ciencias sociales
5	el almuerzo
6	tecnología
7	español
8	educación física
9	ciencias naturales

Modelo Tengo ___*la clase de inglés*___ en ___*la primera hora*___.

1. Tengo _____ en _____.

2. Tengo _____ en _____.

3. Tengo _____ en _____.

4. Tengo _____ en _____.

5. Tengo _____ en _____.

6. Tengo _____ en _____.

7. Tengo _____ en _____.

8. Tengo _____ en _____.

realidades.com

• Web Code: jcd-0201

Realidades **1**

Capítulo 2A

Nombre _____

Fecha _____

Hora _____

Core Practice **2A–3**

¿Cómo son las clases?

Your friend Marcos is curious about which classes you like and which ones you don't like. Answer his questions using adjectives that you have learned in this chapter. Follow the model.

Modelo ¿Te gusta la clase de matemáticas?

Sí, _es interesante_.

1. — ¿Te gusta la clase de tecnología?

   — Sí, _____.

2. — ¿Te gusta la clase de español?

   — Sí, _____.

3. — ¿Te gusta la clase de matemáticas?

   — No, _____.

4. — ¿Te gusta la clase de ciencias sociales?

   — Sí, _____.

5. — ¿Te gusta la clase de ciencias naturales?

   — No, _____.

6. — ¿Te gusta la clase de educación física?

   — No, _____.

7. — ¿Te gusta la clase de inglés?

   — Sí, _____.

8. — ¿Te gusta la clase de arte?

   — Sí, _____.

¿Qué necesitas?

You are getting ready for school, and your mother wants to make sure you have everything. Answer her questions according to the model.

Modelo　MAMÁ: ¿Tienes la tarea?

　　　　　 TÚ: Sí, _tengo la tarea_ .

1. MAMÁ: ¿Tienes un libro?

   TÚ: Sí, _____.

2. MAMÁ: ¿Necesitas una calculadora?

   TÚ: No, _____.

3. MAMÁ: ¿Tienes una carpeta de argollas para la clase de matemáticas?

   TÚ: No, _____.

4. MAMÁ: ¿Necesitas un diccionario para la clase de español?

   TÚ: Sí, _____.

5. MAMÁ: ¿Tienes el cuaderno para la clase de arte?

   TÚ: No, _____.

6. MAMÁ: ¿Tienes un lápiz?

   TÚ: Sí, _____.

7. MAMÁ: ¿Necesitas el horario?

   TÚ: No, _____.

8. MAMÁ: ¿Tienes un bolígrafo?

   TÚ: Sí, _____.

Realidades **1**

Capítulo 2A

Nombre _____

Fecha _____

Hora _____

Core Practice **2A–5**

¡Todo el mundo!

A. How would you talk *about* the following people? Write the correct subject pronoun next to their names. Follow the model.

Modelo Marisol _____ *ella* _____

1. Pablo _____

2. María y Ester _____

3. Marta y yo _____

4. Tú y Marisol _____

5. El doctor Smith _____

6. Jorge y Tomás _____

7. Carmen _____

8. Alicia y Roberto _____

9. Rolando y Elena _____

B. How would you talk *to* the following people? Write the correct subject pronoun next to their names. Follow the model.

Modelo Tu amiga Josefina _____ *tú* _____

1. El profesor Santiago _____

2. Marta y Carmen _____

3. Anita y yo _____

4. Tu amigo Federico _____

5. La señorita Ibáñez _____

6. Ricardo _____

7. La profesora Álvarez _____

Realidades ①

Capítulo 2A

Nombre _____

Fecha _____

Hora _____

Core Practice **2A–6**

El verbo exacto

A. Fill in the chart below with all the forms of the verbs given.

	yo	tú	él/ella/Ud.	nosotros/nosotras	vosotros/vosotras	ellos/ellas/Uds.
hablar	hablo				habláis	hablan
estudiar				estudiamos	estudiáis	
enseñar		enseñas			enseñáis	
usar					usáis	
necesitar			necesita		necesitáis	

B. Now, fill in the blanks in the following sentences with the correct forms of the verbs in parentheses.

1. Ella _____ inglés. (estudiar)

2. Yo _____ mucho. (bailar)

3. Nosotros _____ por teléfono. (hablar)

4. Ellos _____ la computadora durante la primera hora. (usar)

5. ¿Quién _____ un bolígrafo? (necesitar)

6. Tú _____ en bicicleta mucho, ¿no? (montar)

7. Uds. _____ muy bien en la clase de arte. (dibujar)

8. Nosotras _____ hoy, ¿no? (patinar)

9. El profesor _____ la lección. (enseñar)

10. Ana y María _____ el libro de español. (necesitar)

11. Jaime _____ todos los días. (caminar)

12. Dolores y yo _____. (bailar)

13. Tú y tus amigos _____ muy bien. (cantar)

realidades.com ✓
• Web Code: jcd-0204

Realidades ①

Capítulo 2A

Nombre _____

Fecha _____

Hora _____

Core Practice **2A–7**

¿Qué hacen hoy?

A. Today everyone is doing what he or she likes to do. Follow the model to complete sentences about what everyone is doing.

Modelo A Luisa le gusta bailar. Hoy _____*ella baila*_____ .

1. A ti te gusta cantar. Hoy _____ .

2. A mí me gusta hablar por teléfono. Hoy _____ .

3. A Francisco le gusta patinar. Hoy _____ .

4. A Ud. le gusta dibujar. Hoy _____ .

5. A Teresa le gusta practicar deportes. Hoy _____ .

B. Using the pictures to help you, tell what everyone is doing today. Follow the model.

Manuel y Carlos

Modelo Hoy ____*ellos montan en monopatín*____ .

Amelia y yo

1. Hoy _____ .

tú y Roberto

2. Hoy _____ .

Cristina, Miguel y Linda

3. Hoy _____ .

tú y yo

4. Hoy _____ .

Joaquín y Jaime

5. Hoy _____ .

Sofía y Tomás

6. Hoy _____ .

Realidades 1

Capítulo 2A

Nombre _____

Hora _____

Fecha _____

Core Practice **2A–8**

Repaso

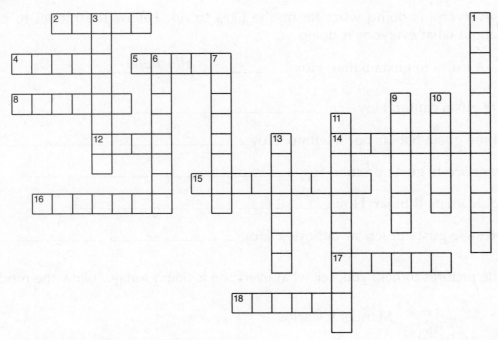

Across

2. No es difícil. Es ____.

4. la ____ de español

5. *homework*

8. educación ____

12. ____ el ____

14. no divertida

15. **ciencias** ____ : *science*

16. ____, octavo, noveno

17. ____ el ____

18. La profesora ____ la clase.

Down

1. ____ las ____

3. ____ **sociales**: *social studies*

6. *lunch*

7. carpeta de ____

9. *schedule*

10. cuarta, ____, sexta

11. ____ la clase de ____

13. primero, segundo, ____

Realidades **1**

Nombre _____

Hora _____

Capítulo 2A

Fecha _____

Core Practice **2A-9**

Organizer

I. Vocabulary

Classes I take in school

_____

_____

_____

_____

_____

Words to talk about the order of things

_____

_____

_____

_____

_____

_____

_____

Words used to refer to people

_____

_____

_____

_____

_____

_____

_____

Words to describe my classes

_____

_____

_____

_____

II. Grammar

1. The following are subject pronouns in Spanish:

   _____, _____, _____, _____, _____,

   _____, _____, _____, _____, _____,

2. Use _____ to address someone formally. Use _____
   to address someone informally.

3. The **-ar** verb endings are: _____ _____ _____ _____ _____ _____

   Now conjugate the verb **hablar**: _____ _____

   _____ _____

Realidades 1

Capítulo 2B

Nombre _____

Fecha _____

Hora _____

Core Practice **2B–1**

En la clase

Label the items in this Spanish class. Make sure to use the correct definite article (**el** or **la**).

1. _____

2. _____

3. _____

4. _____

5. _____

6. _____

7. _____

8. _____

9. _____

10. _____

11. _____

12. _____

realidades.com

• Web Code: jcd-0211

Realidades 1

Capítulo 2B

Nombre _____

Hora _____

Fecha _____

Core Practice **2B–2**

¡Mucha confusión!

You come home after school to find a scene of great confusion in your kitchen. Look at the picture, then describe what you see by filling in the blanks in the sentences below with the appropriate words to indicate location.

1. Paquito está _____ del escritorio.

2. Mamá está _____ de la luz (*the light*).

3. Papá está _____ de la ventana.

4. La papelera está _____ de la puerta.

5. Las hojas de papel están _____ de la mesa.

6. Carmen está _____ de la silla.

7. El reloj está _____ de la mesa.

8. El libro está _____ de la silla.

9. El teclado está _____ de la pantalla.

realidades.com
• Web Code: jcd-0211

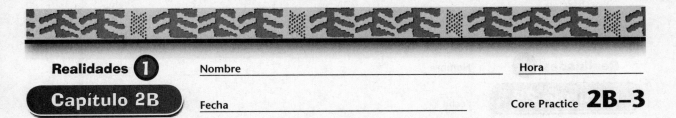

¿Dónde está?

Rosario is describing the room where she studies to a friend of hers on the phone. Using the picture below, write what she might say about where each item is located. There may be more than one right answer. Follow the model.

Modelo   La mochila está _*encima de la silla*_____.

1. El escritorio está _____.

2. La computadora está _____.

3. La papelera está _____.

4. El teclado está _____.

5. Una bandera de los Estados Unidos está _____.

6. La silla está _____.

7. El sacapuntas está _____.

8. Los libros de español están _____.

realidades.com
• Web Code: jcd-0212

¿Qué es esto?

Complete the following conversations that you overhear in school.

1. **A:** ¿_____ estudiantes hay en la clase?

   B: _____ veintidós estudiantes en la clase.

2. **A:** ¿_____?

   B: Es la mochila.

3. **A:** ¿_____ está la computadora?

   B: Está allí, al lado de las ventanas.

4. **A:** ¿_____ una bandera en la sala de clases?

   B: Sí, la bandera está allí.

5. **A:** ¿Dónde están los estudiantes?

   B: Los estudiantes _____ la clase de inglés.

6. **A:** ¿Dónde está el teclado?

   B: Está delante _____ la pantalla.

7. **A:** ¿Dónde está el diccionario?

   B: _____ está, debajo del escritorio.

8. **A:** ¿Qué hay _____ la mochila?

   B: Hay muchos libros.

Realidades ①

Capítulo 2B

Nombre _____

Hora _____

Fecha _____

Core Practice **2B–5**

¿Dónde están?

Spanish teachers are conversing in the faculty room. Fill in their conversations using the correct form of the verb **estar**.

1. — ¡Buenos días! ¿Cómo _____ Ud., Sra. López?

   — _____ bien, gracias.

2. — ¿Dónde _____ Raúl hoy? No _____ en

   mi clase.

   — ¿Raúl? Él _____ en la oficina.

3. — Yo no tengo mis libros. ¿Dónde _____?

   — Sus libros _____ encima de la mesa, profesor Martínez.

4. — ¿Cuántos estudiantes _____ aquí?

   — Diecinueve estudiantes _____ aquí. Uno

   no _____ aquí.

5. — ¿Dónde _____ mi diccionario?

   — El diccionario _____ detrás del escritorio.

6. — ¿Cómo _____ los estudiantes hoy?

   — Teresa _____ bien. Jorge y Bernardo _____

   regulares.

7. — Bien, profesores, ¿_____ nosotros listos (*ready*)? Todos los

   estudiantes _____ en la clase.

realidades.com

• Web Code: jcd-0214

Realidades **1**

Capítulo 2B

Nombre _____

Fecha _____

Hora _____

Core Practice **2B–6**

Muchas cosas

A. Fill in the chart below with singular and plural, definite and indefinite forms of the words given. The first word has been completed.

Definite		Indefinite	
singular	plural	singular	plural
la silla	las sillas	una silla	unas sillas
		un cuaderno	
			unos estudiantes
	las computadoras		
la mochila			
			unos relojes
		una bandera	
la profesora			

B. Now, fill in each sentence below with words from the chart.

1. Pablo, ¿necesitas _____ de los Estados Unidos? Aquí está.

2. Marta, ¿tienes _____? ¿Qué hora es?

3. Hay _____ Macintosh en la sala de clases.

4. _____ está en la sala de clases. Ella enseña la clase de tecnología.

5. Necesito _____ buena. Tengo muchos libros.

• Web Code: jcd-0213

Realidades 1

Capítulo 2B

Nombre _____

Fecha _____

Hora _____

Core Practice **2B–7**

¡Aquí está!

It was a very busy afternoon in your classroom, and things got a little out of order. Write eight sentences describing where things are to help your teacher find everything.

| Modelo | *El escritorio está debajo de la computadora* . |

1. _____

2. _____

3. _____

4. _____

5. _____

6. _____

7. _____

8. _____

realidades.com

• Web Code: jcd-0215

Realidades ❶

Capítulo 2B

Nombre _____

Fecha _____

Hora _____

Core Practice **2B–8**

Repaso

Across

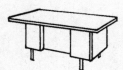

2.

5. la ____ de clases

9.

12.

14.

15. La ____ está detrás del pupitre.

16. La computadora está en la ____ .

17. *window*

19.

Down

1. *pencil sharpener*

3. no está encima de, está ____ de

4.

6.

7. al ____ de: *next to*

8. no delante

10.

11.

13. *mouse*

18. No estás aquí, estás ____ .

Realidades ❶

Capítulo 2B

Nombre _____

Fecha _____

Hora _____

Core Practice **2B–9**

Organizer

I. Vocabulary

Items in my classroom	Words to tell the location of things
_____	_____
_____	_____
_____	_____
_____	_____
_____	_____
_____	_____
_____	_____
_____	_____
_____	_____
_____	

II. Grammar

1. The forms of **estar** are: _____ _____

   _____ _____

   _____ _____

2. _____ and _____ are the singular definite articles in

   Spanish. Their plurals are _____ and _____.

3. The singular indefinite articles are _____ and _____ in

   Spanish. Their plurals are _____ and _____.

realidades.com

• Web Code: jcd-0216

Realidades ①

Capítulo 3A

Nombre _____

Fecha _____

Hora _____

Core Practice **3A–1**

Tus comidas favoritas

You are getting ready to travel as an exchange student to Spain and you are e-mailing your host family your opinions on different foods. Circle the name of the food item that best completes each sentence below.

1. En el desayuno, yo como _____

   a. cereal.   **b.** un sándwich.

2. Mi comida favorita es _____

   a. el té.   **b.** la pizza.

3. Mi fruta favorita es _____

   a. la fresa.   **b.** la sopa.

4. Para beber, yo prefiero _____

   a. los huevos.   **b.** los refrescos.

5. A mí me gusta el jugo de _____

   a. manzana.   **b.** salchicha.

6. En el almuerzo, yo como _____

   a. un sándwich.   **b.** cereal.

7. Cuando hace frío, yo bebo _____

   a. té helado.   **b.** té.

8. Un BLT es un sándwich de verduras con _____

   a. jamón.   **b.** tocino.

9. Cuando voy a un partido de béisbol, yo como _____

   a. la sopa.   **b.** un perrito caliente.

10. En un sándwich, prefiero _____

    a. el queso.   **b.** el yogur.

Realidades ①

Capítulo 3A

Nombre _____

Fecha _____

Hora _____

Core Practice **3A–2**

¿Desayuno o almuerzo?

Your aunt owns a restaurant and is making her breakfast and lunch menus for the day. Help her by writing the foods and beverages that you think she should serve for each meal in the right places on the menus. Some words may be used more than once.

realidades.com

• Web Code: jdd-0301

Realidades 1

Capítulo 3A

Nombre _____

Fecha _____

Hora _____

Core Practice **3A–3**

Tus preferencias

You are asking Corazón, an exchange student from Venezuela, about various food items that she likes to eat. Use the pictures to help you complete Corazón's answers. Follow the model.

Modelo

TÚ: ¿Tú comes galletas?

CORAZÓN: No. _Yo como huevos_ .

1. TÚ: ¿Tú comes salchichas?

CORAZÓN: No. _____ .

2. TÚ: ¿Te gusta más _____ o _____?

CORAZÓN: _____ el café.

3. TÚ: ¿Tú bebes mucha limonada?

CORAZÓN: No. _____ .

4. TÚ: ¿Tú comes mucha sopa de verduras?

CORAZÓN: No. _____ .

5. TÚ: ¿Tú bebes té helado?

CORAZÓN: No. _____ .

6. TÚ: ¿Tú compartes el desayuno con amigos?

CORAZÓN: No. _____ .

realidades.com
• Web Code: jcd-0302

A primera vista — *Videohistoria* **51**

Realidades ❶

Capítulo 3A

Nombre _____

Fecha _____

Hora _____

Core Practice **3A–4**

¿Qué comes?

Carolina, the new exchange student, is having a hard time figuring out the kinds of foods that people like to eat. Answer her questions in complete sentences, using **¡Qué asco!** and **¡Por supuesto!** in at least one answer each.

1. ¿Comes hamburguesas con plátanos?

_____

2. ¿Comes el sándwich de jamón y queso en el almuerzo?

_____

3. ¿Bebes leche en el desayuno?

_____

4. ¿Te gusta la pizza con la ensalada de frutas?

_____

5. ¿Comes papas fritas en el desayuno?

_____

6. ¿Compartes la comida con tu familia?

_____

7. ¿Comes un perro caliente todos los días?

_____

8. ¿Te encantan las galletas con leche?

_____

Realidades ①

Capítulo 3A

Nombre _____

Fecha _____

Hora _____

Core Practice **3A–5**

El verbo correcto

A. Fill in the chart below with all the forms of the verbs given.

	yo	tú	él/ella/Ud.	nosotros/ nosotras	vosotros/ vosotras	ellos/ ellas/Uds.
comer			*come*		*coméis*	
beber		*bebes*			*bebéis*	
comprender	*comprendo*				*comprendéis*	
escribir				*escribimos*	*escribís*	
compartir					*compartís*	*comparten*

B. Now, using the verbs from Part A, write the missing verb to complete each sentence below.

1. Antonio _____ sus papas fritas con Amelia.

2. Uds. _____ los sándwiches de queso.

3. Yo _____ las salchichas en el desayuno.

4. Nosotros _____ el té helado.

5. Ana _____ la tarea.

6. Tú _____ una carta al profesor.

7. Yo _____ el pan con Jorge.

8. Él _____ jugo de naranja en el desayuno.

9. Nosotros _____ con un lápiz.

10. Paula y Guillermo hablan y _____ español.

11. ¿_____ tú leche en el desayuno?

12. Manolo y Federico _____ las galletas con Susana.

• Web Code: jcd-0303

Manos a la obra ▬ *Gramática y vocabulario en uso* **53**

Realidades 1

Capítulo 3A

Nombre _____

Fecha _____

Hora _____

Core Practice **3A–6**

¿Qué te gusta?

A. List your food preferences in the blanks below.

Me gusta	Me gustan	Me encanta	Me encantan
_____	_____	_____	*los sándwiches*
_____	_____	_____	_____
			_____

B. Now, organize your preferences into complete sentences. Follow the model.

Modelo *Me encantan los sándwiches.* _____

1. _____

2. _____

3. _____

4. _____

5. _____

6. _____

7. _____

8. _____

C. Using the words given, write a sentence about each food. Follow the model.

Modelo El té (encantar) *Me encanta el té.* _____

1. los plátanos (gustar) _____

2. la pizza (encantar) _____

3. las papas fritas (encantar) _____

4. el pan (gustar) _____

realidades.com
• Web Code: jdd-0304

Realidades 1

Capítulo 3A

Nombre _____

Fecha _____

Hora _____

Core Practice **3A–7**

Mini-conversaciones

Fill in the blanks in the mini-conversations below with the most logical question or answer.

1. — ¿Comparten Uds. el sándwich de jamón y queso?

   — Sí, nosotros _____ el sándwich.

2. — ¿_____ tú todos los días?

   — No, nunca corro. No me gusta.

3. — ¿_____ en el desayuno?

   — ¡Qué asco! No me gustan los plátanos.

4. — ¿_____?

   — Sí, profesora. Comprendemos la lección.

5. — ¿_____?

   — Mi jugo favorito es el jugo de manzana.

6. — ¿_____?

   — Más o menos. Me gusta más la pizza.

7. — ¿_____?

   — ¡Por supuesto! Me encanta el cereal.

Realidades 1

Capítulo 3A

Nombre _____

Fecha _____

Hora _____

Core Practice **3A–8**

Repaso

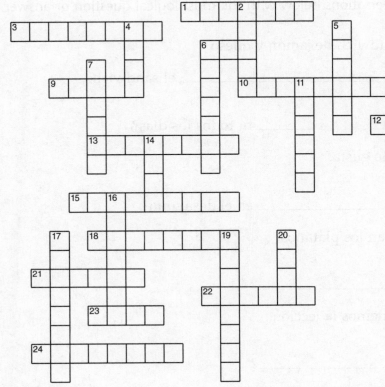

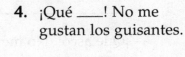

Down ───────────────

2. más o ____
4. ¡Qué ____! No me gustan los guisantes.

5.

6.
7. el té ____
8. las ____ fritas
11. *food*

14.

16. un jugo de ____
17. No como carne. Me gusta la sopa de ____.
19. En los Estados Unidos el ____ es un sándwich y algo de beber.
20. un ____ de naranja

Across ───────────────

1. *always*
3. El Monstruo Comegalletas come muchas ____.
6. el ____ tostado
9. Me gusta el sándwich de jamón y ____.

10.

12.
13. Muchas personas comen cereales con leche en el ____.

15. ¿Te gusta ____ el almuerzo con tus amigos?
18. Me gusta la ____ de frutas, no de lechuga.
21. un yogur de ____

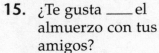

22.

23.
24. el perrito ____

Realidades **1**

Capítulo 3A

Nombre _____

Fecha _____

Hora _____

Core Practice **3A–9**

Organizer

I. Vocabulary

Breakfast foods

_____

_____

_____

_____

_____

Lunch foods

_____

_____

_____

_____

_____

Beverages

_____

_____

_____

Words to express likes/dislikes

_____

_____

_____

_____

II. Grammar

1. The **-er** verb endings are: - _____   - _____

     - _____   - _____

     - _____   - _____

   Now conjugate the verb **beber**: _____   _____

   _____   _____

2. The **-ir** verb endings are: - _____   - _____

     - _____   - _____

     - _____   - _____

   Now conjugate the verb **compartir**: _____   _____

   _____   _____

3. To use **me gusta** and **me encanta** to talk about plural nouns, you add the letter _____ to the end of the verb.

realidades.com
• Web Code: jcd-0306

Nombre _____

Hora _____

Fecha _____

Core Practice **3B–1**

¡A cenar!

A. You are having a party, and you need to make a shopping list. Write at least three items that you might want to buy under each category. You may use vocabulary from other chapters.

La ensalada de frutas:

_____

_____

_____

_____

Las verduras:

_____

_____

_____

_____

La carne:

_____

_____

_____

_____

Bebemos:

_____

_____

_____

_____

B. Now write three things your guests might like to eat after dinner.

_____

_____

_____

Realidades 1

Capítulo 3B

Nombre _____

Fecha _____

Hora _____

Core Practice **3B–2**

Más comida

A. Name the most logical food category to which each group of items belongs.

1. el bistec, el pollo, el pescado   _____

2. las zanahorias, la cebolla, los guisantes   _____

3. las uvas, las manzanas   _____

4. el postre, la mantequilla   _____

B. Now, answer the following questions logically in complete sentences.

1. ¿Debemos comer las uvas, el helado o los pasteles para mantener la salud?

_____

2. ¿Es sabrosa la ensalada de frutas con las papas o con los plátanos?

_____

3. ¿Comemos la mantequilla con el pan tostado o con el bistec?

_____

4. ¿Bebemos los refrescos o el agua para mantener la salud?

_____

C. Using the foods below, write sentences telling whether we should or shouldn't eat or drink each thing to maintain good health. Follow the model.

el agua *Debemos beber el agua para mantener la salud.* _____

1. los tomates _____

2. las grasas _____

3. los plátanos _____

4. las uvas _____

5. la mantequilla _____

6. la leche _____

realidades.com
• Web Code: jcd-0311

Realidades 1

Capítulo 3B

Nombre _____

Fecha _____

Hora _____

Core Practice **3B-3**

La respuesta perfecta

You are learning about fitness and nutrition at school, and your friends want to know more. Answer their questions or respond to their statements in complete sentences.

1. ¿Es el tomate bueno para la salud?

   _____

2. ¿Por qué caminas todos los días?

   _____

3. ¿La mantequilla es buena para la salud?

   _____

4. Creo que las grasas son horribles.

   _____

5. ¿Qué debes hacer para mantener la salud?

   _____

6. ¿Prefieres levantar pesas o caminar?

   _____

7. Creo que los espaguetis son sabrosos. ¿Y tú?

   _____

realidades.com

• Web Code: jcd-0312

Realidades ①

Capítulo 3B

Nombre _____

Fecha _____

Hora _____

Core Practice **3B–4**

¿Qué comes?

Angel is asking his friend Estela about foods she likes. Fill in the blanks with the foods suggested by the pictures, then complete Estela's answers.

1. — ¿Te gustan _____?

   — No, _____.

2. — ¿Prefieres _____ con _____
   en el almuerzo o en la cena?

   — _____ en el almuerzo.

3. — ¿Te gustan _____?

   — Sí, _____.

4. — ¿Prefieres _____ de chocolate o de fruta?

   — _____ de chocolate.

5. — ¿Comes _____?

   — Sí, _____.

6. — ¿Siempre comes _____ en el almuerzo?

   — No, _____.

7. — ¿Te gusta el _____ con _____?

   — Sí, _____.

Realidades 1

Capítulo 3B

Nombre _____

Fecha _____

Hora _____

Core Practice **3B–5**

Las descripciones

A. Fill in the chart below with the singular and plural, masculine and feminine forms of the adjectives given.

Masculine		Feminine	
singular	plural	singular	plural
sabroso			
	prácticos		
		fácil	
	aburridos		
			difíciles
divertido			
		artística	
			buenas
trabajador			

B. Now, complete the sentences below, using some of the words from the chart above. There may be more than one right answer.

1. La ensalada de frutas es _____ para la salud.

2. Me gustan mis clases; son _____.

3. La tarea de matemáticas es _____.

4. Te gustan las computadoras porque son _____.

5. Mi profesor no come pescado porque cree que no es _____.

6. Mis amigos son _____; dibujan muy bien.

7. Tus amigos son muy _____; trabajan mucho.

8. Esquiar y nadar son actividades muy _____.

realidades.com

• Web Code: jcd-0313

Realidades ❶

Capítulo 3B

Nombre _____

Hora _____

Fecha _____

Core Practice **3B–6**

¿Cómo son?

Describe the following people using the pictures as clues. Use a form of **ser** plus an adjective.
Follow the model.

Modelo

¿Cómo _____ es _____ él?

Es popular _____.

1. ¿Cómo _____ él?

_____.

2. ¿Cómo _____ ella?

_____.

3. ¿Cómo _____ ellas?

_____.

4. ¿Cómo _____ ellos?

_____.

5. ¿Cómo _____ nosotras?

_____.

6. ¿Cómo _____ yo?

_____.

Realidades ❶

Capítulo 3B

Nombre _____

Fecha _____

Hora _____

Core Practice **3B–7**

La buena salud

Your cousin Eva has started a new diet and exercise program, and she has sent you an e-mail telling you all about it. Read her e-mail and answer the questions below in complete sentences.

Hola,

Para mantener la salud, como muchas verduras y frutas cada día. ¡Creo que son sabrosas! Yo hago ejercicio también. Me gusta caminar, pero prefiero levantar pesas. Siempre bebo mucha agua, y es mi bebida favorita. No debemos comer los pasteles, porque son malos para la salud. ¿Estás de acuerdo?

1. ¿Qué come Eva para mantener la salud?

_____

2. ¿Eva hace ejercicio?

_____

3. ¿A Eva le gustan las frutas?

_____

4. ¿Qué prefiere hacer Eva para mantener la salud?

_____

5. ¿Cuál es la bebida favorita de Eva?

_____

6. ¿Por qué no debemos comer los pasteles?

_____

realidades.com
• Web Code: jcd-315

Realidades ①

Capítulo 3B

Nombre _____

Fecha _____

Hora _____

Core Practice **3B–8**

Repaso

Across ────────────

3. el ___

5.

6. Prefiero las ensaladas de ___ y tomate.

8. el ___

10. Debes comer bien para mantener la ___.

12. *drinks*

13. el ___

16. *something*

18. Tengo ___. Necesito comer.

20. estoy de ___

22. Los ___ no son buenos para la salud pero son sabrosos.

24. ___ comer bien para mantener la salud.

Down ────────────

1. *meat*

2. un ___

4. las ___ verdes

7. los ___

9. Yo prefiero ___ la salud y comer bien.

11. las ___

14. *carrots*

15. Me gusta la comida de tu mamá. Es muy ___.

17.

19.

21. *dinner*

23. ___ los días; siempre

Realidades **1**

Capítulo 3B

Nombre _____

Fecha _____

Hora _____

Core Practice **3B–9**

Organizer

I. Vocabulary

Fruits and vegetables

_____

_____

_____

_____

Starches

_____

_____

_____

_____

General food terms

_____

_____

_____

_____

Types of exercise

_____

_____

_____

_____

II. Grammar

1. Adjectives are _____ when describing one person or thing, and

    _____ when describing more than one person or thing.

2. To make an adjective plural, add _____ if the last letter is a vowel

    and _____ if the last letter is a consonant.

3. The forms of **ser** are: _____ _____

    _____ _____

    _____ _____

• Web Code: jcd-316

Realidades **1**

Capítulo 4A

Nombre _____

Fecha _____

Hora _____

Core Practice **4A–1**

¿Qué hacen?

What do the people in your neighborhood like to do in their free time? Complete the following sentences based on the pictures.

 **1.** La Sra. García lee un libro en

_____.

 **2.** Jesús levanta pesas en

_____.

 **3.** Los lunes tengo _____

con el Sr. Casals.

 **4.** A Pedro le gusta pasar tiempo en _____

cuando tiene tiempo libre.

 **5.** Elena y Tomás prefieren ir al _____

los viernes.

 **6.** A mí me gusta ir a _____

cuando hace calor.

 **7.** A Sara le gusta caminar en

_____.

 **8.** Me gusta ir al _____

para comer.

realidades.com **V**

• Web Code: jcd-0401

A primera vista ▬ *Vocabulario en contexto* **67**

Realidades ❶

Capítulo 4A

Nombre _____

Fecha _____

Hora _____

Core Practice **4A–2**

¿Adónde vas?

Where do you go to do the following things? Write your answers in complete sentences. Follow the model.

Modelo   esquiar   *Voy a las montañas para esquiar.* _____

1. trabajar   _____

2. leer, estudiar   _____

3. hablar español   _____

4. correr, caminar   _____

5. ir de compras   _____

6. tocar el piano   _____

7. comer, beber   _____

8. ver una película   _____

9. nadar   _____

10. hacer ejercicio   _____

11. estar con amigos   _____

12. levantar pesas   _____

• Web Code: jcd-0401

Realidades ❶

Capítulo 4A

Nombre _____

Fecha _____

Hora _____

Core Practice **4A–3**

¿Qué hacen?

An exchange student from Chile wants to know where people go to do certain activities. Complete each conversation with the verb suggested by the first picture, then answer the questions based on the second illustration.

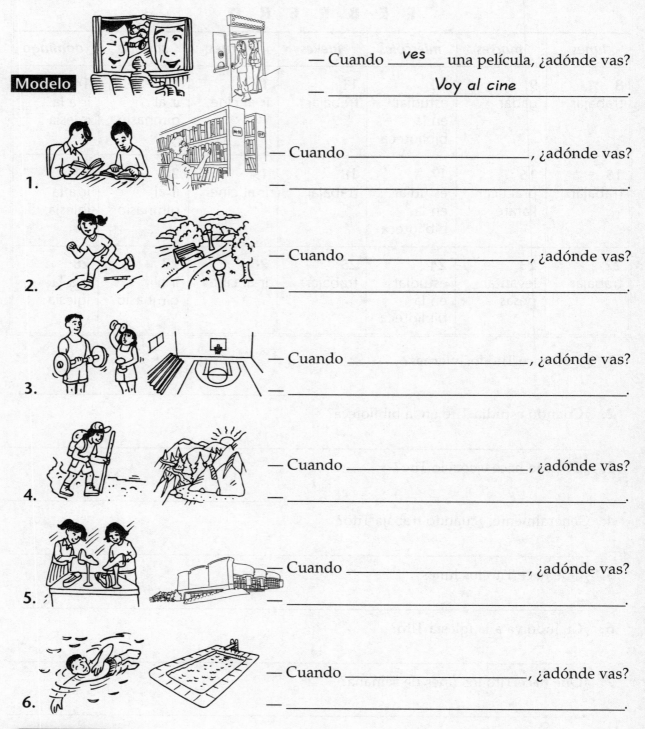

Modelo

— Cuando ___ves___ una película, ¿adónde vas?

— ___Voy al cine___.

1. — Cuando _____, ¿adónde vas?

— _____.

2. — Cuando _____, ¿adónde vas?

— _____.

3. — Cuando _____, ¿adónde vas?

— _____.

4. — Cuando _____, ¿adónde vas?

— _____.

5. — Cuando _____, ¿adónde vas?

— _____.

6. — Cuando _____, ¿adónde vas?

— _____.

Realidades 1

Capítulo 4A

Nombre _____

Fecha _____

Hora _____

Core Practice **4A–4**

El horario de Tito

Look at Tito's schedule for part of the month of February. Then answer the questions about his activities in complete sentences.

F E B R E R O						
lunes	*martes*	*miércoles*	*jueves*	*viernes*	*sábado*	*domingo*
8 trabajar	**9** nadar	**10** estudiar en la biblioteca	**11** trabajar	**12** ir al cine	**13** ir al gimnasio	**14** ir a la iglesia
15 trabajar	**16** practicar karate	**17** estudiar en la biblioteca	**18** trabajar	**19** ir al cine	**20** ir al gimnasio	**21** ir a la iglesia
22 trabajar	**23** levantar pesas	**24** estudiar en la biblioteca	**25** trabajar	**26** ir al cine	**27** ir al gimnasio	**28** ir a la iglesia

1. ¿Qué hace Tito los viernes?

_____

2. ¿Cuándo estudia Tito en la biblioteca?

_____

3. ¿Cuándo hace ejercicio Tito?

_____

4. Generalmente, ¿cuándo trabaja Tito?

_____

5. ¿Qué hace Tito los lunes?

_____

6. ¿Cuándo va a la iglesia Tito?

_____

7. ¿Qué hace Tito los fines de semana?

_____

• Web Code: jcd-0402

Realidades 1

Capítulo 4A

Nombre _____

Fecha _____

Hora _____

Core Practice **4A–5**

Las actividades favoritas

Students are making plans for what they will do after school. Complete their conversations with the correct forms of the verb **ir**.

1. LOLIS: Hoy, (yo) _____ al parque después de las clases.

ELIA: ¡Qué bien! María y yo _____ al cine.

LOLIS: Mi amigo Pablo también _____ al cine hoy.

2. MARTA: Hola, Juan. ¿Adónde _____ ?

JUAN: Pues, _____ a la clase de inglés, pero después

_____ al centro comercial. ¿Y tú?

MARTA: Pues, mis padres _____ a la playa y yo

_____ con ellos.

JUAN: ¡Qué bueno! ¿Cuándo _____ Uds.?

MARTA: Nosotros _____ después de las clases.

3. RODOLFO: ¡Hola, Pablo, Felipe!

PABLO Y FELIPE: ¡Hola, Rodolfo!

RODOLFO: ¿Adónde _____ Uds.?

PABLO: Pues, yo _____ a casa con unos amigos.

FELIPE: Yo no _____ con él. _____ a la mezquita.

¿Y tú?

RODOLFO: Catrina y yo _____ a la piscina. Ella _____

al gimnasio más tarde.

PABLO: Mi amiga Elena _____ al gimnasio con ella. Creo que

ellas _____ a las cinco.

FELIPE: Es muy tarde. Tengo que _____. ¡Hasta luego!

Realidades ❶

Capítulo 4A

Nombre _____

Fecha _____

Hora _____

Core Practice **4A–6**

La pregunta perfecta

A. Complete the following questions with the correct question words.

1. ¿_____ es el chico más alto de la clase?

2. ¿_____ vas al cine? ¿Hoy?

3. ¿_____ es tu número de teléfono?

4. ¿_____ te llamas?

5. ¿_____ vas después de las clases hoy?

6. ¿_____ está mi libro de español?

7. ¿_____ es esto?

8. ¿_____ años tienes?

B. Now, form your own questions using some of the question words above.

1. ¿_____?

2. ¿_____?

3. ¿_____?

4. ¿_____?

5. ¿_____?

6. ¿_____?

7. ¿_____?

realidades.com

• Web Code: jcd-0404

Realidades **1**

Capítulo 4A

Nombre _____

Fecha _____

Hora _____

Core Practice **4A–7**

¿Qué haces?

You are talking with your parents about your plans for the evening. They have lots of questions. Your answers are given below. Write your parents' questions in the spaces provided.

TUS PADRES: ¿_____?

TÚ: Voy a un restaurante.

TUS PADRES: ¿_____?

TÚ: Voy con unos amigos.

TUS PADRES: ¿_____?

TÚ: Ellos se llaman Roberto y Ana.

TUS PADRES: ¿_____?

TÚ: Roberto y Ana son de México.

TUS PADRES: ¿_____?

TÚ: Pues, Roberto es inteligente, trabajador y paciente.

TUS PADRES: ¿_____?

TÚ: Ana es deportista y estudiosa.

TUS PADRES: ¿_____?

TÚ: Después, nosotros vamos al cine.

TUS PADRES: ¿_____?

TÚ: ¿Después? Pues, voy a casa. ¡Uds. hacen muchas preguntas!

Repaso

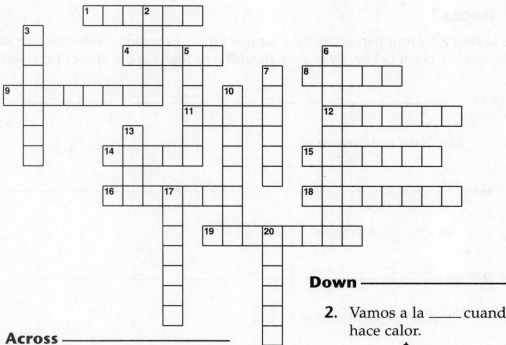

Across

1. *temple*

4.

8. ¡No me ____!

9. *mosque*

11. – ¿Con ____ vas al cine?
    – Con Ana.

12. Tengo que ir a la ____ de piano.

14. No tengo tiempo ____.

15. Para la Navidad todos van de ____.

16. *after*

18. Me gusta la ____ *Desperado*.

19.

Down

2. Vamos a la ____ cuando hace calor.

3.

5. Me gusta caminar en el ____.

6.

7. el ____ comercial

10. Voy al ____ para levantar pesas.

13. Vamos al ____ para ver una película.

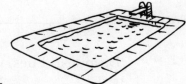

17.

20. Vas al ____ para trabajar.

Realidades 1

Capítulo 4A

Nombre _____

Fecha _____

Hora _____

Core Practice **4A-9**

Organizer

I. Vocabulary

Some of my favorite places

_____
_____
_____
_____
_____
_____

Words to talk about other places

_____
_____
_____
_____
_____
_____

Interrogative words

_____
_____
_____
_____
_____
_____
_____
_____

Phrases related to leisure activities

_____
_____
_____
_____
_____

II. Grammar

1. The forms of the verb **ir** are: _____ _____

   _____ _____

   _____ _____

2. **A.** In order to get information in English, we use the words *who, what, where, when, why,* and *how.* In Spanish these words are: _____ , _____ ,

   _____ , _____ , _____ y _____ .

   B. When asking a question in Spanish, the verb comes _____ the subject.

• Web Code: jcd-0406

Repaso del capítulo ➝ *Vocabulario y gramática* **75**

Realidades 1

Capítulo 4B

Nombre _____

Fecha _____

Hora _____

Core Practice **4B–1**

¿Eres deportista?

Write the name of the sport or activity indicated by the art.

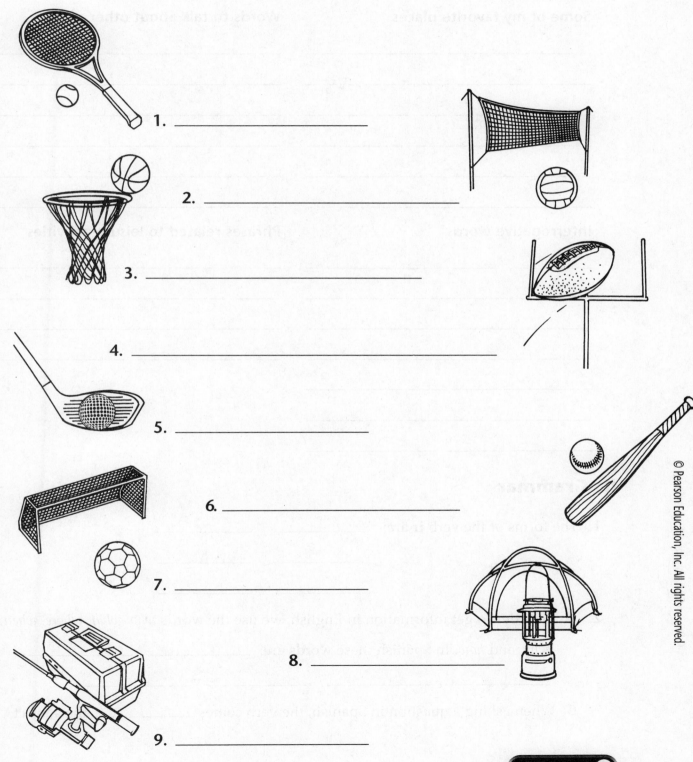

1. _____

2. _____

3. _____

4. _____

5. _____

6. _____

7. _____

8. _____

9. _____

realidades.com
• Web Code: jcd-0411

Realidades 1

Capítulo 4B

Nombre _____

Hora _____

Fecha _____

Core Practice **4B–2**

Las invitaciones

You and your friends are making plans for the weekend. Complete your friends' invitations with the activities suggested by the pictures. Then accept the offers using complete sentences. Follow the model.

Modelo

— ¿Te gustaría ___*ir al cine*___ este fin de semana?

— ___*Sí, me gustaría ir al cine*___ .

1. _____ — ¿Puedes _____ este fin de semana?

— _____ .

2. _____ — ¿Quieres _____ este fin de semana?

— _____ .

3. _____ — ¿Puedes _____ este fin de semana?

— _____ .

4. _____ — ¿Te gustaría _____ este fin de semana?

— _____ .

5. _____ — ¿Quieres _____ este fin de semana?

— _____ .

Nombre _____ Hora _____

Fecha _____ Core Practice **4B–3**

¿Cómo están?

You have just arrived at school and are asking how your friends are doing. Using the pictures to help you, fill in the blanks with the correct form of **estar** and the appropriate adjective. Don't forget to make the adjective agree with the subject!

1. — ¿Cómo está ella?

    — _____ .

2. — ¿Cómo está él?

    — _____ .

3. — ¿Cómo están ellos?

    — _____ .

4. — ¿Cómo están ellas?

    — _____ .

5. — ¿Cómo están los estudiantes?

    — _____ .

6. — ¿Cómo está él?

    — _____ .

realidades.com ⊻

• Web Code: jcd-0412

Realidades ❶

Capítulo 4B

Nombre _____

Fecha _____

Hora _____

Core Practice **4B–4**

¿A qué hora?

Lucía is very busy on the weekends. Answer the questions about her schedule using complete sentences.

| **Modelo** | ¿A qué hora usa la computadora? |

Usa la computadora a las siete y media de la noche.

1. ¿A qué hora tiene que trabajar Lucía?

_____

2. ¿A qué hora va a casa?

_____

3. ¿Qué hacen Lucía y su amiga a las ocho de la mañana?

_____

4. ¿A qué hora come la cena Lucía?

_____

5. ¿Cuándo estudian ella y su amigo?

_____

6. ¿Adónde va Lucía esta noche? ¿A qué hora?

_____

Realidades 1

Capítulo 4B

Nombre _____

Fecha _____

Hora _____

Core Practice **4B–5**

Los planes

It is 10:00 Saturday morning, and you and your friends are making plans for the afternoon and evening. Using a form of **ir** + **a** + *infinitive*, write complete sentences about everyone's plans. Follow the model.

María

Modelo   *María va a ir de compras esta tarde*_____.

Ana y yo

1. _____.

Pablo

2. _____.

Yo

3. _____.

Mis amigos

4. _____.

Tú

5. _____.

Nosotros

6. _____.

Ud.

7. _____.

Ana y Lorena

8. _____.

realidades.com

• Web Code: jcd-0413

Realidades ①   Nombre _____   Hora _____

Capítulo 4B   Fecha _____   Core Practice **4B–6**

Demasiadas preguntas

Your friends are asking you to make plans for this weekend, but you are not able to do anything that they have suggested. Using the pictures to help you, respond to their questions using **ir** + **a** + *infinitive.* Follow the model.

¿Puedes ir al partido mañana?

Modelo

No, no puedo. Voy a correr mañana _____ .

¿Quieres ir al partido esta noche?

1. _____

¿Te gustaría ir al cine conmigo esta noche?

2. _____

¿Quieres jugar al golf esta tarde?

3. _____

¿Puedes jugar videojuegos conmigo el viernes?

4. _____

¿Te gustaría ir de compras mañana por la noche?

5. _____

¿Te gustaría ir al baile conmigo esta noche?

6. _____

¿Quieres ir a la biblioteca conmigo?

7. _____

¿Puedes ir de cámping conmigo este fin de semana?

8. _____

Realidades ❶

Capítulo 4B

Nombre _____

Fecha _____

Hora _____

Core Practice **4B–7**

¿A qué juegas?

Friends are talking about the sports that they enjoy playing. Write the correct form of the verb **jugar** to complete each sentence.

1. — ¿Marta juega al vóleibol?

   — Sí, Rodrigo y ella _____ todos los días.

2. — Oye, ¿puedes jugar al básquetbol con nosotros?

   — Lo siento, pero no _____ bien.

3. — ¿A qué juegan Uds.?

   — Nosotros _____ al golf.

4. — Ellas juegan al tenis muy bien, ¿no?

   — Sí, _____ muy bien.

5. — ¿_____ Ud. al básquetbol a la una?

   — No. Tengo que ir a un concierto.

6. — Yo juego al fútbol hoy.

   — ¡Ay, me encanta el fútbol! ¡_____ contigo!

7. — ¿Tú y Manuel jugáis al béisbol esta tarde?

   — Sí. ¡_____ todos los días!

8. — ¿Qué hace Luz esta noche?

   — Ella _____ al vóleibol a las ocho.

• Web Code: jcd-0414

Realidades 1

Capítulo 4B

Nombre _____

Fecha _____

Hora _____

Core Practice **4B–8**

Repaso

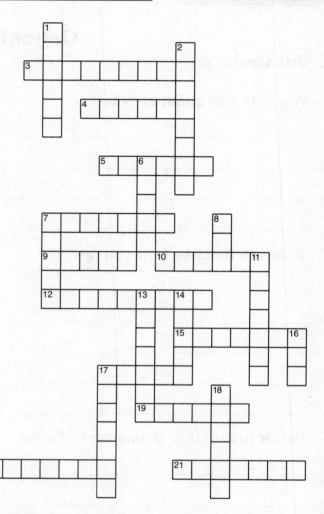

Across

3. No puedo jugar. Estoy ____ ocupado.

4. *sad*

5.

7. Me gusta ver el ____ de béisbol.

9. yo sé, tú ____

10. Lo ____, pero no puedo.

12.  el fútbol ____

15.

17. El *Jitterbug* es un ____.

19. *Great!*

20. Vamos al ____ para escuchar música.

21. *with me*

Down

1. Vamos a la ____ de cumpleaños de Paco.

2.

6. *afternoon;* la ____

7. me gusta ir de *fishing*

8. el ____ de semana

11. Ella trabaja mucho, siempre está ____.

13.

14. Es después de la tarde; la ____.

16. *Hey!*

17.

18. Voy a la escuela a las siete de la ____.

Realidades (1)

Capítulo 4B

Nombre _____

Hora _____

Fecha _____

Core Practice **4B–9**

Organizer

I. Vocabulary

Words to talk about activities

_____

_____

_____

_____

Words to describe how you feel

_____

_____

_____

_____

Words to accept or decline an invitation

_____

_____

_____

_____

_____

Names of sports

_____

_____

_____

_____

_____

Words to say when something happens

_____

_____

_____

_____

_____

II. Grammar

1. The forms of the verb **jugar** are: _____ _____

   _____ _____

   _____ _____

2. The preposition **con** becomes _____ to mean "with me" and _____ to mean "with you."

3. To say you are going to do something, you use the verb _____ + _____ + the action you are going to perform.

• Web Code: jcd-0416

Realidades ①

Capítulo 5A

Nombre _____

Fecha _____

Hora _____

Core Practice **5A–1**

La familia

A. Patricia is telling you about her family. Label each person in her family tree with a word that describes his or her relationship to Patricia. You may use some words more than once.

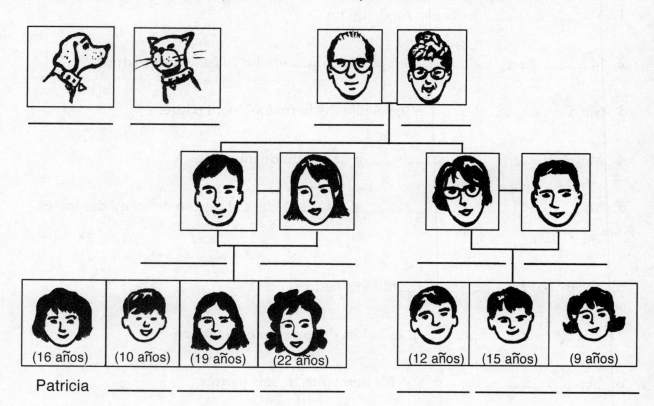

(16 años)   (10 años)   (19 años)   (22 años)   (12 años)   (15 años)   (9 años)

Patricia _____

B. Now, answer the following questions by circling **sí** or **no**.

1. ¿Patricia tiene hermanastros?   Sí   No

2. ¿Patricia tiene hermanas mayores?   Sí   No

3. ¿Patricia tiene dieciséis años?   Sí   No

4. ¿Patricia tiene tres primos menores?   Sí   No

5. ¿Patricia tiene dos abuelas?   Sí   No

Realidades ①

Capítulo 5A

Nombre _____

Fecha _____

Hora _____

Core Practice **5A-2**

¿Quién es?

A. Complete the sentences below with the correct family relationships.

1. Mi ___ ___ (___) es la esposa de mi tío.

2. Mis ___ ___ ___ (___) ___ ___ ___ son los hijos de mis padres.

3. Mi ___ ___ (___) ___ ___ es el hijo del hermano de mi padre.

4. Mi (___) ___ ___ ___ ___ es la madre de mi madre.

5. Mi ___ ___ ___ ___ ___ ___ (___) ___ es el esposo de mi madre (no es mi padre).

6. Yo soy la ___ ___ ___ (___) de mis padres.

7. Mi ___ ___ ___ (___) ___ es la hija de la hermana de mi padre.

8. Mis (___) ___ ___ ___ son los hermanos de mis padres.

9. Mamá y papá son mis ___ ___ (___) ___ ___ ___.

10. Mis ___ ___ (___) ___ ___ ___ ___ (___) ___ ___ ___ ___ son las hijas de la esposa de mi padre (no son mis hermanas).

B. Now, unscramble the circled letters to come up with another member of the family.

___ ___ ___   ___ ___ ___ ___ ___ ___ ___ ___ ___ ___

realidades.com ✔
• Web Code: jcd-0501

Realidades 1

Capítulo 5A

Nombre _____

Fecha _____

Hora _____

Core Practice **5A–3**

¡Una fiesta inesperada (*a surprise party*)!

The Rodríguez family is giving their older son Tomás a surprise birthday party. Complete their conversation, using the most logical word from the word bank.

luces	la piñata	tiene	decoraciones
dulces	pastel	celebrar	sólo
globos	sacar fotos	regalos	

MAMÁ: Vamos a hacer el plan porque vamos a _____ el cumpleaños

de Tomás. Él _____ doce años.

TÍA LULÚ: Sí, ¡vamos a celebrar! Primero, necesitamos un _____ para

comer ¿no? ¡Qué sabroso!

MAMÁ: Sí. Y necesitamos unas _____ perfectas. Vamos a necesitar un

globo y una luz.

TÍA LULÚ: ¿_____ *un* globo y *una* luz? ¡No, necesitamos muchos

_____ y muchas _____! También

necesitamos papel picado.

PABLITO: Oye, ¡yo tengo una cámara fabulosa! Puedo _____ en la fiesta

cuando Tomás abre los _____ .

MAMÁ: Sí, Pablito. ¡Muchas gracias! Y finalmente, pueden romper

_____ . ¿Tenemos _____?

TÍA LULÚ: Sí, tenemos muchos dulces.

PABLITO: ¡Qué buena fiesta!

realidades.com

• Web Code: jcd-0502

A primera vista ━ *Videohistoria* **87**

La celebración

Raúl is explaining how he and his family are preparing for his sister's birthday party. Read his description and answer the questions that follow in complete sentences.

> Hoy es el cumpleaños de mi hermana menor, Gabriela. Mis padres y yo preparamos la fiesta. Mi mamá decora con el papel picado y las luces. Mi papá tiene los regalos y los globos. Yo preparo la mesa con los globos y el pastel. También tengo la cámara porque voy a hacer un video de la fiesta.
>
> Sólo nuestra familia va a estar aquí, pero con todos mis primos, mis tíos y mis abuelos tenemos muchas personas. A las cinco mi hermana va a estar aquí y la fiesta va a empezar.

1. ¿Quién es Gabriela? _____

2. ¿Para quién es la fiesta? _____

3. ¿Qué clase de fiesta es? _____

4. ¿Con qué decora Raúl? _____

5. ¿Qué tiene el papá? _____

6. ¿Qué va a hacer Raúl? _____

7. ¿Quiénes van a estar en la fiesta? _____

_____

8. ¿A qué hora va a empezar la fiesta? _____

realidades.com

• Web Code: jcd-0502

Realidades 1

Capítulo 5A

Nombre _____

Fecha _____

Hora _____

Core Practice **5A–5**

Conversaciones

You overhear a group of students talking. Fill in the blanks in their conversations with the correct forms of the verb **tener**.

1. FRANCO: Hola, Carmen. ¿Qué tienes en la mano?

   CARMEN: (Yo) _____ un regalo para mi primo. Es su cumpleaños.

   FRANCO: Ah, ¿sí? ¿Cuántos años _____?

   CARMEN: _____ doce años.

   FRANCO: Mis primos también _____ doce años.

2. ELENA: ¡Oye, Carlos! ¿Cuántos años _____?

   CARLOS: ¿Yo? Yo _____ quince años. ¿Por qué?

   ELENA: Porque mi hermano y yo _____ una prima de quince

   años que _____ que ir a un baile el viernes. ¿(Tú)

   _____ planes?

   CARLOS: ¿El viernes? No, no _____ otros planes.

3. PABLO: Hola, José. Hola, Manolo. ¿(Uds.) _____ un dólar?

   JOSÉ: Sí, yo _____ un dólar. ¿Por qué?

   PABLO: Porque yo _____ hambre y quiero comprar un perrito

   caliente.

   MANOLO: ¿La cafetería _____ perritos calientes buenos?

   PABLO: Sí. ¿Quieres uno?

   JOSÉ: Sí, pero primero Manolo y yo _____ que ir a clase.

   PABLO: También _____ que ir a clase.

Realidades ❶

Capítulo 5A

Nombre _____

Fecha _____

Hora _____

Core Practice **5A–6**

¿De quién es?

A. Fill in the following chart with the masculine and feminine, singular and plural forms of the possessive adjectives indicated.

hijo	tía	abuelos	hermanas
			mis hermanas
	tu tía		
su hijo			
		nuestros abuelos	
vuestro hijo	vuestra tía	vuestros abuelos	vuestras hermanas

B. Now, complete the following sentences by writing in the possessive adjective that corresponds with the English adjective in parentheses. Follow the model.

Modelo (my) _____Mi_____ abuela es vieja.

1. (our) _____ abuelos van a la casa para hablar con nosotros.

2. (your) Sara, gracias por _____ libro.

3. (my) _____ prima es de Tejas.

4. (your) ¿Tienen mucha tarea en _____ clase de matemáticas?

5. (their) _____ tíos están en la oficina ahora.

6. (my) El perro come _____ galletas.

7. (our) Nosotros vamos a la escuela en _____ bicicletas.

8. (your) Profesor, ¿dónde está _____ oficina?

9. (their) _____ hijo es muy trabajador.

10. (his) _____ hermana está enferma.

realidades.com
• Web Code: jcd-0505

Los regalos perfectos

Using the subjects below and the activities suggested by the pictures, write complete sentences about what your friends and relatives have for the party. Make sure you use the correct possessive adjective. Follow the model.

Mi primo Juan

Modelo *Mi primo Juan tiene su cámara.*

Mis tíos

1. _____

Alicia

2. _____

Tú

3. _____

Nosotros

4. _____

Yo

5. _____

Ud.

6. _____

La profesora Méndez

7. _____

Nosotras

8. _____

Realidades 1

Capítulo 5A

Nombre _____

Hora _____

Fecha _____

Core Practice **5A–8**

Repaso

Across

5. La madre de mi primo es mi ___.

7. El hermano de mi padre es mi ___.

9. *sister*

11.

13. mi papá; el ___

16. La mamá de mi padre es mi ___.

17. Mi hermano y yo somos los ___ de nuestros padres.

19.

20.

21. mi mamá; la ___

Down

1. El esposo de mi madre; no es mi papá, es mi ___.

2. *brother*

3.

4. el papel ___

6.

8. ¡Feliz ___! ¿Cuántos años tienes?

9. Quiero ___ un video.

10. la madre de mi hermanastro; mi ___

12. Los hijos ___ la piñata.

14. Es el hermano de mi prima; mi ___.

15. ¿Quién ___ las fotos de la fiesta?

18. *parents*

21. no menor

Realidades ①

Capítulo 5A

Nombre _____

Fecha _____

Hora _____

Core Practice **5A-9**

Organizer

I. Vocabulary

To describe family relationships

_____

_____

_____

_____

_____

_____

_____

Activities at a party

_____

_____

_____

_____

Items at a party

_____

_____

_____

_____

Words to express possession

_____

_____

_____

_____

II. Grammar

1. The forms of **tener** are: _____ _____

   _____ _____

   _____ _____

2. Possessive adjectives in Spanish are written as follows:

	Singular/Plural		Singular/Plural
my	_____ / _____	our	_____ / _____
your (familiar)	_____ / _____	your (pl., familiar)	_____ / _____
your (formal), his, hers	_____ / _____	your (pl., formal), their	_____ / _____

• Web Code: jcd-0508

Realidades 1

Capítulo 5B

Nombre _____

Hora _____

Fecha _____

Core Practice **5B–1**

Restaurante elegante

Label the following items with the correct word. Don't forget to use the correct definite article (**el** or **la**).

1. _____   5. _____   9. _____

2. _____   6. _____   10. _____

3. _____   7. _____   11. _____

4. _____   8. _____

realidades.com
• Web Code: jcd-0511

Realidades ①

Capítulo 5B

Nombre _____

Fecha _____

Hora _____

Core Practice **5B–2**

Las descripciones

You are telling your friends about some of your family members. Write descriptions of them in complete sentences. Follow the model.

Modelo

6'5"

Paco

Paco es alto y tiene el pelo corto y negro.

6'4"

El tío Roberto

1. _____
_____
_____

5'0"

Melinda, mi madrastra

2. _____
_____
_____

5'2"

El abuelito Jorge

3. _____
_____
_____

6'2"

Los primos Juan y Manuel

4. _____
_____
_____

5'10"

Esperanza

5. _____
_____
_____

realidades.com

• Web Code: jcd-0511

Realidades ①

Capítulo 5B

Nombre _____

Fecha _____

Hora _____

Core Practice **5B–3**

La palabra correcta

Complete the following mini-conversations with the most logical words or phrases from your vocabulary.

1. — ¿Necesita Ud. algo?

   — Sí, me _____ un tenedor.

2. — ¿Te gusta la comida del Sr. Vargas?

   — Sí, es deliciosa. ¡Qué _____!

3. — ¿Quieres otra _____ de café?

   — No, gracias.

4. — ¿Desea Ud. un té helado?

   — Sí, porque tengo _____.

5. — ¿Qué vas a _____ de postre?

   — Yo quiero el flan.

6. — ¿Necesitan _____ más?

   — Sí, la cuenta por favor.

7. — Muchas gracias.

   — De _____.

8. — ¿Qué quisiera Ud. de _____ _____?

   — Me gustaría el arroz con pollo.

9. — ¿Estás cansado?

   — Sí, tengo _____.

10. — ¿Bebes el café?

    — Sí, porque tengo _____.

realidades.com ✔
• Web Code: jcd-0512

Realidades 1

Capítulo 5B

Nombre _____

Fecha _____

Hora _____

Core Practice **5B–4**

Cita (*date*) en español

A. David and Rocío are on a date at a Spanish restaurant. Using the vocabulary you have learned in this chapter, write their possible responses to the waiter's questions. Use complete sentences.

CAMARERO: ¿Qué desean Uds. de plato principal?

DAVID: _____

ROCÍO: _____

CAMARERO: ¿Cómo está la comida?

DAVID: _____

ROCÍO: _____

CAMARERO: ¿Desean algo más?

DAVID: _____

ROCÍO: _____

B. Now, based on the waiter's responses, write what you think David or Rocío may have asked the waiter.

DAVID: ¿ _____?

CAMARERO: Sí, le traigo una servilleta.

ROCÍO: ¿ _____?

CAMARERO: Sí, ahora puede pedir algo de postre.

DAVID: ¿ _____?

CAMARERO: Un café, por supuesto. ¿Tiene sueño?

• Web Code: jcd-0512

Realidades ❶

Capítulo 5B

Nombre _____

Fecha _____

Hora _____

Core Practice **5B–5**

¿Quién viene?

Your class has decided to put on a talent show, and you are in charge of scheduling what time everyone is coming to audition for different skits. Your friend Lola is anxious to know the schedule. Answer her questions using the picture below. Follow the model.

Modelo   ¿Quién viene a las ocho y media?
La Sra. Ramos viene a las ocho y media.

1. ¿Quién viene a las nueve?

   _____

2. ¿Quién viene a las diez?

   _____

3. ¿Quién viene a las once menos cuarto?

   _____

4. ¿Quién viene a las once y media?

   _____

5. ¿Quién viene a las doce?

   _____

6. ¿Quién viene a la una?

   _____

7. ¿Quién viene a las dos y media?

   _____

8. ¿Quién viene a las tres y media?

   _____

realidades.com
• Web Code: jcd-0513

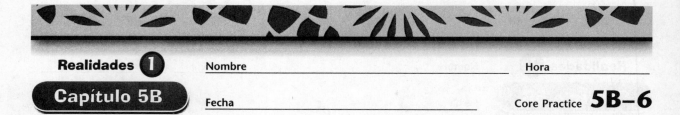

Una carta para mamá

Read the following letter from Rosaura to her mom in Spain. Write the form of **ser** or **estar** that best completes each sentence.

Querida mamá:

    ¡Aquí _____ en Chicago! Chicago _____ una gran ciudad

con muchas personas que _____ muy interesantes. La comida

_____ fantástica. La especialidad _____ la pizza. ¡Qué rica!

    Vivo con una familia muy simpática. Tienen un hijo que siempre

_____ contento y una hija que _____ muy estudiosa.

¡_____ las nueve de la noche y ella _____ en la biblioteca!

    Los chicos de la escuela también _____ estudiosos, pero no muy

serios. Mis compañeros y yo _____ muy buenos amigos y

_____ juntos todos los fines de semana. Una amiga, Vera,

_____ boliviana y _____ divertidísima. Vera y yo

_____ en la misma clase de biología.

    Bueno, mamá, _____ muy tarde. Mañana voy a _____

muy ocupada y necesito dormir. Pero sabes ahora que todo _____

bien aquí y que yo _____ contenta. Besos para ti y para papá.

                                        Un abrazo,

                                        Rosaura

¿Qué van a comer?

The Vázquez family is getting ready to order dinner in a restaurant. Look at the pictures to get an idea of the person's needs. Answer the questions below using vocabulary that would most logically go in each situation.

1.

¿Cómo está la Sra. Vázquez? _____

¿Qué debe pedir de plato principal? _____

¿De postre? _____ ¿Y para beber? _____

2.

¿Cómo están los chicos? _____

¿Qué deben pedir de plato principal? _____

¿De postre? _____ ¿Y para beber? _____

3.

¿Cómo está Elisita? _____

¿Qué debe pedir de plato principal? _____

¿De postre? _____ ¿Y para beber? _____

4.

¿Cómo está el Sr. Vázquez? _____

¿Qué debe pedir de plato principal? _____

¿De postre? _____ ¿Y para beber? _____

realidades.com

• Web Code: jcd-0515

Realidades ①

Capítulo 5B

Nombre _____

Fecha _____

Hora _____

Core Practice **5B–8**

Repaso

Across _____

6. *blond;* el pelo ____

7. Shaquille O'Neal es ____.

8. Uds. ____ cansados.

12. Paquito no es viejo. Es ____.

13. ¡Camarero, la ____ por favor!

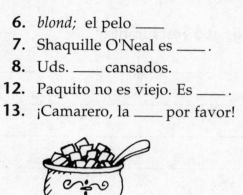

15.

16. Mi abuela tiene el pelo ____.

17. Ella tiene 88 años. Es ____.

18. Necesito un cuchillo y un ____ para comer el bistec.

19. sal y ____

21. Necesito un té. Tengo ____.

Down _____

1. *red-haired (m.)*

2. El Sr. López es un ____.

3. *napkin*

4. Nosotros ____ bajos.

5. *good-looking (f.)*

9. ____ el pelo ____

10. ¿Qué quieres de ____? El flan.

11. Quiero un té helado. Tengo ____.

13. no largo

14.

18. Quiero una ____ de café.

19. el plato ____

20. La Sra. Miranda es una ____.

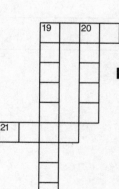

Realidades 1

Capítulo 5B

Nombre _____

Fecha _____

Hora _____

Core Practice **5B–9**

Organizer

I. Vocabulary

To describe people

_____

_____

_____

_____

_____

_____

_____

Things at a restaurant

_____

_____

_____

_____

_____

_____

Words to describe how you're feeling

_____

Words to order food and beverages

_____

_____

_____

_____

_____

II. Grammar

1. The forms of **venir** are: _____ _____

   _____ _____

   _____ _____

2. For physical and personality descriptions, and to tell what time it is, use the verb

   _____ . To talk about location and physical and emotional states,

   use the verb _____ .

realidades.com
• Web Code: jcd-0516

Realidades 1

Capítulo 6A

Nombre _____

Fecha _____

Hora _____

Core Practice **6A–1**

Un dormitorio nuevo para mí

Ignacio is moving into his sister's room when she goes away to college. His parents have told him that he can bring anything into his new room that he can carry by himself. Make a list of eight things that he would definitely be able to bring with him, and five things that he definitely wouldn't be able to bring. Use the examples given to help you.

Traer conmigo

_____El lector DVD_____

_____

_____

_____

_____

_____

_____

_____

No traer conmigo

_____La pared_____

_____

_____

_____

_____

Realidades 1

Capítulo 6A

Nombre _____

Fecha _____

Hora _____

Core Practice **6A–2**

Muchos colores

Write the names of the color or colors that you associate with the following things. Don't forget to make the colors agree in gender and number.

1. el jugo de naranja _____

2. la limonada _____

3. el 14 de febrero _____

4. el 25 de diciembre _____

5. el sol _____

6. la nieve _____

7. unas zanahorias _____

8. la bandera de los Estados Unidos _____

9. un tomate _____

10. la piscina _____

11. la noche _____

12. el Día de San Patricio _____

realidades.com

• Web Code: jcd-0601

Realidades 1

Capítulo 6A

Nombre _____

Fecha _____

Hora _____

Core Practice **6A–3**

La experiencia nueva

A. Read the letter that Gloria wrote to her friend in Spain about her host family in Chile.

Querida Sandra,

Lo paso muy bien aquí con la familia Quijano. Desde el primer día aquí, tengo mi propio dormitorio. Hay una cama, una mesita, una lámpara, un escritorio con una silla pequeña y un espejo. También hay una ventana con cortinas amarillas. La mejor cosa del cuarto es la lámpara. Es roja, negra y marrón y es muy artística. Creo que es la lámpara más bonita del mundo.

El cuarto también es bonito. Las paredes son moradas. Sólo quiero mi equipo de sonido y mis discos compactos.

Abrazos,

Gloria

B. Now, answer these questions in complete sentences.

1. ¿A Gloria le gusta la familia?

_____

2. ¿Comparte Gloria el dormitorio con otro estudiante?

_____

3. ¿De qué color son las paredes en el dormitorio de Gloria?

_____

4. ¿Tiene Gloria su equipo de sonido en su dormitorio?

_____

5. ¿Cómo es la lámpara en el dormitorio de Gloria? ¿A ella le gusta?

_____

6. ¿De qué color son las cortinas en el dormitorio de Gloria?

_____

Realidades ①

Capítulo 6A

Nombre _____

Fecha _____

Hora _____

Core Practice **6A–4**

¿Dónde está todo?

Movers just finished putting everything into Marcela's new room. Help her locate everything by describing where the items are in the picture below. Follow the model.

| Modelo | *Una lámpara está al lado del televisor.* |

_____

_____

_____

_____

_____

_____

realidades.com

• Web Code: jcd-0602

Realidades ①

Capítulo 6A

Nombre _____

Fecha _____

Hora _____

Core Practice **6A–5**

Las comparaciones

Felipe and Mónica are brother and sister who are very different from each other. Using their pictures and the model to help you, write comparisons of the two siblings. Remember to make the adjectives agree in gender with the subject.

Modelo Mónica / alto   *Mónica es más alta que Felipe.*

1. Felipe / serio _____

2. Mónica / sociable _____

3. Mónica / rubio _____

4. Felipe / estudioso _____

5. Felipe / alto _____

6. Mónica / viejo _____

7. Felipe / rubio _____

8. Felipe / joven _____

9. Mónica / serio _____

realidades.com ⓥ
• Web Code: jcd-0603

Realidades 1

Capítulo 6A

Nombre _____

Fecha _____

Hora _____

Core Practice **6A–6**

Los premios Óscar

The following chart rates movies according to certain categories. Four stars is the best rating, one star is the worst rating. Using the chart as a guide, write complete sentences comparing the three movies. Follow the model.

	Una tarde en agosto	*Mi vida*	*Siete meses en Lima*
Actores – talentosos	****	**	***
Fotografía – artística	****	*	***
Ropa – bonita	***	****	***
Director – creativo	****	***	**
Cuento – interesante	****	**	*

Modelo   actores / "Una tarde en agosto"

Los actores de "Una tarde en agosto" son los más talentosos.

1. fotografía / "Una tarde en agosto"

_____

2. fotografía / "Mi vida"

_____

3. director / "Una tarde en agosto"

_____

4. actores / "Una tarde en agosto"

_____

5. director / "Siete meses en Lima"

_____

6. ropa / "Mi vida"

_____

7. cuento / "Siete meses en Lima"

_____

8. actores / "Mi vida"

_____

9. cuento / "Una tarde en agosto"

_____

realidades.com

• Web Code: jcd-0604

Realidades 1

Capítulo 6A

Nombre _____

Fecha _____

Hora _____

Core Practice **6A–7**

Las mini-conversaciones

A. Fill in the rest of these conjugations.

	DORMIR	PODER
yo		
tú		*puedes*
él, ella, Ud.	*duerme*	
nosotros		
vosotros	*dormís*	*podéis*
ellos, ellas, Uds.		

B. Write the correct forms of either **dormir** or **poder** in the blanks to complete the mini-conversations below.

1. — ¿Quieres ir al cine?

   — No _____. Tengo que trabajar.

2. — ¿Cuántas horas _____ cada noche?

   — Generalmente, ocho horas.

3. — ¿Uds. _____ venir a nuestra fiesta?

   — Sí. ¿A qué hora es?

4. — Nosotros no _____ trabajar hoy.

   — Está bien. Van a trabajar mañana.

5. — Cuando ellas van de cámping, ¿dónde _____?

   — Pues, en sus sacos de dormir, por supuesto.

6. — ¿Qué haces a las once y media de la noche?

   — ¡Yo _____!

7. — ¿_____ (tú) hablar con tu abuela por teléfono?

   — No, no _____ porque estoy ocupado.

8. — ¿Qué hace una chica cansada?

   — _____ mucho.

Realidades ❶

Capítulo 6A

Nombre _____

Hora _____

Fecha _____

Core Practice **6A–8**

Repaso

Down

1. Tengo que ____ por la noche.

2.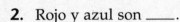

3. el ____ DVD

4. no pequeño

5.

6. un ____ compacto

8. no es a la derecha; es a la ____

11. Un plátano es de color ____.

13. *dresser*

17. La nieve es de color ____.

18. no mejor

Across

2. Rojo y azul son ____.

7.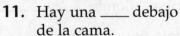

9.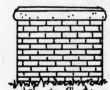

10. el ____ de sonido

11. Hay una ____ debajo de la cama.

12. Uds. tienen mucha ropa en el ____.

14. Los libros están en el ____.

15. *brown*

16. no es fea, es ____

19. Duermo en la ____.

20. *mirror*

Realidades 1

Capítulo 6A

Nombre _____

Fecha _____

Hora _____

Core Practice **6A–9**

Organizer

I. Vocabulary

To talk about things in a bedroom

_____

_____

_____

_____

_____

_____

_____

Words to describe things

_____

_____

_____

_____

Electronic equipment

_____

_____

_____

_____

_____

Words to talk about colors

_____

_____

_____

_____

II. Grammar

1. To compare peoples' ages, use either _____ + **que** or _____ + **que**. To say that something is "better than" use _____ + **que**; to say that something is "worse than" use _____ + **que**.

2. To say that something is the "best" or "worst" use the following construction: article + _____ / _____ + noun. To say "most" or "least" the construction is article + noun + _____ / _____ + adjective.

3. The forms of **poder** are:

_____ _____

_____ _____

_____ _____

The forms of **dormir** are:

_____ _____

_____ _____

_____ _____

Realidades 1

Capítulo 6B

Nombre _____

Fecha _____

Hora _____

Core Practice **6B–1**

Los cuartos

The Suárez family has just moved into a new house. Tell what rooms are on each floor of the house.

En la planta baja hay: _____

_____

_____

En el primer piso hay: _____

_____

_____

_____

realidades.com

• Web Code: jcd-0611

Realidades ❶

Capítulo 6B

Nombre _____

Fecha _____

Hora _____

Core Practice **6B–2**

Los quehaceres

Each person below has been given a location from which to do his or her chores. In the spaces provided, list at least two chores each person could logically be doing. Follow the model.

Modelo   Alberto y Antonio están en el garaje.

lavan el coche

sacan la basura

limpian el garaje

1. Dolores está en el baño.

_____

_____

2. Eugenio está en el dormitorio.

_____

_____

3. Carolina y Catarina están en la sala.

_____

_____

4. Vladimir está en el comedor.

_____

_____

5. Ana Gracia está en la cocina.

_____

_____

Realidades ①

Capítulo 6B

Nombre _____

Fecha _____

Hora _____

Core Practice **6B-3**

La lista de quehaceres

Melisa's mom has left her a list of the things that she has to do before her relatives come over for a dinner party. Complete the list with the appropriate word or phrase. Follow the model.

Modelo _____Arregla_____ tu cuarto.

1. _____ la mesa del comedor.

2. Tienes que _____ porque no tienes ropa limpia.

3. _____ porque no tenemos platos limpios.

4. ¿Puedes _____? Hay demasiada basura.

5. _____ los platos en la cocina.

6. Necesitas _____ porque el coche está sucio.

7. Hay que _____ porque hay mucho polvo en el primer piso.

8. _____ las camas.

9. ¿Puedes _____ por las alfombras?

10. El baño no está limpio. Necesitas _____ .

11. _____ de comer al perro.

12. Si tienes tiempo, _____ todos los quehaceres.

realidades.com ✓

• Web Code: jcd-0612

Realidades

Capítulo 6B

Nombre _____

Fecha _____

Hora _____

Core Practice **6B–4**

No es correcto

The following statements do not make sense. Rewrite the sentences by replacing the underlined words or phrases with words or phrases that make sense. Follow the model.

Modelo　Nunca <u>haces</u> en casa cuando tienes quehaceres.
　　　　　Nunca ayudas en casa cuando tienes quehaceres .

1. Tengo que <u>dar</u> la aspiradora por las alfombras.

　　_____

2. El cuarto está <u>limpio</u>. Voy a limpiarlo.

　　_____

3. Papá va a lavar platos en <u>el dormitorio</u>.

　　_____

4. No te <u>recibo</u> dinero porque no estás haciendo nada.

　　_____

5. ¡<u>Haz la cama!</u> Vamos a comer.

　　_____

6. Mamá lava <u>el coche</u> en la cocina.

　　_____

7. ¿Cuáles son los <u>dinero</u> que tienes que hacer?

　　_____

8. Doy <u>dinero</u> al perro todos los días.

　　_____

9. Debes cortar <u>el polvo</u>, está bastante largo.

　　_____

10. Ernesto quita <u>el coche</u> de la sala.

　　_____

11. Las hermanas <u>cocinan</u> la basura por la noche.

　　_____

Realidades (1)

Capítulo 6B

Nombre _____

Fecha _____

Hora _____

Core Practice **6B–5**

Los mandatos

A. Write the affirmative **tú** command forms of the following verbs in the spaces provided.

1. correr _____

2. poner _____

3. hacer _____

4. comer _____

5. hablar _____

6. leer _____

7. limpiar _____

8. ver _____

9. cortar _____

10. abrir _____

11. escribir _____

B. Now, write the chore your parents might tell you to do in each of the following situations. Follow the model.

| Modelo | Tu dormitorio no está limpio. | _Arregla tu dormitorio_ . |

1. El coche está sucio. _____.

2. El perro tiene hambre. _____.

3. No hay platos limpios. _____.

4. Hay mucha basura en el garaje. _____.

5. La camisa blanca ahora es gris. _____.

6. Necesitamos cenar. _____.

7. El baño no está limpio. _____.

8. Hay mucho polvo en la sala. _____.

realidades.com
• Web Code: jcd-0613

Realidades ❶

Capítulo 6B

Nombre _____

Fecha _____

Hora _____

Core Practice **6B–6**

¿Qué están haciendo?

The Duarte family is getting ready for a barbecue. Look at the picture, then write what each of the family members is doing. Follow the model.

| Modelo | La madre *está cocinando las hamburguesas* . |

1. Manolo y José _____.

2. Ana María _____.

3. El padre _____.

4. Tito y Ramón _____.

5. Graciela _____.

6. Lola y Elia _____.

7. Todos _____.

Realidades ❶

Capítulo 6B

Nombre _____

Fecha _____

Hora _____

Core Practice **6B–7**

Mucho trabajo

The Escobar family is getting ready to have guests over. Fill in the blanks in their conversation below with the appropriate form of the following verbs: **cortar, ayudar, hacer, lavar, pasar, sacar.**

PABLO: Mamá, ¿qué estás _____ tú?

MAMÁ: Estoy _____ los platos, hijo. ¿Y tú?

PABLO: Nada.

MAMÁ: Vale. ¿Qué están _____ tus hermanos?

PABLO: Juan está _____ el baño y Marta está arreglando

su dormitorio.

MAMÁ: Bien, hijo. Ahora, quita el polvo de la sala y luego _____

la aspiradora por las alfombras.

PABLO: Pero, mamá …

MAMÁ: ¡Ahora! Y después _____ la basura …

¡María! ¿Qué estás _____, hija?

MARÍA: Isabel y yo _____ el césped. ¿Por qué?

MAMÁ: Porque tus primos vienen a comer hoy y necesito ayuda para poner la mesa.

MARÍA: ¿Por qué no te está _____ papá?

MAMÁ: Papá, cariño, ¿dónde estás?

PAPÁ: Estoy en el garaje. Estoy _____ el coche.

MAMÁ: Ah, sí. Después, arregla nuestro cuarto y _____ tu ropa sucia.

PAPÁ: ¿Por qué?

MAMÁ: ¡Vienen tu hermano y su familia!

realidades.com ▼

• Web Code: jcd-0615

Realidades ①

Capítulo 6B

Nombre _____

Hora _____

Fecha _____

Core Practice **6B–8**

Repaso

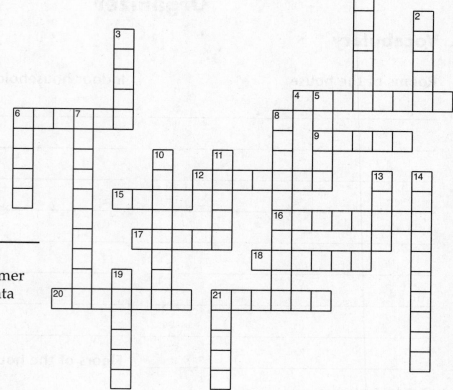

Across

4. cómo pasas al primer piso desde la planta baja; la ____

6. Yo ____ el baño.

9.

12. *to cook*

15. El hijo ____ la aspiradora cada fin de semana.

16.

____ el cuarto

17. La hija debe ____ los platos ahora.

18. un cuarto donde puedes poner el coche

20. cuarto donde come la familia; el ____

21. el piso más bajo de la casa

Down

1. el cuarto donde preparas la comida

2. Tengo que ____ la cama hoy.

3.

quitar el ____

5.

____ la basura

6. no cerca

7. Después de subir la escalera, estás en el ____ ____.

8. Cuando entras en la casa, estás en la ____ ____.

10. la oficina en la casa

11. ¿Quién va a ____ la mesa?

13. el cuarto donde ves la tele

14. el cuarto donde duermes

19. Mateo tiene que cortar el ____.

21. no limpio

Realidades 1

Capítulo 6B

Nombre _____

Hora _____

Fecha _____

Core Practice **6B–9**

Organizer

I. Vocabulary

Rooms of the house

_____

_____

_____

_____

_____

_____

_____

_____

Outdoor chores

_____

_____

_____

Indoor household tasks

_____

_____

_____

_____

_____

_____

Floors of the house

_____

_____

_____

_____

II. Grammar

1. To talk about actions in progress, use the _____ tense. This is formed by adding -_____ to the roots of **-ar** verbs and -_____ to the roots of **-er** and **-ir** verbs.

2. **Tú** commands are the same as the _____ form of the _____ tense of verbs. But the **tú** command form of **poner** is _____ and of **hacer** is _____.

realidades.com
• Web Code: jcd-0616

Realidades 1

Capítulo 7A

Nombre _____

Fecha _____

Hora _____

Core Practice **7A–1**

En el escaparate (*store window*)

You are window shopping at a large department store and you decide to make a list of what they have and what everything costs. Using the picture, list seven items and their prices below. Follow the model.

Modelo   *Los pantalones cuestan 35 dólares.*

1. _____

2. _____

3. _____

4. _____

5. _____

6. _____

7. _____

• Web Code: jcd-0701

Realidades 1

Capítulo 7A

Nombre _____

Fecha _____

Hora _____

Core Practice **7A–2**

Tienda de la Gracia

A. Write the numbers below in Spanish.

1. 100 _____

2. 500 _____

3. 909 _____

4. 222 _____

5. 767 _____

6. 676 _____

7. 110 _____

8. 881 _____

B. Read the following statistics about the chain of stores **Tienda de la Gracia**. Then answer the questions that follow.

TIENDA DE LA GRACIA	
Tiendas	100
Trabajadores	324
Promedio diario (*daily average*) de clientes	760
Camisas	612
Pantalones	404

1. ¿Cuántas Tiendas de la Gracia hay?

_____

2. ¿Cuál es el promedio diario de clientes en cada tienda?

_____

3. ¿Cuántos trabajadores hay en las Tiendas de la Gracia?

_____

4. ¿Cuántos pantalones hay en cada tienda?

_____

5. ¿Y camisas?

_____

realidades.com

• Web Code: jcd-0701

Realidades 1

Nombre _____

Hora _____

Capítulo 7A

Fecha _____

Core Practice **7A–3**

En el centro comercial

Tatiana and Mariana are in the local mall. Write the words that most logically complete their conversation as they go from store to store.

TATIANA: Vamos a esta tienda de ropa. Aquí tienen _____ elegante.

MARIANA: Bien. ¿Qué _____ comprar?

TATIANA: Necesito un vestido para la fiesta de mi primo.

DEPENDIENTA: ¿En qué puedo _____, señorita?

TATIANA: _____ un vestido elegante.

DEPENDIENTA: ¿Va Ud. a _____ el vestido a una fiesta o un baile formal?

TATIANA: A una fiesta. Me gusta este vestido.

MARIANA: ¿Cómo te _____?

TATIANA: ¡Me queda fantástico! Quiero comprarlo.

MARIANA: Vamos a otra tienda. Necesito _____ unos zapatos nuevos.

              Vamos a esa tienda, tienen buenos precios allí.

TATIANA: Mira estos zapatos aquí.

MARIANA: ¿Cuánto cuestan?

TATIANA: Trescientos dólares. ¿Es un buen _____?

MARIANA: Sí. Y me quedan _____. Voy a comprar estos zapatos.

TATIANA: Bien. Pasamos a otra tienda.

MARIANA: La tienda de música está a la derecha. ¿Entramos?

TATIANA: Sí, ¡ _____!

Realidades ①

Capítulo 7A

Nombre _____

Fecha _____

Hora _____

Core Practice **7A–4**

¿Qué llevan?

In complete sentences, describe two articles of clothing that each of the people below is wearing.

Pedro

A. _____

_____

B. _____

1. _____

Las hermanas Guzmán

A. _____

_____

B. _____

2. _____

La profesora Jones

A. _____

_____

B. _____

3. _____

El Dr. Cambambia

A. _____

_____

B. _____

4. _____

Anita

A. _____

_____

B. _____

5. _____

realidades.com
• Web Code: jcd-0702

Realidades ❶

Capítulo 7A

Nombre _____

Fecha _____

Hora _____

Core Practice **7A–5**

Algunos verbos nuevos

A. Fill in the chart below with the forms of the stem-changing verbs indicated.

	PENSAR	QUERER	PREFERIR
yo	*pienso*		
tú			*prefieres*
él, ella, Ud.		*quiere*	
nosotros			*preferimos*
vosotros	*pensáis*	*queréis*	*preferís*
ellos, ellas, Uds.		*quieren*	

B. Now, complete each sentence below by choosing the correct form of the verb **pensar**, **querer**, or **preferir**.

1. ¿ _____ (tú) la camisa roja o la camisa azul?

2. Nosotros _____ comprar un suéter nuevo.

3. Ellas _____ ir de compras hoy.

4. Vivian _____ llevar ropa elegante.

5. ¿Uds. _____ trabajar en la tienda de Mónica?

6. Yo _____ comprar los zapatos ahora.

7. Mis amigos y yo _____ jugar al fútbol cuando llueve.

8. Eduardo _____ ir a la fiesta con Brenda.

9. ¿Qué _____ (tú) hacer después de la escuela?

10. Marcelo y Claudio _____ ir al gimnasio después de la escuela.

11. Yo _____ buscar una bicicleta nueva.

12. ¿Tomás va a la tienda o _____ quedarse en casa?

• Web Code: jcd-0704

Manos a la obra ➡ *Gramática y vocabulario en uso* **125**

Realidades 1

Capítulo 7A

Nombre _____

Fecha _____

Hora _____

Core Practice **7A–6**

¿Cuál prefieres?

A. Fill in the chart below with the singular and plural, masculine and feminine forms of the demonstrative adjectives.

este		estos	
	esa		esas

B. Complete the following questions about the clothing items pictured by writing in the appropriate demonstrative adjectives from the chart above. Then answer the questions by saying that you prefer the item indicated by the arrow.

1. — ¿Prefieres _____ camisa o _____ suéter?

— _____

2. — ¿Prefieres _____ pantalones cortos o _____ jeans?

— _____

3. — ¿Te gustan más _____ sudaderas aquí o _____ suéteres?

— _____

4. — ¿Te gusta más _____ vestido o _____ falda?

— _____

5. — ¿Quieres _____ zapatos negros o _____ botas negras?

— _____

6. — ¿Prefieres _____ chaqueta o _____ abrigo?

— _____

realidades.com
• Web Code: jcd-0703

Realidades 1

Capítulo 7A

Nombre _____

Fecha _____

Hora _____

Core Practice **7A–7**

¿Quién?

Two sales associates are discussing some of the clients in their busy store. Fill in the blanks with the appropriate demonstrative adjectives based on the picture.

CELIA: ¿Qué hace _____ mujer allá?

YOLANDA: Pues, está mirando las botas, pero no quiere pagar mucho.

CELIA: ¿Qué quieren _____ mujeres aquí?

YOLANDA: Piensan comprar unos calcetines.

CELIA: ¿Y _____ hombre solo allí?

YOLANDA: ¿_____ hombre? Prefiere mirar los pantalones.

CELIA: A la derecha de él hay unos niños, ¿no? ¿Qué hacen _____ niños?

YOLANDA: Pues, _____ niños quieren unos suéteres nuevos.

CELIA: Oye, ¿ves a _____ hombres al lado de la puerta?

YOLANDA: Sí, piensan comprar _____ abrigos. ¿Por qué?

CELIA: Pues, son muy guapos, ¿no?

YOLANDA: Ah, sí. Creo que necesitan ayuda.

CELIA: ¡Hasta luego!

Realidades ❶

Capítulo 7A

Nombre _____

Fecha _____

Hora _____

Core Practice **7A–8**

Repaso

Across

2. Llevas ____ debajo de los zapatos.

3. ____ de baño

6. ¿Te ____ bien ese suéter?

7.

8. los ____ cortos

10. Yo llevo ____ en los pies.

12. No cuestan tanto. Es un buen ____.

14. En esta tienda, quiero ____ unas botas.

15. Jaime es informal. Siempre lleva camiseta y los ____.

17. Ella tiene que comprar un ____ para la fiesta.

18.

Down

1.

2.

4. ¿Cuánto ____ las botas?

5. Mi padre es inteligente. Siempre tiene ____.

6. 5000 ÷ 10

8. ____, señorita. Necesito ayuda.

9. Llevo una ____ en la cabeza.

11. Cuando hace frío, llevo un ____.

13. la ____ de ropa

16. 500 x 2

Organizer

I. Vocabulary

Clothing for warm weather

_____

_____

_____

_____

_____

Clothing for cold weather

_____

_____

_____

_____

_____

_____

Other words to talk about clothing

_____

_____

_____

Numbers in the hundreds

_____

_____

_____

_____

_____

_____

_____

_____

II. Grammar

1. The forms of the verb **pensar** are: _____ _____

   _____ _____

   _____ _____

   The forms of the verb **querer** are: _____ _____

   _____ _____

   _____ _____

   The forms of the verb **preferir** are: _____ _____

   _____ _____

   _____ _____

2. To refer to something close, use _____ / _____, _____ / _____; to refer to something further away, use _____ / _____, _____ / _____.

Realidades ❶

Capítulo 7B

Nombre _____

Fecha _____

Hora _____

Core Practice **7B–1**

Los regalos

Marcela is writing a list of gifts she wants to buy for her family. Help her by writing the names of the items suggested by the pictures in the blanks provided.

1. Para mi novio:

_____   _____   _____   _____

2. Para mi mejor amiga:

_____   _____

3. Para mi hermana:

_____   _____   _____   _____

4. Para mi padre:

 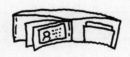 

_____   _____   _____

5. Para mi madre:

_____   _____   _____

realidades.com

• Web Code: jcd-0711

¡Tantas tiendas!

Write the names of the items pictured in the first blank, and where each person would find the items in the second blank.

1. Yo busco _____
   en una _____.

2. Germán busca _____
   en una _____.

3. Tú buscas _____
   en la _____.

4. Mi hermano busca _____
   en la _____.

5. Bárbara busca _____
   en un _____.

6. Buscamos _____
   en la _____.

7. Esteban y Luis buscan un _____
   en la _____.

8. Susana y Paulina buscan _____
   en una _____.

9. — ¿En dónde puedo comprar _____?
   — En un _____.

realidades.com ⓥ
• Web Code: jcd-0711

Realidades ①

Capítulo 7B

Nombre _____

Fecha _____

Hora _____

Core Practice **7B–3**

¿El regalo perfecto?

Valentine's Day is coming and Pepe and Laura are deciding what gifts to give each other.

A. Read the conversations below.

(*En una tienda de descuentos*)

PEPE: Necesito comprar un regalo para mi novia.

DEPENDIENTE: ¿Qué piensa comprar?

PEPE: No sé. Tiene que ser algo barato porque no tengo mucho dinero.

DEPENDIENTE: Pero, ¿no quiere un anillo bonito o un collar elegante para su novia?

PEPE: No. Es demasiado.

DEPENDIENTE: Puede comprar un reloj pulsera que no cuesta tanto.

PEPE: Oiga, el mes pasado compré software nuevo para mi computadora, para poder jugar videojuegos en la Red. ¡Pagué unos 90 dólares!

DEPENDIENTE: Entonces quiere este llavero de veinte dólares.

PEPE: ¡Genial!

(*En un almacén*)

LAURA: Quiero el regalo perfecto para mi novio.

DEPENDIENTA: ¿Él trabaja? ¿Quizás una corbata bonita?

LAURA: Estoy pensando en un regalo más romántico . . .

DEPENDIENTA: ¿Unos guantes para las noches de frío?

LAURA: No creo. Él nunca tiene frío. ¿Ud. tiene algo romántico?

DEPENDIENTA: ¡Mire! ¿Qué piensa de este anillo de cincuenta dólares?

LAURA: ¡Perfecto! Quiero uno, por favor.

B. Answer the questions about the dialogues in complete sentences.

1. ¿A qué tienda va Pepe? _____

    ¿Qué busca allí? ¿Por qué? _____

    _____

2. ¿Qué quiere venderle el dependiente? ¿Por qué Pepe no quiere comprarlos?

    _____

    _____

3. ¿Qué compra por fin Pepe? _____

4. ¿Qué quiere comprar Laura? _____

5. ¿Por qué Laura no quiere ni una corbata ni unos guantes? _____

    _____

6. ¿Qué va a comprar Laura? _____ ¿Es más

    caro o más barato que el regalo de Pepe? _____

realidades.com ✓

• Web Code: jcd-0712

Realidades

Capítulo 7B

Nombre _____

Fecha _____

Hora _____

Core Practice **7B–4**

Oraciones desordenadas

Put the scrambled sentences below into logical order.

1. compré / hace / lo / semana / una

   _____

2. yo / por / ayer / unos / pagué / un / guantes / dólar

   _____

3. lector / caro / DVD / un / es / muy / no

   _____

4. joyas / en / venden / almacén / el

   _____

5. pasada / la / compré / yo / semana / suéter / nuevo / un

   _____

6. anoche / una / compré / computadora / yo / nueva

   _____

7. pagaste / el / collar / cuánto / por

   ¿_____?

8. lo / año / el / tú / compraste / pasado

   _____

9. joyas / por / venden / tienda / esta / veinte / en / dólares

   _____

10. cuánto / por / el / pagaste / reloj

    ¿_____?

Realidades ①

Capítulo 7B

Nombre _____

Fecha _____

Hora _____

Core Practice **7B–5**

Hablamos del pasado

A. Fill in the chart below with the preterite forms of the verbs indicated.

	COMPRAR	HABLAR	PREPARAR	USAR	MIRAR
yo	compré				
tú					miraste
él, ella, Ud.		habló			
nosotros				usamos	
vosotros	comprasteis	hablasteis	preparasteis	usasteis	mirasteis
ellos, ellas, Uds.			prepararon		

B. Fill in the blanks in the following postcard with the correct preterite forms of the verbs given.

¡Hola, mamá!

  ¿Cómo estás? Estoy muy bien aquí en Quito.
Primero, José y yo _____ (preparar) unos
sándwiches ricos y _____ (hablar) con su
mamá un poco. Después, decidimos ir al centro
comercial. José y su mamá _____ (mirar)
unas chaquetas en la tienda de Smith y yo
_____ (comprar) algunas cosas para la
semana.

  A las cinco, la mamá de José _____
(llamar) por teléfono al padre, y él _____
(regresar) del trabajo un poco después. Nosotros
_____ (cenar) y _____ (usar) la
computadora antes de dormir.

  ¿Y tú? ¿_____ (caminar) esta semana?
¿_____ (comprar) el regalo para el
cumpleaños de papi? Pues, nos vemos en una semana.
¡Mañana me voy a Lima!

          Un abrazo,
           Víctor

La Sra. Guiraldo
Vía Águila 1305
Col. Cuauhtémoc
06500 México, D.F.

realidades.com ▾
• Web Code: jcd-0713

Realidades **1**

Capítulo 7B

Nombre _____

Fecha _____

Hora _____

Core Practice **7B–6**

Mini-conversaciones

A. Fill in the following charts with the preterite forms of the verbs given.

	PAGAR	BUSCAR	JUGAR	PRACTICAR	TOCAR
yo	*pagué*			*practiqué*	
tú			*jugaste*		
él, ella, Ud.		*buscó*			
nosotros					*tocamos*
vosotros	*pagasteis*	*buscasteis*	*jugasteis*	*practicasteis*	*tocasteis*
ellos, ellas, Uds.				*practicaron*	

B. Now, complete the mini-conversations below with preterite verb forms from the chart above.

1. — Juan, ¿cuánto _____ por tu suéter?

— Yo _____ 25 dólares.

2. — ¿Qué hizo Marta anoche?

— Ella _____ al fútbol con sus hermanos.

3. — Hija, ¿_____ el piano?

— Sí, mamá. _____ por una hora.

4. — Busco un apartamento nuevo.

— Yo _____ por un año antes de encontrar el apartamento perfecto.

5. — ¿Uds. _____ un instrumento en el pasado?

— Sí, nosotros _____ el violín.

6. — ¿Marcos va a practicar el básquetbol hoy?

— No, él _____ toda la semana pasada.

7. — ¿Con quién _____ (tú) al golf?

— _____ con mis dos hermanos y con mi padre.

Objeto directo

A. Rewrite the following sentences about shopping using direct object pronouns in place of the appropriate nouns.

1. Compré los zapatos. _____
2. ¿Tienes el vestido verde? _____
3. Escribo el cuento. _____
4. Mi mamá recibe el dinero. _____
5. Las mujeres llevan las faldas nuevas. _____
6. ¿Rosario va a comprar el regalo? _____
7. Las amigas compraron aretes nuevos. _____
8. Llevo los dos abrigos. _____

B. Ramona's mother is talking to her about their trip to the mall. Answer her questions using direct object pronouns. Follow the model.

Modelo ¿Llevas tu vestido nuevo a la escuela?

Sí, lo llevo mucho.

1. ¿Dónde vas a poner tu camisa nueva?

_____

2. ¿Compraste los zapatos azules?

_____

3. ¿Usas el reloj pulsera negro?

_____

4. ¿Cuándo vas a llevar tus guantes nuevos?

_____

5. ¿Tienes las camisetas nuevas?

_____

 realidades.com • Web Code: jcd-0715

Realidades 1

Capítulo 7B

Nombre

Fecha

Hora

Core Practice **7B–8**

Repaso

Across

5. donde las mujeres ponen las llaves, bolígrafos, etc.
7. la ___ de electrodomésticos
8. tienda donde venden zapatos

13.
14. los ___ de sol
17. Una tienda de ropa es donde ___ ropa.
18. no caro
20. tienda donde venden joyas

Down

1. Llevo los ___ durante el invierno porque tengo las manos frías.
2. Sancho quiere ___ las fotos de tu viaje.

3.
4. donde pones el dinero y a veces unas fotos; la ___
6. tienda donde venden libros
9. joya que llevas en las orejas
10. tienda donde venden todo
11. tipo de reloj que llevas en el cuerpo; reloj ___
12. donde pones las llaves
15. joya que llevas en el dedo
16. Los hombres llevan una camisa con ___ al trabajo.
19. *last night*

Realidades

Capítulo 7B

Nombre _____

Fecha _____

Hora _____

Core Practice **7B–9**

Organizer

I. Vocabulary

Types of stores

_____

_____

_____

_____

_____

Words to talk about jewelry

_____

_____

_____

_____

_____

Other gifts

_____

_____

_____

Words to talk about the past

_____

_____

_____

II. Grammar

1. The preterite endings of **-ar** verbs are: -_____   -_____

   -_____   -_____

   -_____   -_____

   Now conjugate the verb **pasar** in the preterite: _____ _____

   _____ _____

   _____ _____

2. The preterite ending of the **yo** form of verbs ending with **-car** is -_____. For **-gar** verbs it is -_____.

3. The direct object pronouns are _____ , _____ , _____ , and

   _____ .

realidades.com

• Web Code: jcd-0717

¿Adónde van?

Complete the mini-conversations. Use the drawing to fill in the first blank and to give you a clue for the second blank. Follow the model.

Modelo

— ¿Viste el ___monumento___ nuevo de Cristóbal Colón?

— Sí, ¡es fantástico! Está enfrente del ___museo___.

1.

— Mamá, quiero ver _____.

— Sí, Marisol. Vamos al _____.

2.

— ¿Uds. van de vacaciones en _____ este verano?

— No, vamos a la _____.

3.

— ¿Vas a ver _____ hoy?

— Sí, mis padres y yo vamos al _____.

4.

— ¿Quieres _____ hoy?

— Sí, pero ¿en dónde? ¿En el _____?

5.

— ¿Dónde es el _____?

— Pues, en el _____, por supuesto.

6.

— ¿Cómo te gusta ir de _____?

— Siempre viajamos en _____.

Asociaciones

A. Write the names of the places from your vocabulary that you associate with the following things or actions.

1. la historia, el arte __ __ __ Ⓞ __ __ __ __ Ⓞ __

2. las atracciones, los monos __ __ __ Ⓞ __ __ __ __ __

3. pintar, dibujar, el arte __ __ Ⓞ __ __ __

4. divertido, personas atrevidas, jugar __ __ Ⓞ __ __ __ __ __ __

   __ __ __ Ⓞ __ __ __ __ Ⓞ __

5. los deportes, un partido, ver Ⓞ __ __ __ Ⓞ __ __ __

6. la obra, el actor __ Ⓞ __ __ __ __

7. el hotel, muchas personas Ⓞ __ __ __ __ __ __

8. pasear en bote, mucha agua __ __ __ Ⓞ __

B. Now, unscramble the circled letters to find a related word.

__ __ __ __ __ __ __ __ __ __

realidades.com
• Web Code: jcd-0801

Realidades ❶

Capítulo 8A

Nombre _____

Fecha _____

Hora _____

Core Practice **8A–3**

¡Vamos al parque nacional!

The Carreras family went on vacation to Rocky Mountain National Park in Colorado. Read the postcard they sent to their friends back home and fill in the blanks with the words suggested by the pictures.

¡Saludos desde Colorado!

Llegamos al _____ el lunes pasado. Yo fui directamente

a la playa para _____ El _____

es precioso y ¡los _____ son enormes! El martes paseamos

en _____ por el lago y miramos los _____

_____. ¡Yo vi un oso en el bosque!

Para mañana tenemos muchos planes. Vamos a _____

por las montañas y por la noche vamos al _____ para ver

una obra musical.

Regresamos a la _____ el viernes. ¡Nos vemos

este fin de semana!

Abrazos,

Familia Carreras

Realidades 1

Capítulo 8A

Nombre _____

Fecha _____

Hora _____

Core Practice **8A–4**

¿Qué te pasó?

A. Read the dialogue between Aníbal and Carmen about Aníbal's trip to the beach.

CARMEN: Dime, ¿fuiste a la playa con tus primos?

ANÍBAL: ¡Ay, amiga; fue un desastre! Salí muy temprano para pasar todo el día allí.

Durante el día tomamos el sol y buceamos en el mar.

CARMEN: ¿No fue un día tremendo para descansar y pasarlo bien con tus amigos?

ANÍBAL: Por dos horas, sí. Pero después de mucha lluvia, todo salió mal.

CARMEN: Lo siento. Va a hacer buen tiempo este sábado. . .

ANÍBAL: Bueno, tú y yo podemos salir de la ciudad.

CARMEN: ¡Genial!

B. Now, answer the questions in complete sentences.

1. ¿Adónde fue Aníbal? _____

_____

2. ¿Qué hizo allí? _____

_____

3. ¿Con quién fue Aníbal? _____

_____

4. ¿Qué tiempo va a hacer el sábado? _____

_____

5. ¿Qué van a hacer Aníbal y Carmen? _____

_____

Realidades 1

Capítulo 8A

Nombre _____

Fecha _____

Hora _____

Core Practice **8A–5**

¿Qué hicieron?

A. Fill in the chart with the preterite forms of the verbs given.

	COMER	ESCRIBIR	CORRER	SALIR	VER	BEBER
yo	comí				vi	
tú			corriste	saliste	viste	bebiste
él, ella, Ud.				salió		bebió
nosotros		escribimos				
vosotros	comisteis	escribisteis	corristeis	salisteis	visteis	bebisteis
ellos/as, Uds						

B. Now, complete the mini-conversations below by filling in the appropriate forms of one of the verbs from Part A.

1. — Pablo, ¿vas a correr hoy?

— No, _____ ayer.

2. — ¿Elena _____ toda la leche?

— Sí, toda.

3. — ¿Uds. salieron anoche?

— Sí, _____ a las once.

4. — ¿_____ la nueva película de Almodóvar?

— Sí, la vi anoche.

5. — ¡Qué buenos niños!

— Sí, _____ todas las zana-horias.

6. — Juan, escribe la tarea.

— Ya la _____ , mamá.

7. — ¿Uds. comieron en el hotel anoche?

— No, _____ en el restaurante.

8. — ¿Quién va a correr en el maratón este año?

— Todos, porque sólo dos personas _____ el año pasado.

9. — ¿Con quién saliste, Marta?

— _____ con Toño.

10. — ¿El autor va a escribir un cuento nuevo?

— No, él _____ uno el mes pasado.

realidades.com

• Web Code: jcd-0803

¿Adónde fueron?

Some friends are talking about where they went on vacation. Write where they went, using the pictures below to help you. Follow the model.

Modelo   La familia Madrigal *fue al zoológico* _____.

1. Carlos _____.

2. Yo _____.

3. Lola y Tina _____.

4. Nosotros _____.

5. Elisa _____.

6. Tú _____.

7. Uds. _____.

BIENVENIDOS a YELLOWSTONE

realidades.com
• Web Code: jcd-0804

Realidades ①

Capítulo 8A

Nombre _____

Fecha _____

Hora _____

Core Practice **8A–7**

Qué viste?

Alicia saw many things at the park yesterday. Use the drawing and the location clues to say whom or what she saw. Pay attention to the use of the personal **a** in your statements. Follow the model.

Modelo   En el parque ayer, yo vi ___*a unos amigos*___ corriendo.

1. Yo vi _____ dándoles de comer a unos pájaros.

2. Yo vi _____ jugando al fútbol.

3. Yo vi _____ en la mesa.

4. En el lago, yo vi _____ paseando.

5. En el bote, yo vi _____ con una señorita.

6. En un árbol yo vi _____.

7. Al lado del árbol vi _____.

8. Debajo del árbol vi _____ con pelo largo.

9. En la playa vi _____.

realidades.com
• Web Code: jcd-0805

Manos a la obra ━ *Gramática y vocabulario en uso*   **145**

Repaso

Down ──────────────────

1. Me gusta ___ en el sofá.
2. donde puedes pasear en bote; el ___
3. Yo quiero ___ la tele.
4. medio de transporte que va por el agua; el ___
5. un edificio con muchos cuadros; el ___
8. medio de transporte que usan los estudiantes para ir a la escuela; el ___
10. la ___ de teatro
12. *the train*; el ___
13. *the sea*; el ___
14. sinónimo de **vacaciones**; un ___

17.
20. Chicago es una ___ donde hace mucho viento.

22.

Across ──────────────────

2. *place*; un ___
6. En el monumento, compramos ___.
7. el ___ de diversiones

9.

11. donde se juegan los partidos de fútbol; el ___
15. España es un ___ donde hablan español.
16. medio de transporte que va por el aire; el ___
18. pasear en ___
19. donde hay atracciones de animales; el ___
21. no tarde

Realidades 1

Capítulo 8A

Nombre _____

Fecha _____

Hora _____

Core Practice **8A–9**

Organizer

I. Vocabulary

Places to visit

_____

_____

_____

_____

Modes of transportation

_____

_____

_____

_____

Leisure activities

_____

_____

_____

_____

Phrases to discuss experiences

_____

_____

_____

_____

II. Grammar

1. The preterite endings of **-er** and **-ir** verbs are:

   yo   -_____   nosotros -_____

   tú   -_____   vosotros -_*isteis*___

   Ud. -_____   Uds.   -_____

2. The preterite forms of **ir** (and **ser**) are: _____ _____

   _____ _____

   _____ _____

3. _____ is inserted before the direct object of a sentence if the direct object is

   a person. This is called the _____.

Realidades 1

Capítulo 8B

Nombre _____

Fecha _____

Hora _____

Core Practice **8B–1**

La comunidad

Your new friend in Costa Rica is showing you around her community. Label each place or point of interest in the picture with the appropriate word.

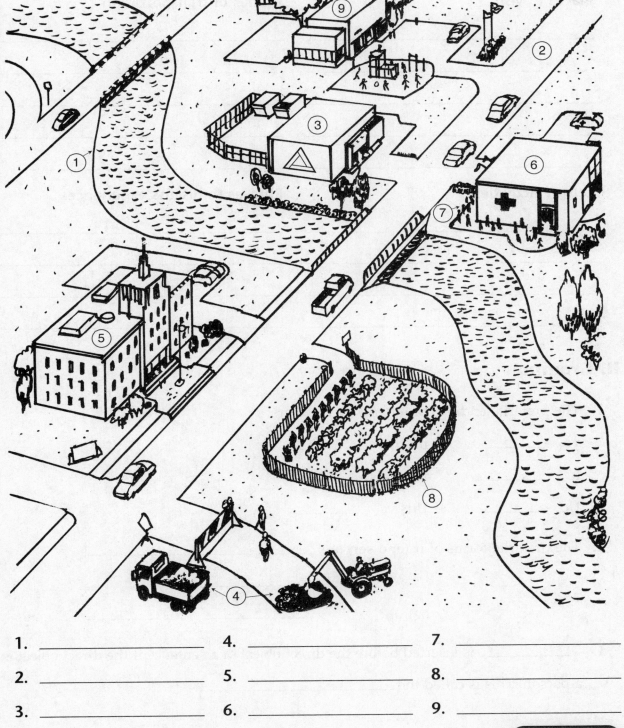

1. _____
2. _____
3. _____
4. _____
5. _____
6. _____
7. _____
8. _____
9. _____

realidades.com

• Web Code: jcd-0811

Realidades 1

Capítulo 8B

Nombre

Fecha

Hora

Core Practice **8B–2**

El reciclaje

A. Your community is starting a recycling program. Label each item below with words from your vocabulary.

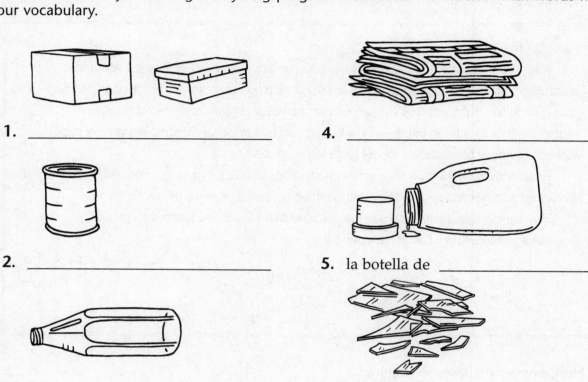

1. _____

2. _____

3. _____

4. _____

5. la botella de _____

6. la botella de _____

B. Now, write sentences to say whether or not it is necessary to recycle the items below. Follow the model.

Modelo Los tomates *No es necesario reciclar los tomates.*

1. El helado _____

2. El plástico _____

3. El vidrio _____

4. La sala _____

5. Las latas _____

realidades.com
• Web Code: jcd-0811

A primera vista ▬ *Vocabulario en contexto* **149**

Realidades ①

Capítulo 8B

Nombre _____

Fecha _____

Hora _____

Core Practice **8B–3**

El voluntario

A. Read the letter below from Álvaro, who is working as an AmeriCorps volunteer.

Querida familia:

¡Qué experiencia! Hacemos tantas cosas para ayudar a los demás. La semana pasada ayudamos en un proyecto de construcción con otro grupo de voluntarios. Ellos van a terminar el proyecto. Después de eso, fuimos a un centro de reciclaje. Allí aprendimos a reciclar el papel y el vidrio. También nos enseñaron cómo separar el papel normal (como el papel de los libros) de los periódicos.

Esta semana nosotros recogimos mucha ropa usada de varias partes de la ciudad y la llevamos a un centro para pobres. Allí le dimos la ropa a la gente pobre del barrio.

Hoy vamos a un centro para ancianos para ayudar a personas mayores. Estoy cansado, pero es importante hacer esto.

¡Hasta pronto!

Álvaro

B. Now, answer the questions below.

1. ¿Cuántas cosas hace Álvaro para ayudar a los demás? ¿Cuáles son? _____

_____

_____

2. ¿Qué aprendió Álvaro en el centro de reciclaje? _____

_____

3. ¿Adónde llevaron Álvaro y los voluntarios la ropa usada? _____

_____

4. ¿A quiénes le dieron la ropa? _____

_____

5. ¿Qué hace Álvaro hoy? _____

realidades.com ⊻
• Web Code: jcd-0812

Realidades ❶

Capítulo 8B

Nombre _____

Fecha _____

Hora _____

Core Practice **8B–4**

¿Qué haces en la comunidad?

You overhear two friends telling their teacher about what they do to help out in their communities. You can't hear what the teacher is asking. Fill in the teacher's questions. Follow the model.

Modelo	—¿Uds. ayudan en la comunidad?

　　　　　　— Sí, trabajamos como voluntarios en la comunidad.

— ¿_____?

— Trabajamos en una escuela primaria. Les enseñamos a los niños a leer.

— ¿_____?

— También recogemos ropa usada.

— ¿_____?

— Recogemos la ropa usada del barrio.

— ¿_____?

— Hay que separar la ropa y después lavarla.

— ¿_____?

— Le damos la ropa usada a la gente pobre del barrio.

— ¿_____?

— Sí, ayudamos en el hospital.

— ¿_____?

— Trabajamos como voluntarios en un hospital para niños. Nos encanta el trabajo voluntario.

¿Quién dice qué?

The people in the chart below are concerned citizens. Tell what each says by combining the subject on the left with the phrase on the right using **decir** + **que**. Follow the model.

Subjects	Phrases
Smokey the Bear	Hay que tener cuidado en el campamento.
Los directores del centro de reciclaje	Es necesario separar el plástico y el vidrio.
Gloria	La gente tiene que limpiar el barrio.
Yo	Todos deben participar en las actividades de la comunidad.
La profesora	Es esencial hacer trabajo voluntario.
La Cruz Roja	Es importante ayudar a los enfermos.
Tú	Es importante llevar la ropa usada a centros para los pobres.
Mi familia y yo	Es importante reciclar las botellas y latas.

Modelo *Smokey the Bear dice que hay que tener cuidado en el campamento.*

1. _____

2. _____

3. _____

4. _____

5. _____

6. _____

7. _____

realidades.com
• Web Code: jcd-0813

Realidades **1**

Capítulo 8B

Nombre _____

Fecha _____

Hora _____

Core Practice **8B–6**

Más trabajo voluntario

A. Write the indirect object pronouns that correspond to the following phrases.

1. A Javier y a Sara _____
2. A Diego y a mí _____
3. A la Dra. Estes _____
4. A Uds. _____
5. A Tito _____

6. A Luz y a ti _____
7. A ti _____
8. A nosotros _____
9. Al Sr. Pérez _____
10. A mí _____

B. Now, fill in the blanks in the following sentences with the correct indirect object pronouns.

1. La Cruz Roja _____ ayuda a las personas de la comunidad.

2. Nuestros padres _____ hablaron a mi hermano y a mí del reciclaje.

3. Mi profesora _____ ayudó a decidir qué trabajo voluntario me gustaría

   hacer.

4. _____ dice el profesor al estudiante que es importante separar las latas

   y el plástico.

5. Las personas _____ escriben al director del centro de reciclaje para

   recibir información sobre el reciclaje.

6. ¿Tus padres _____ dicen que debes ayudar a los demás?

7. _____ traigo unos juguetes a los niños en el hospital.

8. Los ancianos están muy contentos cuando _____ decimos que

   volvemos mañana.

Realidades ❶

Capítulo 8B

Nombre

Fecha

Hora

Core Practice **8B–7**

¿Hacer o dar?

A. Fill in the chart below with the correct forms of **hacer** and **dar** in the preterite.

	HACER	DAR
yo	hice	di
tú		
él, ella, Ud.		
nosotros		
vosotros	hicisteis	disteis
ellos, ellas, Uds.		

B. Now, fill in the blanks in the telephone conversation below with the appropriate forms from the chart above.

LEYDIN: ¡Mamá, estoy aquí en los Estados Unidos!

MADRE: Hola, hija. ¿Cómo estás?

LEYDIN: Bien, mamá. Yo _____ muchas cosas ayer después de llegar.

MADRE: ¿Qué _____?

LEYDIN: Pues, primero les _____ los regalos a toda la familia.

MADRE: ¿Y la abuelita te _____ un regalo a ti, también?

LEYDIN: Sí, ¡una bicicleta nueva! Estoy muy contenta.

MADRE: Y, ¿qué _____ Uds. después?

LEYDIN: Los primos _____ la tarea y la abuelita y yo le _____ la lista de cosas que comprar para la cena. Después le _____ la lista al abuelo, quien _____ las compras en el supermercado.

MADRE: ¿_____ Uds. algo más?

LEYDIN: Sí. Después de comer, yo _____ un postre especial para todos: ¡tu famoso pastel de tres leches!

MADRE: ¡Qué coincidencia! Yo _____ uno también y les _____ un poco a nuestros amigos, los Sánchez. ¿Qué más . . .?

realidades.com

• Web Code: jcd-0814

Realidades ①

Capítulo 8B

Nombre _____

Fecha _____

Hora _____

Core Practice **8B-8**

Repaso

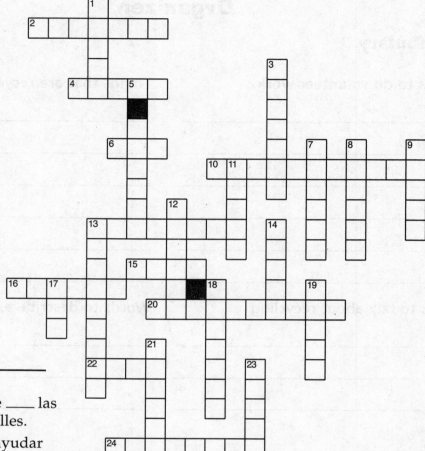

Across

2. Es importante ____ las latas de las calles.

4. Es necesario ayudar a los ____.

6. otra ____

10. *unforgettable*

13. el ____ de construcción

15.

16. lugar donde recogen las verduras y las plantas; el ____

20. AmeriCorps hace el trabajo ____.

22. Esa ____ es de cartón.

24. *problem*

Down

1. *poor*

3. Puedes reciclar una ____ de vidrio o de plástico.

5. *often*; ____ ____

7. Puedes reciclar las botellas de ____ y de plástico.

8. Es importante reciclar las cajas de ____.

9. sinónimo de **las personas**; la ____

11. Los ____ son nuestro futuro.

12. el ____ de reciclaje

13.

14. El profesor ____ las botellas al centro de reciclaje.

17. el ____ Grande

18. *toy*; un ____

19. Mis padres me ____ la verdad.

21. sinónimo de **la comunidad**; el ____

23.

Realidades 1

Capítulo 8B

Nombre _____

Fecha _____

Hora _____

Core Practice **8B–9**

Organizer

I. Vocabulary

Places to do volunteer work

_____

_____

_____

_____

_____

Things that are recyclable

_____

_____

_____

_____

_____

Verbs to talk about recycling

_____

_____

_____

Words to describe experiences

_____

_____

_____

II. Grammar

1. The forms of **decir** in the present are: _____ _____

   _____ _____

   _____ _____

2. The indirect object pronouns are: _____ _____

   _____ _____

   _____ _____

3. The preterite forms of **dar** are: The preterite forms of **hacer** are:

   _____ _____   _____ _____

   _____ _____   _____ _____

   _____ _____   _____ _____

realidades.com

• Web Code: jcd-0817

Realidades **1**

Capítulo 9A

Nombre _____

Fecha _____

Hora _____

Core Practice **9A–1**

Las películas

A. You love movies, but always forget to check the newspaper for the showings. You constantly have to ask your friends what movies are showing and at what time. Complete each dialogue by filling in the words that best identify the picture.

1. — ¿Cuándo empieza la _____?

— Empieza a las nueve y media. Son casi las nueve. ¡Vamos ahora!

2. — ¿Va a ser larga la _____?

— Sí. Empieza a las dos y media y termina a las cinco menos cuarto.

3. — ¿A qué hora dan la _____?

— A las seis.

4. — ¿Cuánto dura el _____?

— Dura menos de tres horas.

5. — ¿Cuándo va a empezar la _____?

— Empieza a las cuatro y media.

6. — Ya es la una y veinte. ¿Qué podemos hacer?

— Podemos ir al cine a ver una _____

B. Now, say the following time expressions another way using new vocabulary phrases.

1. Son las cinco menos diez. _____.

2. Son las dos y treinta. _____.

3. Dura una hora y cincuenta minutos. Dura _____.

4. Termina a las once y cuarenta. Termina _____.

realidades.com
• Web Code: jcd-0901

A primera vista — *Vocabulario en contexto* **157**

Realidades 1

Capítulo 9A

Nombre _____

Fecha _____

Hora _____

Core Practice **9A–2**

¿Qué programas les gustan?

Read the information about each person below. Then decide which TV program would be best for him or her and write it in the blank.

1. Pedro es gracioso. Siempre cuenta chistes y hace cosas cómicas. A él le gustan

   los programas _____.

2. Mi padre lee el periódico todos los días. Le interesa la política. A él le gustan

   los programas _____.

3. La profesora tiene dos hijos y quiere enseñarles mucho. También busca información

   para usar en la clase. Ella prefiere los programas _____.

4. Abuela no trabaja y tiene que estar en casa. Le interesan mucho los

   juegos, especialmente cuando la gente gana dinero. A ella le gustan los programas

   _____.

5. Javi toca la guitarra y Juanita canta. Pasan casi todo el tiempo practicando la

   música. A ellos les gustan los programas _____.

6. Rosa estudia inglés. Un día quiere trabajar para un periódico. Para aprender más

   de la gente, ella ve los programas _____.

7. Ronaldo es deportista. Juega al fútbol, al béisbol y al básquetbol. Cuando no está

   practicando un deporte está viendo programas _____.

8. A Cristina le gustan las historias. Lee novelas románticas y a veces escribe cuentos

   de amor. A ella le gustan las _____.

realidades.com

• Web Code: jcd-0901

Realidades ①

Capítulo 9A

Nombre _____

Fecha _____

Hora _____

Core Practice **9A–3**

¿Cómo son las cosas allí?

Luzma is writing a letter to her pen pal in the U.S. She is telling her pen pal about TV and movies in her country. Fill in the blanks with the words that best complete her thoughts.

> Querida Valerie,
>
> ¿Qué tal? ¿Cómo fue la _____ que viste la semana pasada? En
>
> mi país me encanta ir al cine. Me gustan más las películas _____ .
>
> Mi hermano es policía y _____ yo sé mucho _____
>
> los policías. También me interesa esta clase de películas porque son más
>
> _____ que una comedia o la ciencia ficción. Las comedias
>
> _____ aburren y a veces son infantiles. No me gustan las películas
>
> de _____ porque son demasiado violentas. ¿Qué _____
>
> película te gusta más a ti?
>
> Ahora te hablo de los _____ de televisión aquí. Bueno, no son
>
> muy diferentes de los programas de allí. Tenemos programas de dibujos
>
> animados como *Rin, ran, run,* programas de _____ como *¡Una*
>
> *fortuna para ti!* y tenemos las noticias. Yo veo las noticias pero sólo me
>
> interesan los programas que dan sobre la policía en el _____ 56.
>
> Eso es todo. Adiós, amiga.
>
> *Luzma*

Tus programas favoritos

Read the TV listings below, then answer the questions that follow in complete sentences.

EVENING — NOCHE

Hora	Canal	Programa
6PM	2	Noticias
	18	Amigos
	26	Noticias
	30	Pepito y Paquito
	33	Mi casa
	42	Deportivas
	60	Música cubana
7pm	2	Los monos
	18	Noticias
	26	Entre tú y yo
	30	Noticias
	33	Noticias
	42	Deportes
	60	La salsa y la samba
8PM	2	¡Niágara!
	18	Amigos
	26	Película: El monstruo verde
	30	El mundo real
	33	Hoy día
	42	Fútbol . . . .
	60	¿Puedes cantar?
9PM	2	El zoológico
	18	Mi Amiga Sara
	26	. . . .
	30	El día en Alaska
	33	¡Ganar un coche!
	42	. . . .
	60	Baile en vivo

1. ¿Cuántos programas de noticias empiezan a las seis? __________

2. ¿Qué clase de programas tiene el canal 42? __________

   ¿Y el canal 60? __________

   ¿Y el canal 2? __________

3. ¿Qué programa deportivo puedes ver a las ocho? __________

4. Para ver un programa educativo, ¿vas a ver el canal 2 o el 18 a las nueve? __________

5. ¿Qué clase de programa empieza a las nueve en el canal 33? __________

   ¿Y a las nueve en el canal 30? __________

6. ¿Qué clase de programa dan a las siete en el canal 26? __________

7. ¿Dan una película de horror a las ocho en el canal 26? __________

realidades.com
• Web Code: jcd-0902

Realidades ❶

Capítulo 9A

Nombre _____

Fecha _____

Hora _____

Core Practice **9A–5**

Acabo de . . .

Write what the following people just finished doing and are now going to do, based on the pictures. Follow the model.

Modelo Marta <u>acaba de estudiar. Ahora va a dormir.</u>

1. Anabel _____

   _____

2. Nosotros _____

   _____

3. Ellas _____

   _____

4. Yo _____

   _____

5. Tú _____

   _____

6. Juan y el Sr. Lebredo _____

   _____

7. Roberto _____

   _____

8. Ana María _____

   _____

Realidades ❶

Capítulo 9A

Nombre _____

Fecha _____

Hora _____

Core Practice **9A–6**

Más gustos

A. Complete the sentences below with the correct forms of the verbs given.

1. Al Presidente le _____ (interesar) la política.

2. ¡Qué terrible! Me _____ (doler) el pie izquierdo.

3. A los estudiantes les _____ (aburrir) las presentaciones largas.

4. A nosotros nos _____ (encantar) ver comedias.

5. A tus hermanos les _____ (gustar) las películas de horror.

6. A ti te _____ (interesar) el teatro.

7. Me _____ (quedar) bien los pantalones pero me

   _____ (faltar) el dinero para comprarlos.

B. Now, complete each sentence below with the correct form of the verb given and the appropriate indirect object pronoun. Follow the model.

Modelo   A Carlos _____*le aburre*_____ (aburrir) la política.

1. A mí _____ (faltar) un lápiz.

2. A ellas _____ (aburrir) las clases de arte.

3. A Carmen _____ (quedar) bien la falda, ¿no?

4. A ti _____ (encantar) los programas deportivos.

5. ¿A ti y a Pedro _____ (gustar) leer revistas?

6. A mi papá _____ (doler) los pies.

7. ¿A Ud. _____ (faltar) los cuadernos?

8. A nosotros _____ (interesar) las obras de teatro.

9. A Lola y a Roberto _____ (interesar) el programa musical y el programa educativo.

realidades.com

• Web Code: jcd-0904

Realidades 1

Capítulo 9A

Nombre _____

Fecha _____

Hora _____

Core Practice **9A-7**

Frases revueltas

The following sentences are mixed up. Rearrange them so that they are grammatically correct and make sense. Don't forget to conjugate verbs where appropriate. Follow the model.

Modelo   ir al cine / me / a mí / y al centro comercial / gustar

A mí me gusta ir al cine y al centro comercial.

1. le / leer / a Elena / poemas / encantar / y escribir

_____

2. negros / unos zapatos / te / para / faltar / a ti / ir a la fiesta

_____

3. diez kilómetros / a mí / doler / después de / me / los pies / correr

_____

4. al Sr. Mirabal / interesar / americano / le / el fútbol

_____

5. los programas / les / a mis padres / de entrevistas / aburrir

_____

6. importar / voluntario / a nosotros / el trabajo / nos

_____

7. a Uds. / los boletos para el cine / les / para comprar / faltar / el dinero

_____

8. interesar / les / a José y a Felipe / policíacas / las películas

_____

9. el trabajo / a Angélica / aburrir / le

_____

10. la comida / italiana / encantar / a Vanessa y a mí / nos

_____

Nombre _____

Hora _____

Fecha _____

Core Practice **9A–8**

Repaso

Down

1. Yo veo mis programas favoritos en el ____ cinco.
2. Es más que interesante; es ____.
4. *already*
5. No es actor, es ____.
7. No es interesante, es ____.
9. Me van a ____ zapatos. Necesito comprarlos.
10. Puedes leer las ____ o verlas en la tele.
11.
    película ____
14. *really?*
16. A Paco le gusta el fútbol. Ve programas ____.
18. No sé mucho ____ eso.

Across

3. Cuando vas al cine, ves una ____.

6.

8. un programa en la tele que cuenta las historias románticas de la gente; la ____

12. *therefore*
13. Una comedia es ____.
15. No es actriz, es ____.
16. Los programas ____ una hora.
17. *Entre tú y yo* es un programa de ____.
19. Cuando la gente gana dinero, es un programa de ____.

Realidades ❶

Capítulo 9A

Nombre _____

Hora _____

Fecha _____

Core Practice **9A–9**

Organizer

I. Vocabulary

Types of television programs

_____

_____

_____

_____

_____

_____

Types of movies

_____

_____

_____

_____

_____

_____

Words to describe movies/programs

_____

_____

_____

_____

_____

Words to express opinions

_____

_____

_____

_____

_____

II. Grammar

1. Use _____ + _____ to say what you or others have just finished doing.

2. **Me gusta** is literally translated as "_____." So, the construction is formed by putting the _____ first, followed by the _____ , and finally the _____ .

Realidades ❶

Capítulo 9B

Nombre _____

Fecha _____

Hora _____

Core Practice **9B–1**

El laboratorio

Label the computer lab below with the appropriate words.

1. _____

2. _____

3. _____

4. _____

5. _____

6. _____

realidades.com ✓
• Web Code: jcd-0911

Realidades ❶

Capítulo 9B

Nombre _____

Fecha _____

Hora _____

Core Practice **9B–2**

Las asociaciones

Write the words from your vocabulary that you associate with each of the following definitions.

1. Una sala de clases con muchas computadoras _____

2. Lugar para hablar con otras personas en línea _____

3. Comunicarse con otros por computadora _____

4. Lo que haces si quieres aprender más _____

5. Buscar información _____

6. Un lugar de la Red dedicado a algún tema _____

7. Hacer actividades electrónicas divertidas _____

8. Una comunicación *no* por correo electrónico _____

9. Una carta que envías para una fecha especial _____

10. Expresar y comprender ideas de otra persona _____

11. Si quieres hacer un disco compacto _____

12. Un artista puede hacerlos en la computadora _____

El sitio Web

Sara has just purchased a laptop computer. She is so excited that she just has to tell her friend Ramón. In the e-mail below write the words that best complete her thoughts.

Ramón,

   Ay, amigo, tienes que comprarte una computadora

_____. ¡Son los mejores juguetes del mundo!

Cuando vas de vacaciones puedes llevarla en tu mochila y

cuando estás en el hotel puedes _____ en la

Red, escribir por _____ o

_____ información de la Red. ¿Y quieres

sacar fotos? Con una cámara _____ puedes

sacarlas y ponerlas en la computadora. También puedes

mandar las fotos a otra _____ electrónica

si quieres. ¿Qué te _____? ¿Es difícil?

Puedes _____ un curso para aprender más

sobre cómo usar esta clase de cámara y cómo crear

_____ en la computadora. No debes tener

_____ de buscar información sobre

cámaras digitales porque hay muchas personas que

_____ usarlas o que escribieron unos

_____ sobre estas cámaras.

   Bueno, podemos hablar más de esto_____

porque no tengo tiempo ahora. Hasta luego.

Sara

realidades.com
• Web Code: jcd-0912

¡Una computadora muy buena!

Your local newspaper recently ran an ad for a new computer and many of your friends bought one. Read some of the computer's capabilities in the ad below. Then, based on the information you are given about each person that bought this computer, say what he or she uses the new computer for. Follow the model.

> **CON LA COMPUTADORA ES POSIBLE:**
>
> • Grabar un disco compacto
> • Preparar presentaciones
> • Escribir por correo electrónico
> • Usar una cámara digital
> • Visitar salones de chat
> • Navegar en la Red
> • Crear documentos
> • Estar en línea

Modelo A Juan le gusta bajar información.

Juan usa la computadora para estar en línea.

1. A Alejandro le gusta escribir cuentos y composiciones.

   _____

2. A Diego le gusta sacar fotos.

   _____

3. A Caridad le gusta tocar y escuchar música.

   _____

4. A Ramiro le gusta buscar los sitios Web.

   _____

5. A Esperanza le gusta conocer y hablar con otras personas.

   _____

6. A Lucita le gusta escribir tarjetas y cartas a su familia que vive en otra ciudad.

   _____

7. A Rodrigo le gusta enseñar a los niños.

   _____

Realidades 1

Capítulo 9B

Nombre _____

Fecha _____

Hora _____

Core Practice **9B–5**

¿Pedir o servir?

A. Fill in the charts below with the present tense forms of the verbs **pedir** and **servir**.

	PEDIR	**SERVIR**
yo	pido	
tú		
él, ella, Ud.		sirve
nosotros		
vosotros	pedís	servís
ellos, ellas, Uds.		

B. Complete the mini-conversations below with the correct forms of **pedir** or **servir**.

1. — Cuando vas al restaurante Marino para comer, ¿qué _____ tú?

   — Normalmente _____ una ensalada y una pasta.

2. — ¿Para qué _____ esto?

   — _____ para grabar discos compactos, hijo.

3. — ¿Los camareros les _____ rápidamente en el restaurante Guzmán?

   — Sí, son muy trabajadores.

4. — No puedo ver esos gráficos.

   — (Nosotros) _____ ayuda, entonces.

5. — Bienvenida a la fiesta. ¿Le _____ algo?

   — Sí, un refresco, por favor.

6. — Vamos al restaurante. Esta noche ellos _____ pollo con salsa y pasta.

   — Yo siempre _____ el pollo.

7. — ¿Para qué _____ el menú?

   — _____ para conocer la comida del restaurante. ¿Y qué vas a

   _____ del menú?

   — Yo siempre _____ la misma cosa. . . el bistec.

realidades.com
• Web Code: jcd-0913

Realidades ①

Capítulo 9B

Nombre _____

Fecha _____

Hora _____

Core Practice **9B–6**

¿Saber o conocer?

A. Write either **saber** or **conocer** in the blanks under the items below.

1. Mi número de teléfono

_____

2. Usar una computadora

_____

3. El profesor de la clase de español

_____

4. La película *Casablanca*

_____

5. Leer música

_____

6. La ciudad de Nueva York

_____

7. Mi madre

_____

8. Tu mejor amigo

_____

9. Navegar en la Red

_____

10. El sitio Web

_____

B. Fill in the missing forms of **saber** and **conocer** in the charts below.

	SABER	CONOCER
yo		
tú		
él, ella, Ud.	sabe	conoce
nosotros		
vosotros	sabéis	conocéis
ellos, ellas, Uds.		

C. Complete the following sentences using the correct forms of **saber** or **conocer**.

1. Juan, ¿ _____ la fecha de hoy?

2. ¿Alguien _____ a un médico bueno?

3. Mis padres _____ bailar muy bien.

4. Nosotros _____ todas las palabras de la obra.

5. ¿ _____ dónde está el Museo del Prado?

Web Code: jcd-0914

Manos a la obra ● *Gramática y vocabulario en uso* **171**

Planes para la noche

The Miranda family is planning to go out to eat. Fill in their conversation using forms of **conocer**, **saber**, **pedir**, or **servir**.

PADRE: Vamos al restaurante Vista del Mar. ¿Lo _____ Uds.? Me gusta

mucho.

TERESA: Yo no lo _____ pero _____ dónde está. ¡Quiero ir

a ese restaurante!

TOMÁS: Por supuesto que _____ dónde está, Tere, el nombre es Vista del Mar.

TERESA: Sí. ¿_____ Uds. que tienen el mejor pescado de la ciudad?

Es muy sabroso.

MADRE: ¿Y ellos _____ otra comida también?

TERESA: Yo no _____ . ¿Sabes tú, Tomás?

TOMÁS: Sí. Allí _____ mucha comida rica.

PADRE: Yo _____ el pescado porque me encanta.

TOMÁS: Sí, me encanta el pescado también.

TERESA: Es verdad Tomás, pero siempre _____ la misma cosa cuando

comemos pescado.

PADRE: Por eso vamos a este restaurante. Puedes _____ de todo y va a ser

sabrosísimo.

TERESA: ¡Yo quiero _____ ese restaurante!

MADRE: Pues, estamos de acuerdo. Vamos a Vista del Mar.

realidades.com

• Web Code: jcd-0915

Realidades **1**

Capítulo 9B

Nombre _____

Fecha _____

Hora _____

Core Practice **9B–8**

Repaso

Down

1.

2. El cliente ___ un té helado porque tiene calor.

3. Voy a visitar Nueva York porque quiero ___ la.

4. ___ un disco compacto

6. Los estudiantes hacen un ___ del presidente Lincoln.

8. Quiero escribirte una carta. ¿Cuál es tu ___ electrónica?

9. Yo escribo por ___ electrónico.

11. Estoy en línea. Quiero ___ en ___ ___.

12. *song;* la ___

13. El ___ Web para este libro es **realidades.com.**

14. No tengo ese programa. Lo voy a ___ de la Red.

16. Necesito ___ información para mi informe.

18. La artista sabe muy bien hacer ___ en la computadora.

19. Necesito una computadora que puede ___ documentos.

21. *slide;* la ___

Across

1. Quiero ___ un curso.

5. No debes tener ___ de la tecnología.

7. Para navegar en la Red, hay que estar ___ ___.

10. Si quieres hablar con personas inmediatamente, vas a un ___ de chat.

13. ¿Para qué ___?

15. *to communicate (with)*

17. Mi amiga me escribió una ___.

20. No me gusta hablar por teléfono. Me gusta hablar ___ ___ ___.

22. Voy a la escuela porque quiero ___ cómo hacer cosas.

23. Vamos al ___ para usar las computadoras de la escuela.

24. la computadora ___

Realidades 1

Capítulo 9B

Nombre _____

Fecha _____

Hora _____

Core Practice **9B–9**

Organizer

I. Vocabulary

Words to talk about the Web

_____

_____

_____

Words to name other electronics

_____

_____

_____

_____

Verbs related to online activities

_____

_____

_____

_____

_____

II. Grammar

1. The present tense of **pedir** is: The present tense of **servir** is:

_____ _____   _____ _____

_____ _____   _____ _____

_____ _____   _____ _____

2. Use the verb _____ for information or activities that you know. Use

the verb _____ to talk about familiarity with people, places, or things.

realidades.com
• Web Code: jcd-0916

Table of Contents

Realidades 1

Nombre

Hora

Capítulo 5B

Fecha

Vocabulary Check, Sheet 3

Tear out this page. Write the English words on the lines. Fold the paper along the dotted line to see the correct answers so you can check your work.

el postre

_____

rico, rica

_____

el azúcar

_____

la cuchara

_____

el cuchillo

_____

la pimienta

_____

el plato

_____

la sal

_____

la servilleta

_____

la taza

_____

el tenedor

_____

el vaso

_____

el camarero

_____

la camarera

_____

la cuenta

_____

el menú

_____

Fold In

Tear out this page. Write the Spanish words on the lines. Fold the paper along the dotted line to see the correct answers so you can check your work.

dessert _____

rich, tasty _____

sugar _____

spoon _____

knife _____

pepper _____

plate, dish _____

salt _____

napkin _____

cup _____

fork _____

glass _____

waiter _____

waitress _____

bill _____

menu _____

Fold In

To hear a complete list of the vocabulary for this chapter, go to www.realidades.com and type in the Web Code jcd-0599. Then click on **Repaso del capítulo**.

The verb *venir* (p. 256)

- The forms of **venir** are similar to the forms of **tener** that you just learned. Notice that the **yo** forms of both verbs end in **-go**.

yo	**vengo**	nosotros/nosotras	**venimos**
tú	**vienes**	vosotros/vosotras	**venís**
usted/él/ella	**viene**	ustedes/ellos/ellas	**vienen**

A. Circle all the forms of **venir** you see in this conversation.

RAÚL: ¿Vienes a la fiesta?

ANA: Si, vengo a las ocho y media.

Mis padres vienen también.

RAÚL: Muy bien. Mis amigos no vienen, pero mi hermano sí viene.

ANA: ¿Cuándo vienen?

RAÚL: Venimos a las nueve.

B. Now, write the forms of **venir** that you circled in **part A** in the correct row of the table. Write only one form of **venir** for each subject pronoun. The first one has been done for you.

Subject pronoun	Form of *venir*
1. yo	
2. tú	*Vienes*
3. usted/él/ella	
4. nosotros	
5. ustedes/ellos/ellas	

C. Complete the following conversation by circling the correct forms of **venir**.

ISABEL: ¿(**Vienes / Vienen**) ustedes a la fiesta?

MÍA: Sí, Marcos y yo (**vienen / venimos**). Pero Luis no (**vienes / viene**).

ISABEL: ¿Por qué no (**viene / vengo**) Luis?

MÍA: Tiene que trabajar. ¿(**Venimos / Vienes**) tú?

ISABEL: Sí. (**Vengo / Vienen**) a las ocho.

MÍA: ¡Qué bien! Nosotros (**venimos / vienes**) a las ocho también.

• **Venir** is used to say that someone is coming to a place or an event.

D. Write forms of **venir** to say when people are coming to the party.

1. Nosotras _____ a las ocho y cuarto.

2. Tú _____ a las nueve menos cuarto.

3. Elena y Olga _____ a las nueve y media.

4. Yo _____ a las ocho.

5. Marcos _____ a las diez y cuarto.

6. Usted _____ a las diez menos cuarto.

7. Ustedes _____ a las diez.

E. This agenda shows when people have appointments. Complete each sentence to say when each person is coming. Follow the model.

```
8:00  8:30 La Sra. Ramos
9:00  Marta
10:00 Raúl y Josefina
      10:45 Yo
11:00 11:30 tú
12:00 Carmen y yo
      Pedro
1:00
2:00  2:30 Roberto y tú
3:00  3:30 Lucía y Ramón
4:00
5:00
```

| **Modelo** | _La Sra. Ramos viene_ a las ocho y media. |

1. _____ a las nueve.

2. _____ a las diez.

3. _____ a las once menos cuarto.

4. _____ a las once y media.

5. _____ a las doce.

6. _____ a la una.

7. _____ a las dos y media.

8. _____ a las tres y media.

F. Answer each question by completing the sentences. Follow the model.

| **Modelo** | ¿A qué hora vienes a la clase de español? |

Yo ____vengo___ a la clase de español ___a las diez y media___ .

1. ¿A qué hora vienes a la escuela?

   Yo _____ a la escuela _____ .

2. ¿A qué hora vienes a la clase de español?

   Yo _____ a la clase de español _____ .

3. ¿A qué hora vienes a casa?

   Yo _____ a casa _____ .

realidades.com ⓥ
• Web Code: jcd-0513

Realidades **1**

Capítulo 5B

Nombre _____

Fecha _____

Hora _____

Guided Practice Activities 5B-3

The verbs *ser* and *estar* (p. 258)

- There are two Spanish verbs that mean "to be": **ser** and **estar**.
- Review their forms in the present tense.

ser			
yo	**soy**	nosotros/nosotras	**somos**
tú	**eres**	vosotros/vosotras	**sois**
usted/él/ella	**es**	ustedes/ellos/ellas	**son**

estar			
yo	**estoy**	nosotros/nosotras	**estamos**
tú	**estás**	vosotros/vosotras	**estáis**
usted/él/ella	**está**	ustedes/ellos/ellas	**están**

A. Circle the form of **ser** or **estar** that is used in each sentence.

1. Mi madre es profesora.

2. Ellas son de México.

3. Las decoraciones están en mi casa.

4. Nosotras somos artísticas.

5. Yo estoy enferma.

6. Los libros están en la mesa.

7. Tú estás en la oficina.

8. Yo soy la prima de Ana.

B. Look at the forms of **ser** and **estar** that you circled in **part A**. Decide why **ser** or **estar** was used in each. Write the reason using the chart in the explanation on page 258 in your textbook to find the reason why **ser** or **estar** was used in each sentence. Write each reason in the right-hand side of the chart. The first one has been done for you.

Forms of *ser* and *estar*	Reason
1. *es*	*who a person is*
2.	
3.	
4.	
5.	
6.	
7.	
8.	

The verbs *ser* and *estar* (continued)

C. Circle the correct form of the verb **ser** in each sentence.

1. Mis padres (**son / somos**) profesores.

2. Yo (**soy / eres**) muy atrevida.

3. La comida (**es / eres**) de un restaurante.

D. Circle the correct form of the verb **estar** in each sentence.

1. Tú (**estoy / estás**) muy cansado hoy.

2. La computadora (**está / estamos**) en la oficina.

3. Nosotros (**estamos / están**) muy ocupados.

E. Circle the correct form of **ser** or **estar** in these sentences. Look back at the chart with the uses of **ser** and **estar** if you need help.

1. Mis abuelos (**son / están**) profesores de matemáticas.

2. Yo (**soy / estoy**) enfermo hoy.

3. Tú (**eres / estás**) en la clase de historia.

4. Tomás (**es / está**) de Argentina.

5. Ustedes (**son / están**) argentinos también.

6. Nosotras (**somos / estamos**) muy cansadas.

7. Los libros (**son / están**) muy interesantes.

8. Los libros (**son / están**) en la biblioteca.

F. Write the correct form of **ser** or **estar** to complete each sentence.

1. Tú _____ en la oficina.

2. Nosotras _____ muy ocupadas hoy.

3. Yo _____ estudiante.

4. Mi padre _____ profesor.

5. El video _____ interesante.

6. Los videos _____ en la biblioteca.

7. Nosotros _____ de Guatemala.

8. Tú _____ muy simpático.

realidades.com

• Web Code: jcd-0514

Realidades 1

Capítulo 5B

Nombre _____

Hora _____

Fecha _____

Guided Practice Activities 5B-5

Lectura: Una visita a Santa Fe (pp. 262–263)

A. The reading in your textbook is about the city of Santa Fe. What kinds of information would you expect to find in such a reading? List three ideas below.

1. _____

2. _____

3. _____

B. As you skim the reading you will come across some new cognates. Write the English word for each Spanish cognate listed below.

1. visita _____

2. historia _____

3. museo _____

4. típica _____

5. histórico _____

6. tradicional _____

C. Did you find some activities when you skimmed the reading? If not, look again to find three activities that the cousins are going to do during their visit to Santa Fe. Write the three activities in Spanish below.

1. _____

2. _____

3. _____

D. Now, read the paragraph below from your textbook and answer the questions in English that follow.

> *Durante los días de su visita, el Rancho va a celebrar "un fandango", un baile histórico y típico, con una cena tradicional. Toda la comida es riquísima, pero nuestro plato favorito es el chile con carne y queso. Después de comer, vamos a bailar.*

1. What is a "fandango"? _____

2. What kind of meal will they have to accompany the "fandango"?

   _____

3. What is their favorite dish at the restaurant? _____

4. Which comes first, the meal or dancing? _____

Presentación escrita (p. 265)

Task: Pretend your town needs a Spanish-language community guide for restaurants written. Write a review of your favorite local restaurant in Spanish.

❶ **Prewrite.** Compile the information you will need in order to write about your favorite restaurant. Fill in the information on the lines next to each category.

1. nombre _____

2. descripción general _____

   _____

3. platos principales _____

4. postres _____

❷ **Draft.**

A. In order to prepare your first draft, write sentences with the information you compiled in **section 1** (**Prewrite**).

1. El restaurante se llama _____.

2. Es un restaurante _____ con

   _____.

3. Los _____ son riquísimos.

4. Hay _____, _____ y _____ también.

B. Read the model below to give you an idea of what a complete review could look like.

> *Café Beló es un café tranquilo con un ambiente intelectual donde puedes pasar el tiempo en la compañía de un buen amigo o un buen libro. Los precios son baratos. Puedes comer un sándwich, una ensalada, un postre o simplemente beber un café. Los postres son riquísimos. Un "plus" es la presentación de grupos musicales los fines de semana.*

C. Use the sentences you wrote in **part A** above and add anything useful from the model to construct your complete review.

❸ **Revise.** Read through your review. Then you will share it with a partner. You should each check for:

_____ adjective agreement (masculine words with masculine endings, feminine words with feminine endings)

_____ correct use of verb forms

_____ correct spelling

_____ persuasiveness of your review

Realidades 1

Capítulo 6A

Nombre _____

Hora _____

Fecha _____

Vocabulary Flash Cards, Sheet 1

Write the Spanish vocabulary word below each picture. If there is a word or phrase, copy it in the space provided. Be sure to include the article for each noun.

_____

_____

_____

_____

_____

_____

_____

_____

_____

_____

_____

_____

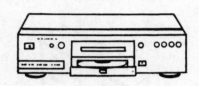

_____

_____

_____

_____

_____

_____

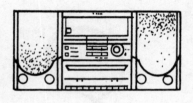

_____

_____

_____

_____

_____

_____

**el
video**

_____

_____

_____

_____

_____

_____

_____

_____

_____

_____

_____

poder

_____

¿De qué color...?

_____ _____

_____

gris

_____

los colores

_____

_____

azul

_____

marrón

_____

amarillo, amarilla

_____,

_____

blanco, blanca

_____,

_____

morado, morada

_____,

_____

rojo, roja _____, _____	**anaranjado, anaranjada** _____, _____	**importante** _____
rosado, rosada _____, _____	**feo, fea** _____, _____	**mismo, misma** _____, _____
verde _____	**grande** _____	**pequeño, pequeña** _____, _____

Realidades 1

Capítulo 6A

Nombre _____

Fecha _____

Hora _____

Vocabulary Flash Cards, Sheet 5

propio, propia	el/la mejor	la cosa
_____ _____	_____ _____	____ _____
a la derecha (de)	menos... que	para mí
____ ____ _____	_____ 	_____ ____
a la izquierda (de)	el/la peor	para ti
____ ____ 	_____ 	_____ _____

Realidades ❶

Capítulo 6A

Nombre _____

Hora _____

Fecha _____

Vocabulary Flash Cards, Sheet 6

el
dormitorio

_____

_____

la
posesión

_____

_____

bonito,
bonita

_____ ,

_____

peor(es)
que

_____

_____

los/las
mejores

_____

_____

mejor(es)
que

_____

_____

negro,
negra

_____

_____

los/las
peores

_____

_____

Realidades ①

Capítulo 6A

Nombre _____

Hora _____

Fecha _____

Vocabulary Check, Sheet 1

Tear out this page. Write the English words on the lines. Fold the paper along the dotted line to see the correct answers so you can check your work.

la alfombra _____

el armario _____

la cama _____

la cómoda _____

las cortinas _____

el cuadro _____

el despertador _____

el dormitorio _____

el espejo _____

el estante _____

_____

la lámpara _____

la mesita _____

la pared _____

el equipo de sonido _____

_____

el lector DVD _____

el televisor _____

Fold In

Realidades 1

Capítulo 6A

Nombre

Hora

Fecha

Vocabulary Check, Sheet 2

Tear out this page. Write the Spanish words on the lines. Fold the paper along the dotted line to see the correct answers so you can check your work.

rug _____

closet _____

bed _____

dresser _____

curtains _____

painting _____

alarm clock _____

bedroom _____

mirror _____

shelf,
bookshelf _____

lamp _____

night table _____

wall _____

sound (stereo)
system _____

DVD player _____

television set _____

Fold In

Realidades ❶

Capítulo 6A

Nombre _____

Fecha _____

Hora _____

Vocabulary Check, Sheet 3

Tear out this page. Write the English words on the lines. Fold the paper along the dotted line to see the correct answers so you can check your work.

amarillo,
amarilla   _____

anaranjado,
anaranjada   _____

azul   _____

blanco, blanca   _____

gris   _____

marrón   _____

morado, morada   _____

rojo, roja   _____

rosado, rosada   _____

verde   _____

bonito, bonita   _____

feo, fea   _____

grande   _____

importante   _____

mismo, misma   _____

pequeño,
pequeña   _____

Fold In →

Tear out this page. Write the Spanish words on the lines. Fold the paper along
the dotted line to see the correct answers so you can check your work.

yellow   _____

_____

orange   _____

_____

blue   _____

white   _____

gray   _____

brown   _____

purple   _____

red   _____

pink   _____

green   _____

pretty   _____

ugly   _____

large   _____

important   _____

same   _____

small   _____

_____

To hear a complete list of the vocabulary for this chapter,
go to www.realidades.com and type in the Web Code jcd-0689.
Then click on **Repaso del capítulo**.

Fold In

Making comparisons (p. 278)

- Use **más** + adjective + **que** to compare two people, things, or actions:

  El libro es **más interesante que** el video.

  *The book is **more interesting than** the video.*

- Use **menos** + adjective + **que** to compare two people, things, or actions:

  Correr es **menos divertido que** montar en bicicleta.

  *Running is **less fun than** riding a bike.*

A. Below are six comparisons. Write a + (plus sign) next to the ones that give the idea of "greater than" or "more than." Write a – (minus sign) next to the ones that give the idea of "worse than" or "less than." Follow the models.

| Modelos | más simpático que | _+_ |
| | menos ordenada que | _–_ |

1. menos divertido que _____   4. más interesante que _____

2. más simpático que _____   5. menos paciente que _____

3. más reservada que _____   6. menos atrevida que _____

B. The sentences below are marked with a + (plus sign) or a – (minus sign). Write in **más** if there is a + and **menos** if there is a –.

1. + El perro es _____ simpático que el gato.

2. – Luisa es _____ artística que Beatriz.

3. – Tomás es _____ trabajador que Marcos.

4. + La bicicleta es _____ grande que el monopatín.

- Some adjectives have special forms for comparisons. See the chart below.

Adjective		Comparative	
bueno / buena	*good*	**mejor (que)**	*better than*
malo / mala	*bad*	**peor (que)**	*worse than*
viejo / vieja	*old*	**mayor (que)**	*older than*
joven	*young*	**menor (que)**	*younger than*

C. Choose the correct comparative to complete each sentence.

1. Lorena tiene catorce años. Lidia tiene quince años. Lorena es (**mayor / menor**) que Lidia.

2. El restaurante grande es malo. El restaurante pequeño es bueno. El restaurante grande es (**mejor / peor**) que el restaurante pequeño.

3. Mi abuela tiene sesenta años. Tu abuela tiene cincuenta y ocho años. Mi abuela es (**mayor / menor**) que tu abuela.

Realidades ①

Capítulo 6A

Nombre _____

Fecha _____

Hora _____

Guided Practice Activities 6A-2

The superlative (p. 280)

- To say someone or something is the *most* or the *least*:

    el / la / los / las + noun + **más / menos** + adjective

    Es **el libro más interesante** de la biblioteca.

- To say someone or something is the *best* or the *worst*:

    el / la / los / las + **mejor(es) / peor(es)** + noun

    Es **el peor libro** de la biblioteca.

A. Below are eight superlative expressions. Write a + (plus sign) next to the ones that give the idea of the *most* or the *best*. Write a – (minus sign) next to the ones that give the idea of the *least* or the *worst*.

1. la lámpara más grande   _____

2. la mesita más fea   _____

3. el peor video   _____

4. las mejores cortinas   _____

5. el espejo menos feo   _____

6. la alfombra menos bonita   _____

7. los peores cuadros   _____

8. los mejores despertadores   _____

B. Look at each sentence and see whether it is marked with a + or a –. Write in **más** if there is a + and **menos** if there is a –.

1. + Mi tío es la persona _____ simpática de mi familia.

2. – La cama es la _____ grande de todas.

3. – Marzo es el mes _____ bonito del año.

4. + Sandra es la persona _____ divertida de la familia.

C. Choose the correct superlative to complete each sentence. Circle the word you have chosen.

1. Me gusta mucho nadar y montar en bicicleta. Para mí, julio es el (**mejor / peor**) mes del año.

2. Todos mis primos son inteligentes, pero Alberto es el (**más / menos**) inteligente de todos. Es muy estudioso y trabajador también.

3. Me gusta mucho esquiar. Para mí, julio es el (**mejor / peor**) mes del año.

4. No me gustan los libros aburridos. Tu libro es el (**más / menos**) aburrido de todos. Es bastante interesante.

5. Mis abuelos son muy divertidos. Son las personas (**más / menos**) divertidas de la familia.

6. No me gusta esta cama. Es la cama (**más / menos**) grande de la casa.

Stem-changing verbs: *poder* and *dormir* (p. 284)

- **Poder** (*to be able to do something*) and **dormir** (*to sleep*) are both stem-changing verbs like **jugar**, which you learned previously. Just like **jugar**, only the **nosotros/nosotras** and **vosotros/vosotras** forms of **poder** and **dormir** do not change their stems.
- Here are the forms of **poder** and **dormir**:

yo	**puedo**	nosotros/nosotras	**podemos**
tú	**puedes**	vosotros/vosotras	**podéis**
usted/él/ella	**puede**	ustedes/ellos/ellas	**pueden**

yo	**duermo**	nosotros/nosotras	**dormimos**
tú	**duermes**	vosotros/vosotras	**dormís**
usted/él/ella	**duerme**	ustedes/ellos/ellas	**duermen**

A. Circle the forms of **poder** and **dormir** in each sentence. Then underline the stem in each verb you circled. The first one has been done for you.

1. <u>Dormim</u>os ocho horas al día.
2. ¿<u>Pued</u>es montar en bicicleta?
3. No <u>pued</u>o trabajar hoy.
4. Mis hermanos <u>duerm</u>en mucho.
5. <u>Podem</u>os traer la comida.
6. <u>Duerm</u>o mucho los fines de semana.
7. No <u>podem</u>os hablar francés.
8. Ud. <u>duerm</u>e en una cama grande.

B. Now, write the words you circled in **part A** next to each subject pronoun below.

1. nosotros ____*dormimos*____
2. tú ____*puedes*____
3. yo ____*puedo*____
4. ellos ____*duermen*____
5. nosotros ____*podemos*____
6. yo ____*duermo*____
7. nosotros ____*podemos*____
8. Ud. ____*duerme*____

C. Circle the correct form of **poder** or **dormir** to complete each sentence.

1. Mis amigos y yo (**dormimos** / **duermen**) diez horas al día.
2. Roberto no (**puedo** / **puede**) ir a la fiesta.
3. Ustedes (**dormimos** / **duermen**) en la cama más grande de la casa.
4. Tú y yo (**puedes** / **podemos**) traer unos discos compactos.
5. Linda y Natalia (**duermo** / **duermen**) en un dormitorio grande.
6. Nosotros no (**podemos** / **puedes**) usar el lector DVD.
7. Tú (**dormimos** / **duermes**) en el dormitorio con la alfombra azul.

Realidades 1

Nombre _____

Hora _____

Capítulo 6A

Fecha _____

Guided Practice Activities 6A-4

Stem-changing verbs: *poder* and *dormir (continued)*

D. Complete the sentences with forms of **poder** and **dormir**. Follow the models.

Modelos Paco (**poder**) ir a la biblioteca.

Paco ___*puede*___ ir a la biblioteca.

Mónica (**dormir**) en el dormitorio grande.

Mónica ___*duerme*___ en el dormitorio grande.

1. Olivia (**poder**) montar en monopatín.

   Olivia _____ montar en monopatín.

2. Javier (**dormir**) ocho horas al día.

   Javier _____ ocho horas al día.

3. Tú (**dormir**) en un dormitorio con tu hermano.

   Tú _____ en un dormitorio con tu hermano.

4. Yo (**poder**) usar el televisor.

   Yo _____ usar el televisor.

5. Nosotros (**poder**) comprar unas cortinas para el dormitorio.

   Nosotros _____ comprar unas cortinas para el dormitorio.

6. Nosotros (**dormir**) en un dormitorio pequeño.

   Nosotros _____ en un dormitorio pequeño.

7. Ustedes (**dormir**) mucho los fines de semana.

   Ustedes _____ mucho los fines de semana.

E. Write sentences about yourself and your friends using forms of **poder**. Follow the models. Use ideas from the list or other words you know.

montar en bicicleta / esquiar / patinar / montar en monopatín / hablar español / nadar / patinar / tocar la guitarra / jugar a ¿...?

Modelos Yo ___*puedo montar en bicicleta*___ .

Mis amigos y yo ___*podemos nadar*___ .

1. Yo _____ .

2. Yo no _____ .

3. Mis amigos y yo _____ .

4. Mis amigos y yo no _____ .

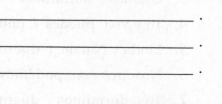

Realidades ①

Capítulo 6A

Nombre _____

Fecha _____

Hora _____

Guided Practice Activities 6A-5

Lectura: El desastre en mi dormitorio (pp. 288–289)

A. Try to guess the meaning of the following cognates. If you are having difficulty, skim through the reading in your textbook to find these words in context. Write your answers in the spaces below.

1. desastre _____
2. posesiones _____
3. desorden _____
4. situación _____
5. recomendar _____
6. considerar _____

B. The statements below refer to one of the roommates from the reading in your textbook. The roommates' names are Rosario and Marta. After each statement, circle **M** if it describes **Marta** or **R** if it describes **Rosario**.

1. **M R** Le gusta el orden.
2. **M R** Le gusta el desorden.
3. **M R** Su color favorito es el negro.
4. **M R** Su color favorito es el amarillo.
5. **M R** Hay comida en el suelo.
6. **M R** Hay postre en el escritorio.

C. The second part of the reading in your textbook is the response from the advice columnist, Magdalena, to Marta's letter. Read the final piece of advice below that Magdalena gives to Rosario. Answer the questions in English that follow.

> *Si la situación no es mejor después de unas semanas, tienes que considerar la posibilidad de separar el dormitorio con una cortina. ¡Pero no debe ser una cortina ni negra ni amarilla!*

1. How long does Magdalena tell Rosario to wait before considering another possibility?

   _____

2. According to Magdalena, with what should Rosario separate the room?

   _____

3. What colors should not separate the two rooms?

   _____ and _____

D. In your own words, explain what the disaster in Rosario's bedroom is.

_____

_____

Presentación oral (p. 291)

Task: Use a photograph or drawing of a bedroom to talk about what its contents and colors tell about the personality of the owner.

A. Bring in a picture of a bedroom. It can be a photo, a picture cut out from a magazine, or a picture that you drew. Use the following four questions to organize your thoughts about the room. Write your answers to the questions on the line beneath each question.

1. ¿Qué hay en el dormitorio?

   _____

2. ¿Cómo es el dormitorio?

   _____

3. ¿De qué color es?

   _____

4. ¿Qué cosas hay en las paredes?

   _____

B. Using the information you just compiled in **part A**, answer the questions below in the spaces provided.

- En tu opinión, ¿cómo es la persona que vive (*lives*) en el dormitorio?
- ¿Qué le gusta hacer?

Es una persona _____ porque el dormitorio _____

_____.

Le gusta _____ porque en el dormitorio hay _____

_____.

C. Go through your presentation several times. Make sure you:

_____ support your statements with examples

_____ use complete sentences

_____ speak clearly

Realidades ①

Capítulo 6B

Nombre _____

Fecha _____

Hora _____

Vocabulary Flash Cards, Sheet 1

Write the Spanish vocabulary word below each picture. If there is a word or phrase, copy it in the space provided. Be sure to include the article for each noun.

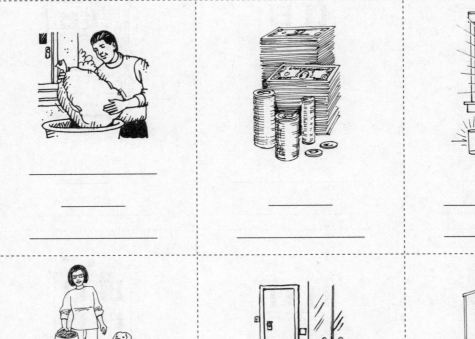

_____

_____

_____

_____

_____,

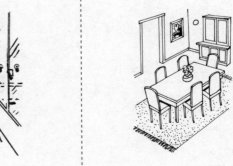

_____

_____

_____

_____

_____

_____

_____

_____

_____

_____

_____

_____

Realidades **1**

Capítulo 6B

Nombre _____

Hora _____

Fecha _____

Vocabulary Flash Cards, Sheet 2

_____

_____

_____

_____

_____

_____

_____

_____

_____

_____

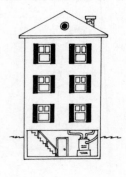

_____

_____

el piso

_____

_____

_____

_____

_____

_____

Realidades 1

Capítulo 6B

Nombre _____

Fecha _____

Hora _____

Vocabulary Flash Cards, Sheet 3

_____

_____

_____

_____

_____

_____

_____

_____

_____

_____

_____

_____

_____

_____

Realidades ①

Capítulo 6B

Nombre

Hora

Fecha

Vocabulary Flash Cards, Sheet 4

ayudar

cerca
(de)

los
quehaceres

dar

lejos
(de)

el
apartamento

poner

vivir

el
cuarto

**sucio,
sucia**

_____ ,

_____

**¿Qué
estás
haciendo?**

_____

_____

_____

si

_____

bastante

_____

**un
momento**

_____

_____

_____

_____

¿Cuáles?

_____

recibir

_____

_____

_____

_____
_____

_____
_____

_____
_____

_____
_____

_____
_____

_____
_____

_____
_____

_____
_____

_____
_____

Tear out this page. Write the English words on the lines. Fold the paper along the dotted line to see the correct answers so you can check your work.

cerca (de)   _____

lejos (de)   _____

vivir   _____

el apartamento   _____

la cocina   _____

el comedor   _____

el despacho   _____

la escalera   _____

el garaje   _____

la planta baja   _____

el primer piso   _____

el segundo piso   _____

la sala   _____

el sótano   _____

arreglar el cuarto   _____

ayudar   _____

cocinar   _____

cortar el césped   _____

Fold In

Tear out this page. Write the Spanish words on the lines. Fold the paper along the dotted line to see the correct answers so you can check your work.

close (to), near _____

far (from) _____

to live _____

apartment _____

kitchen _____

dining room _____

home office _____

stairs, stairway _____

garage _____

ground floor _____

second floor _____

third floor _____

living room _____

basement _____

to straighten up
the room _____

_____

to help _____

to cook _____

to cut the lawn _____

Fold In

Realidades ①

Capítulo 6B

Nombre _____

Fecha _____

Hora _____

Vocabulary Check, Sheet 3

Tear out this page. Write the English words on the lines. Fold the paper along the dotted line to see the correct answers so you can check your work.

dar de comer
al perro   _____

hacer la cama   _____

lavar los platos   _____

limpiar el baño   _____

                        _____

pasar la
aspiradora   _____

poner la mesa   _____

los quehaceres   _____

quitar el polvo   _____

sacar la basura   _____

                        _____

limpio, limpia   _____

sucio, sucia   _____

bastante   _____

el dinero   _____

recibir   _____

Fold In

Realidades **1**

Capítulo 6B

Nombre _____

Fecha _____

Hora _____

Vocabulary Check, Sheet 4

Tear out this page. Write the Spanish words on the lines. Fold the paper along the dotted line to see the correct answers so you can check your work.

to feed the dog _____

_____

to make the bed _____

to wash the dishes _____

to clean the
bathroom _____

to vacuum _____

_____

to set the table _____

chores _____

to dust _____

to take out
the trash _____

clean _____

dirty _____

enough; rather _____

money _____

to receive _____

Fold In

To hear a complete list of the vocabulary for this chapter,
go to www.realidades.com and type in the Web Code jcd-0699.
Then click on **Repaso del capítulo.**

Realidades ❶

Capítulo 6B

Nombre _____

Fecha _____

Hora _____

Guided Practice Activities 6B-1

Affirmative *tú* commands (p. 305)

- **Tú** commands are used to tell friends, family members, or peers to do something.
- **Tú** command forms are the same as the regular present-tense forms for **Ud./él/ella.**

Infinitive	*Ud./él/ella* form	Affirmative *tú* command
-**ar** verb: **hablar**	habla	¡Habla!
-**er** verb: **leer**	lee	¡Lee!
-**ir** verb: **escribir**	escribe	¡Escribe!

- Two verbs you have learned already, **hacer** and **poder**, have irregular affirmative **tú** command forms:

    poner → **pon**   ¡**Pon** la mesa!

    hacer → **haz**   ¡**Haz** la cama!

- You can tell the difference between a command form and an **Ud., él,** or **ella** verb form from the context of the sentence. A comma after the person's name indicates they are being talked to directly. Possessive adjectives can also help you decide if the person is being addressed directly (**tu**) or referred to in the third person (**su**).

    Marcos lee **su** libro. (**él** verb form)

    Marcos, lee **tu** libro. (command form)

A. Circle the command form in each sentence.

1. María, habla con tu hermano, por favor.
2. Tomasina, escribe tu tarea.
3. Marcos, come el almuerzo.
4. Silvia, practica la guitarra.
5. Elena, haz la cama.
6. Sandra, pon la mesa.
7. Alfonso, lee el libro.
8. Carlos, lava el coche.

B. Now look at each sentence. Write **C** if the verb is a command form. Write **no** if it is not a command form. Follow the models.

Modelos Javier estudia en su dormitorio. ___no___

     Javier, estudia en tu dormitorio. ___C___

1. Alfonso lee el libro. _____
2. Paula, ayuda a tu madre. _____
3. Roberto escucha a su madre. _____
4. Pablo hace la tarea. _____
5. Ana, lava los platos. _____
6. Isa juega con su hermana. _____
7. David, limpia la casa. _____
8. Elena, pon la mesa. _____

Affirmative *tú* commands *(continued)*

C. Circle the correct form of the verb to complete each sentence.

1. ¡(**Plancha** / **Planchan**) la ropa, por favor!

2. Gerardo, (**prepara** / **preparas**) la comida, por favor.

3. Alberto, (**hace** / **haz**) la tarea ahora.

4. Rosa, (**pone** / **pon**) los platos en la mesa, por favor.

5. ¡(**Lavas** / **Lava**) el coche, por favor!

6. Linda, (**juega** / **juegas**) con tu hermana esta tarde.

D. Write the affirmative **tú** command forms to complete the following conversations. Follow the model.

Modelo   RAÚL: Ana, (poner) ____*pon*____ los libros en la mesa.

   ANA: Sí, pero (tomar) ____*toma*____ mi mochila.

1. SEBASTIÁN: Roberto, (lavar) _____ los platos, por favor.

   ROBERTO: Claro. (Traer) _____ los platos sucios aquí.

2. TERESA: Susana, (preparar) _____ el almuerzo.

   SUSANA: Sí, pero (hablar) _____ con mamá para ver qué necesitamos.

3. EDUARDO: Elena, (hacer) _____ los quehaceres.

   ELENA: Claro. (Escribir) _____ una lista.

4. ISABEL: Margarita, (planchar) _____ la ropa, por favor.

   MARGARITA: Claro, pero (sacar) _____ la plancha, por favor.

E. Write **tú** command forms to complete each sentence. Use verbs from the list.

hacer	lavar	poner	sacar

1. ¡_____ la basura!

2. ¡_____ el coche!

3. ¡_____ la mesa!

4. ¡_____ la cama!

realidades.com
• Web Code: jcd-0613

Realidades ①

Capítulo 6B

Nombre _____

Fecha _____

Hora _____

Guided Practice Activities 6B-3

The present progressive tense (p. 308)

- Use the present progressive tense to say what people are doing or what is happening right now.

  Estamos lavando el coche.   *We are washing the car.*

- The present progressive tense uses forms of **estar** with the present participle.

- Review the forms of **estar**:

yo	**estoy**	nosotros/nosotras	**estamos**
tú	**estás**	vosotros/vosotras	**estáis**
usted/él/ella	**está**	ustedes/ellos/ellas	**están**

- You form the present participle for **-ar** verbs by removing the **-ar** ending and adding **-ando: preparar → preparando, hablar → hablando.**

- You form the present participle for **-er** and **-ir** verbs by removing the **-er** or **-ir** ending and adding **-iendo: comer → comiendo, escribir → escribiendo.**

- The forms of **estar** change to match the subject of the sentence. The present participle always stays the same, regardless of who the subject is.

  Francisco está limpiando la mesa.   *Francisco is cleaning the table.*

  Tú y yo estamos limpiando el baño.   *We are cleaning the bathroom.*

A. Look at each sentence. Underline the form of **estar**. Circle the present participle. Follow the model.

Modelo   Enrique <u>está</u> lavando los platos.

1. Tú y yo estamos pasando la aspiradora.

2. Mis abuelos están cortando el césped.

3. Mi hermana está quitando el polvo en la sala.

4. Yo estoy dando de comer al perro.

5. Ustedes están sacando la basura de la cocina.

6. Tú estás poniendo la mesa con los platos limpios.

7. Ella está haciendo las camas del segundo piso.

B. Complete each sentence with the appropriate form of **estar**.

1. Yo _____ poniendo la mesa.

2. Tú _____ sacando la basura.

3. Ella _____ lavando la ropa.

4. Nosotros _____ preparando el almuerzo.

5. Ustedes _____ cortando el césped.

The present progressive tense (continued)

C. Write the present participles of the verbs shown. Follow the models. Remember to use **-ando** for **-ar** verbs and **-iendo** for **-er** and **-ir** verbs.

Modelos ayudar _____*ayudando*_____

hacer _____*haciendo*_____

escribir _____*escribiendo*_____

1. dar _____

2. abrir _____

3. comer _____

4. romper _____

5. sacar _____

6. lavar _____

7. jugar _____

8. poner _____

D. Look at the drawing. Then write forms of the present progressive (**estar** + present participle) to complete each sentence. Follow the models.

Modelos Graciela (**dar**)____*está dando*____ de comer al perro.

Lola y Elia (**hablar**)____*están hablando*____.

1. El padre (**sacar**) _____ la basura.

2. La madre (**cocinar**) _____ unas hamburguesas.

3. Ana María (**cortar**) _____ el césped.

4. Manolo y José (**lavar**) _____ el coche.

5. Tito y Ramón (**poner**) _____ la mesa.

realidades.com

• Web Code: jcd-0614

Realidades ①

Capítulo 6B

Nombre _____

Fecha _____

Hora _____

Guided Practice Activities 6B-5

Lectura: Cantaclara (pp. 312–313)

A. The reading in your textbook is similar to the story of Cinderella. Write four facts that you can remember about the Cinderella story in the spaces below. If you are not familiar with the story you will need to find out from someone who is.

1. _____
2. _____
3. _____
4. _____

B. Skim through the reading and the pictures in your textbook to find similarities between the story of Cantaclara and Cinderella. Check off any similarities in your list above.

C. Since you know that the story in your textbook is like the story of Cinderella, you know that Cantaclara lives with her stepmother and two stepsisters. Below is a dialogue with all four of them. Read the dialogue and answer the questions that follow.

> –Cantaclara, saca la basura. Y después, pon la mesa –dice la madrastra.
> –Cantaclara, haz mi cama y limpia el baño –dice Griselda.
> –Haz mi cama también –dice Hortencia.
> –Un momento. Estoy lavando los platos ahora mismo –dice Cantaclara.

1. Circle the names of the four people who are speaking.
2. How is a dialogue written differently in Spanish than in English?

_____

3. Which person does NOT say she wants Cantaclara to make her bed?

D. Now, read what takes place at the end of the story. Answer the questions in English that follow.

> Son las ocho de la noche. La madrastra y las dos hermanastras están en la sala y ven su programa favorito. Pero, ¿qué es esto? ¡Ven a Cantaclara en la pantalla!
> –Mira, mamá. ¡Es Cantaclara! –dice Hortencia.
> –¡Oh, no! Si Cantaclara es la nueva estrella del futuro, ¿quién va a hacer los quehaceres? –pregunta Griselda.

1. At what time do the stepmother and stepsisters sit down to watch their favorite show? _____
2. Whom do they see on TV? _____
3. What problem does Griselda think of at the end? _____

Presentación escrita (p. 315)

Task: Pretend that your family is selling their house, apartment, or that you are selling an imaginary dream home. Create a flyer in Spanish to promote the sale of your home.

❶ **Prewrite.** You are going to prepare an informative flyer about your home. In order to provide the most information to potential buyers, you will need to anticipate their questions. Read the potential questions below and write answers about your home in the spaces provided.

a) En general, ¿cómo es la casa o apartamento? (¿Es grande o pequeño?)

_____.

b) ¿De qué color es la casa o apartamento?

_____.

c) ¿Cuántos cuartos hay en la casa o apartamento? ¿Cuáles son?

_____.

d) ¿Cómo son los cuartos? (¿grandes o pequeños?)

_____.

e) ¿De qué color son los cuartos?

_____.

f) ¿Cuál es la dirección (*address*) y el precio (*price*) de la casa o apartamento?

_____.

❷ **Draft.** Now, compile the answers you wrote above on a separate sheet of paper to create your rough draft. Organize your answers in a way that will be easy for anyone to read. Your flyer should also include illustrations and colored ink to make it more attractive to potential buyers. The first line on your flyer should read: **Se vende casa** (or **Se vende apartamento**).

❸ **Revise.** Read through your ad to see that you have included all the information that a potential buyer might want. Share your draft with a partner who will check the following:

_____ Are all words spelled correctly?

_____ Is the flyer neat and attractive?

_____ Does the flyer need a visual?

_____ Is the key information provided?

_____ Does the flyer make me want to look at the property?

❹ **Publish.** Write a new, final copy of your flyer making any necessary corrections or adding to it anything your partner suggested.

Realidades ①

Capítulo 7A

Nombre _____

Hora _____

Fecha _____

Vocabulary Flash Cards, Sheet 1

Write the Spanish vocabulary word below each picture. If there is a word or phrase, copy it in the space provided. Be sure to include the article for each noun.

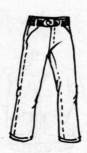

_____

_____

_____

_____

_____

_____

_____

_____

_____

_____

_____

_____

_____

_____

_____

_____

_____

_____

Realidades 1

Capítulo 7A

Nombre _____

Hora _____

Fecha _____

Vocabulary Flash Cards, Sheet 3

buscar

_____

_____

la
tienda

_____

comprar

_____

la tienda
de ropa

_____

entrar

_____

¿En qué
puedo
servirle?

_____ _____

_____

llevar

_____

Realidades ❶

Capítulo 7A

Nombre _____

Hora _____

Fecha _____

Vocabulary Flash Cards, Sheet 4

nuevo, nueva _____, _____	**Me queda(n) mal.** ____ _____ _____	**¡Vamos!** _____
¿Cómo te queda(n)? _____ ____ _____	**quizás** _____	**costar** _____
Me queda(n) bien. ____ _____ _____	**Perdón.** _____	**¿Cuánto cuesta(n)...?** _____ _____

Realidades **1**

Capítulo 7A

Nombre

Hora

Fecha

Vocabulary Flash Cards, Sheet 5

el
precio

————————
————————

trescientos,
trescientas

————————,
————————

seiscientos,
seiscientas

————————,
————————

tanto

————————

cuatrocientos,
cuatrocientas

————————,
————————

setecientos,
setecientas

————————,
————————

doscientos,
doscientas

————————,
————————

quinientos,
quinientas

————————,
————————

ochocientos,
ochocientas

————————,
————————

novecientos, novecientas

_____,

_____

los dos

_____

_____

estos, estas

_____,

_____

mil

_____

las dos

_____

_____

ese, esa

_____,

_____

tener razón

_____

_____

este, esta

_____,

_____

esos, esas

_____,

_____

Realidades 1

Capítulo 7A

Nombre _____

Hora _____

Fecha _____

Vocabulary Check, Sheet 1

Tear out this page. Write the English words on the lines. Fold the paper along the dotted line to see the correct answers so you can check your work.

buscar   _____

comprar   _____

el dependiente,   _____
la dependienta

entrar   _____

la tienda de ropa   _____

el abrigo   _____

la blusa   _____

las botas   _____

los calcetines   _____

la camiseta   _____

la chaqueta   _____

la falda   _____

la gorra   _____

los jeans   _____

los pantalones   _____
cortos

la sudadera   _____

el suéter   _____

Fold In

Tear out this page. Write the Spanish words on the lines. Fold the paper along the dotted line to see the correct answers so you can check your work.

to look for   _____

to buy   _____

salesperson   _____

_____

to enter   _____

clothing store   _____

coat   _____

blouse   _____

boots   _____

socks   _____

T-shirt   _____

jacket   _____

skirt   _____

cap   _____

jeans   _____

shorts   _____

_____

sweatshirt   _____

sweater   _____

Fold In →

Tear out this page. Write the English words on the lines. Fold the paper along the dotted line to see the correct answers so you can check your work.

el traje de baño   _____

el vestido   _____

los zapatos   _____

llevar   _____

nuevo, nueva   _____

costar   _____

el precio   _____

doscientos   _____

trescientos   _____

cuatrocientos   _____

quinientos   _____

seiscientos   _____

setecientos   _____

ochocientos   _____

novecientos   _____

mil   _____

tener razón   _____

Fold In

Realidades ❶

Capítulo 7A

Nombre _____

Hora _____

Fecha _____

Vocabulary Check, Sheet 4

Tear out this page. Write the Spanish words on the lines. Fold the paper along the dotted line to see the correct answers so you can check your work.

swimsuit   _____

dress   _____

shoes   _____

to wear   _____

new   _____

to cost   _____

price   _____

two hundred   _____

three hundred   _____

four hundred   _____

five hundred   _____

six hundred   _____

seven hundred   _____

eight hundred   _____

nine hundred   _____

a thousand   _____

to be correct   _____

To hear a complete list of the vocabulary for this chapter, go to www.realidades.com and type in the Web Code jcd-0789. Then click on **Repaso del capítulo.**

Fold In

Realidades ①

Capítulo 7A

Nombre _____

Fecha _____

Hora _____

Guided Practice Activities 7A-1

Stem-changing verbs: *pensar, querer,* and *preferir* (p. 330)

- Like the other stem-changing verbs you've learned (**jugar, poder,** and **dormir**), **pensar, querer,** and **preferir** use the regular present-tense endings. These endings attach to a new stem for all forms except for the **nosotros** and **vosotros** forms, which use the existing stem.

- Here are the forms of **pensar, querer,** and **preferir.** Note that in all cases, the **e** in the stem changes to **ie.**

yo	**pienso**	nosotros/nosotras	**pensamos**
tú	**piensas**	vosotros/vosotras	**pensáis**
usted/él/ella	**piensa**	ustedes/ellos/ellas	**piensan**

yo	**quiero**	nosotros/nosotras	**queremos**
tú	**quieres**	vosotros/vosotras	**queréis**
usted/él/ella	**quiere**	ustedes/ellos/ellas	**quieren**

yo	**prefiero**	nosotros/nosotras	**preferimos**
tú	**prefieres**	vosotros/vosotras	**preferís**
usted/él/ella	**prefiere**	ustedes/ellos/ellas	**prefieren**

A. Circle the forms of **pensar, querer,** or **preferir** in each sentence. Then underline the stem in each verb you circled. The first one has been done for you.

1. <u>Prefier</u>en comprar unos zapatos.
2. Queremos ir de compras.
3. Pensamos ir a la tienda de ropa.
4. ¿Prefiere Ud. el vestido o la falda?

5. Pienso comprar una sudadera.
6. ¿Quieres hablar con la dependienta?
7. Preferimos ir a una tienda grande.
8. Quieren entrar en la tienda.

B. Now, write the forms of **pensar, querer,** and **preferir** that you circled in **part A** next to each subject pronoun.

1. ellos (preferir) _____
2. nosotros (querer) _____
3. nosotros (pensar) _____
4. Ud. (preferir) _____

5. yo (pensar) _____
6. tú (querer) _____
7. nosotros (preferir) _____
8. ellos (querer) _____

Realidades 1

Nombre _____

Hora _____

Capítulo 7A

Fecha _____

Guided Practice Activities 7A-2

Stem-changing verbs (continued)

C. Circle the correct form of **pensar, querer,** or **preferir** to complete each sentence.

1. Yo (**quiere** / **quiero**) comprar unas botas nuevas.

2. Ella (**prefiere** / **prefieren**) los pantalones cortos a la falda.

3. Nosotros (**prefieren** / **preferimos**) ir de compras en una tienda grande.

4. Ellos (**pienso** / **piensan**) comprar dos abrigos nuevos.

5. Tú y yo (**pensamos** / **piensas**) buscar una tienda con precios buenos.

6. Ustedes (**quieres** / **quieren**) hablar con la dependienta.

7. Nosotros (**queremos** / **quieres**) entrar en la tienda de ropa.

8. Tú y yo no (**piensan** / **pensamos**) comprar ropa hoy.

D. Complete the sentences with forms of **pensar, querer,** or **preferir.** Follow the models.

Modelos Tú (**pensar**) comprar un suéter.

Tú _____*piensas*_____ comprar un suéter.

Tú y yo (**preferir**) comprar el vestido azul.

Tú y yo ___*preferimos*___ comprar el vestido azul.

1. Elena (**pensar**) comprar una sudadera.

Elena _____ comprar una sudadera.

2. Sandra y yo (**querer**) ir a una tienda de ropa grande.

Sandra y yo _____ ir a una tienda de ropa grande.

3. Yo (**preferir**) hablar con un dependiente.

Yo _____ hablar con un dependiente.

4. Nosotras (**pensar**) que es un precio bueno.

Nosotras _____ que es un precio bueno.

5. Tú (**querer**) entrar en una tienda de ropa grande.

Tú _____ entrar en una tienda de ropa grande.

6. Tú y yo (**querer**) comprar unas camisetas nuevas.

Tú y yo _____ comprar unas camisetas nuevas.

7. Tomás y Sebastián (**preferir**) no comprar ropa hoy.

Tomás y Sebastián _____ no comprar ropa hoy.

8. Yo (**pensar**) comprar una gorra y un suéter.

Yo _____ comprar una gorra y un suéter.

realidades.com

• Web Code: jcd-0704

Realidades 1

Nombre _____

Hora _____

Capítulo 7A

Fecha _____

Guided Practice Activities 7A-3

Demonstrative adjectives (p. 332)

- Demonstrative adjectives are the equivalent of **this, that, these,** and **those** in English. You use them to point out nouns: **this hat, those shoes**.
- In Spanish, the demonstrative adjectives agree with the noun they accompany in both gender and number.

	Close		**Farther away**	
Singular masculine	**este** suéter	(*this* sweater)	**ese** suéter	(*that* sweater)
Singular feminine	**esta** falda	(*this* skirt)	**esa** falda	(*that* skirt)
Plural masculine	**estos** suéteres	(*these* sweaters)	**esos** suéteres	(*those* sweaters)
Plural feminine	**estas** faldas	(*these* skirts)	**esas** faldas	(*those* skirts)

A. Circle the demonstrative adjective in each sentence below. Write **C** next to the sentence if the object referred to is *close* (**este, esta, estos, estas**). Write **F** if the object referred to is *farther away* (**ese, esa, esos, esas**).

1. Me gustan estos zapatos. _____
2. Quiero comprar esas camisetas. _____
3. ¿Prefieres esta falda? _____
4. Esa camisa es muy bonita. _____
5. No me gustan esos vestidos. _____
6. ¿Te gustan estas chaquetas? _____

B. Circle the correct demonstrative adjective in each sentence.

1. ¿Cómo me quedan (**esto** / **estos**) pantalones?
2. Me gustan (**esas** / **esos**) sudaderas.
3. ¿Prefieres (**esta** / **este**) chaqueta?
4. Pienso comprar (**estos** / **este**) calcetines.
5. No me gusta (**ese** / **esa**) abrigo.
6. ¿Cómo me queda (**este** / **esta**) traje?
7. (**Eso** / **Esas**) botas son muy bonitas.
8. ¿Vas a comprar (**esos** / **esas**) pantalones cortos?

- Web Code: jcd-0703

Demonstrative adjectives *(continued)*

C. Choose the correct form of the demonstrative adjective and write it next to each noun. Follow the models.

Close: este, esta, estos, estas   **Farther: ese, esa, esos, esas**

| **Modelos** | calcetines (close): | ___*estos*___ | calcetines |
| | camisa (farther): | ___*esa*___ | camisa |

1. abrigo (farther): _____ abrigo
2. botas (farther): _____ botas
3. jeans (close): _____ jeans
4. falda (close): _____ falda
5. traje de baño (close): _____ traje de baño
6. zapatos (farther): _____ zapatos
7. chaquetas (farther): _____ chaquetas
8. pantalones (close): _____ pantalones
9. vestido (farther): _____ vestido
10. suéter (close): _____ suéter

D. In each drawing below, the item of clothing that is larger is closer to you. The one that is smaller is farther away. Write the correct demonstrative adjective to indicate the item that is marked with an arrow. Follow the model.

Modelo  ___*esta*___ camisa

1.  _____ pantalones   4.  _____ zapatos

2.  _____ sudaderas   5.  _____ abrigo

3.  _____ vestido

realidades.com ⊙
• Web Code: jcd-0703

Lectura: Tradiciones de la ropa panameña (pp. 336–337)

A. You will find out a lot about the contents of the reading in your textbook by looking at the title and the photos. In the spaces below, write three main topics that you would expect a reading on Panamanian culture to cover.

1. _____

2. _____

3. _____

B. Read the paragraph below on **polleras** and answer the questions that follow in Spanish.

> *Una tradición panameña de mucho orgullo (pride) es llevar el vestido típico de las mujeres, "la pollera". Hay dos tipos de pollera, la pollera montuna y la pollera de gala, que se lleva en los festivales.*

1. Según la lectura, ¿cómo se llama el vestido típico de las mujeres en Panamá?

   _____

2. ¿Cuáles son los dos tipos de pollera?

   _____ y _____

3. ¿Cuándo se lleva la pollera de gala? _____

C. Look through the reading in your textbook again to find whether the following statements are true or false. Then, circle **cierto** for true or **falso** for false.

1. **cierto   falso**   Hay un Día Nacional de la Pollera en la ciudad de Las Tablas.

2. **cierto   falso**   Las Tablas es famosa por ser el mejor lugar para celebrar los carnavales.

3. **cierto   falso**   El canal de Panamá conecta el océano Pacífico con el lago Titicaca.

4. **cierto   falso**   Panamá es un istmo.

5. **cierto   falso**   El segundo tipo de ropa auténtico de Panamá que se menciona es la gorra de Panamá.

Realidades ①

Capítulo 7A

Nombre _____

Fecha _____

Hora _____

Guided Practice Activities 7A-6

Presentación oral (p. 339)

Task: You and a partner will play the roles of a customer and a salesclerk. The customer will look at various items in the store, talk with the clerk, and then decide if he or she would like to buy anything.

A. Work with a partner to prepare the skit. You will be the customer. You and your partner will need to discuss what type of clothing your store is selling. You will then need a name for your store and some samples of merchandise to use in your skit. You may bring in clothes or use cutouts from a magazine. Complete the following in the spaces below:

Type of clothing: _____

Store name: _____

B. Now, make a list below of five different expressions and questions that will help you play your role. You may want to look back in the *A primera vista* and *Videohistoria* sections in your textbook for ideas to help you get started.

1. _____
2. _____
3. _____
4. _____
5. _____

C. Work with your partner to put together and practice your presentation. Keep in mind the following things:

_____ to answer questions using complete sentences

_____ to speak clearly

_____ to keep the conversation going

_____ to finish the conversation at a logical point

D. When you present your skit, the clerk will begin the conversation. That means that you will need to respond as your first action. As your last action, you will need to decide whether or not to buy something. Your teacher will grade you based on the following:

• how well you keep the conversation going
• how complete your presentation is
• how well you use new and previously learned vocabulary

Realidades ①

Capítulo 7B

Nombre _____

Fecha _____

Hora _____

Vocabulary Flash Cards, Sheet 1

Write the Spanish vocabulary word below each picture. If there is a word or phrase, copy it in the space provided. Be sure to include the article for each noun.

_____	_____	_____
_____ _____	_____	_____
_____	_____	_____

Realidades ①

Capítulo 7B

Nombre _____

Hora _____

Fecha _____

Vocabulary Flash Cards, Sheet 2

_____

_____

_____

_____

en la Red

_____

_____

_____

_____

_____

_____

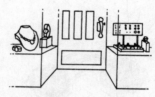

_____

_____

_____

_____

"Almacén Galerías"

_____

_____

_____

_____

Realidades ①

Capítulo 7B

Nombre _____

Fecha _____

Hora _____

Vocabulary Flash Cards, Sheet 3

La tienda de descuentos	**el novio**	**caro, cara**
_____ _____	_____	_____ , _____
	la novia	**mirar**
_____ _____	_____	_____
	barato, barata	**pagar (por)**
_____ _____	_____ , _____	_____

Realidades 1

Capítulo 7B

Nombre _____

Hora _____

Fecha _____

Vocabulary Flash Cards, Sheet 4

vender

_____

ayer

_____

hace
+ *time
expression*

_____

_____

_____

anoche

_____

la semana
pasada

_____ _____

_____

_____

_____

el año
pasado

_____

_____

¡Uf!

_____

_____

Realidades ①

Capítulo 7B

Nombre _____

Hora _____

Fecha _____

Vocabulary Check, Sheet 1

Tear out this page. Write the English words on the lines. Fold the paper along the dotted line to see the correct answers so you can check your work.

el almacén _____
_____

en la Red _____

la joyería _____

la librería _____

la tienda de _____
descuentos

la tienda de _____
electrodomésticos _____

la zapatería _____

el anillo _____

los anteojos de sol _____

los aretes _____

el bolso _____

la cadena _____

la cartera _____

el collar _____

la corbata _____

los guantes _____

el llavero _____

Fold In

Tear out this page. Write the Spanish words on the lines. Fold the paper along the dotted line to see the correct answers so you can check your work.

department store _____

online _____

jewelry store _____

bookstore _____

discount store _____

_____

household appliance store _____

_____

shoe store _____

ring _____

sunglasses _____

earrings _____

purse _____

chain _____

wallet _____

necklace _____

tie _____

gloves _____

key chain _____

Fold In

Tear out this page. Write the English words on the lines. Fold the paper along the dotted line to see the correct answers so you can check your work.

el perfume _____

la pulsera _____

el reloj pulsera _____

el software _____

el novio _____

la novia _____

barato,
barata _____
_____

caro, cara _____

mirar _____

pagar (por) _____

vender _____

Fold In →

Tear out this page. Write the Spanish words on the lines. Fold the paper along the dotted line to see the correct answers so you can check your work.

perfume _____

bracelet _____

watch _____

software _____

boyfriend _____

girlfriend _____

inexpensive, cheap _____

expensive _____

to look (at) _____

to pay (for) _____

to sell _____

Fold In

To hear a complete list of the vocabulary for this chapter, go to www.realidades.com and type in the Web Code jcd-0799. Then click on **Repaso del capítulo.**

The preterite of *-ar* verbs (p. 354)

- The preterite is a Spanish past tense that is used to talk about actions that were completed in the past: *I went to the store. I bought a jacket.*
- To form the preterite of **-ar** verbs, you take the stem of the verb (the same stem you used to form the present tense) and add the following endings:

hablar → habl- + endings

yo	**hablé**	nosotros/nosotras	**hablamos**
tú	**hablaste**	vosotros/vosotras	**hablasteis**
usted/él/ella	**habló**	ustedes/ellos/ellas	**hablaron**

- Notice the accents on the **yo** and **usted/él/ella** forms: **hablé, habló**.

A. Underline the preterite verb forms in the following conversations. **¡Ojo!** Not all the verb forms are preterite forms.

1. ELENA: ¿Hablaste con Enrique ayer?

    ANA: Sí, hablamos por teléfono anoche. Él trabajó ayer.

    ELENA: ¿Ah, sí? ¿Dónde trabaja?

    ANA: Trabaja en un restaurante. Ayer lavó muchos platos y limpió las mesas.

2. MARCOS: ¿Estudiaste para el examen?

    TOMÁS: Sí, estudié mucho, pero estoy nervioso.

    MARCOS: Yo también. Pasé dos horas en la biblioteca.

    TOMÁS: Yo estudié en casa y usé la computadora.

B. Now, fill in the conversations from **part A** with the missing preterite forms.

1. ELENA: ¿_____ con Enrique ayer?

    ANA: Sí, _____ por teléfono anoche. Él _____ ayer.

    ELENA: ¿Ah, sí? ¿Dónde trabaja?

    ANA: Trabaja en un restaurante. Ayer _____ muchos platos

    y _____ las mesas.

2. MARCOS: ¿_____ para el examen?

    TOMÁS: Sí, _____ mucho, pero estoy nervioso.

    MARCOS: Yo también. _____ dos horas en la biblioteca.

    TOMÁS: Yo _____ en casa y _____ la computadora.

The preterite of -ar verbs (continued)

C. Circle the correct preterite form to complete each sentence.

1. Yo (**caminó / caminé**) por dos horas ayer.

2. Ellos (**hablaste / hablaron**) por teléfono anoche.

3. Nosotros (**cocinamos / cocinaron**) la cena.

4. Tú (**cantaron / cantaste**) en la ópera.

5. Ella (**escuchó / escucharon**) música en su dormitorio.

6. Ustedes (**levantaron / levantamos**) pesas en el gimnasio.

D. Write the missing preterite forms in the chart.

	cantar	bailar	escuchar	lavar	nadar
yo	canté				
tú		bailaste			
Ud./él/ella			escuchó		
nosotros/nosotras				lavamos	
Uds./ellos/ellas					nadaron

E. Write the correct preterite form of the verb indicated next to each subject pronoun. Follow the model.

Modelo   tú (bailar) _____*bailaste*_____

1. yo (cantar) _____
2. ella (nadar) _____
3. Ud. (esquiar) _____
4. ellos (lavar) _____
5. nosotros (dibujar) _____
6. ellos (pasar) _____
7. tú (hablar) _____
8. yo (limpiar) _____

F. Use verbs from the list to say what you and your friends did last night.

> estudiar   trabajar   hablar por teléfono   bailar   cantar   cocinar
> escuchar música   esquiar   lavar la ropa   levantar pesas   limpiar el baño

1. Anoche yo _____ .

2. Yo no _____ .

3. Anoche mis amigos _____ .

4. Nosotros no _____ .

realidades.com ▾
• Web Code: jcd-0713

The preterite of verbs ending in *-car* and *-gar* (p. 356)

- Verbs that end in **-car** and **-gar** use the same preterite endings as regular **-ar** verbs, except in the **yo** form.
- Here are the preterite forms of **buscar** (*to look for*) and **pagar** (*to pay*).

c → qu

yo	**busqué**	nosotros/nosotras	**buscamos**
tú	**buscaste**	vosotros/vosotras	**buscasteis**
usted/él/ella	**buscó**	ustedes/ellos/ellas	**buscaron**

g → gu

yo	**pagué**	nosotros/nosotras	**pagamos**
tú	**pagaste**	vosotros/vosotras	**pagasteis**
usted/él/ella	**pagó**	ustedes/ellos/ellas	**pagaron**

- Other verbs you know follow this pattern. **Jugar** is like **pagar** (g → gu). **Practicar, sacar,** and **tocar** are like **buscar** (c → qu).

A. Fill in the missing **yo** forms in the chart.

	buscar	pagar	jugar	practicar	sacar	tocar
yo						
tú	buscaste	pagaste	jugaste	practicaste	sacaste	tocaste
Ud./él/ella	buscó	pagó	jugó	practicó	sacó	tocó
nosotros/nosotras	buscamos	pagamos	jugamos	practicamos	sacamos	tocamos
Uds./ellos/ellas	buscaron	pagaron	jugaron	practicaron	sacaron	tocaron

B. Write the correct forms of the verb indicated next to each subject pronoun. Follow the model.

Modelo (pagar): tú _____*pagaste*_____

1. (pagar): ellos _____
2. (pagar): yo _____
3. (pagar): él _____
4. (jugar): tú y yo _____
5. (jugar): yo _____
6. (jugar): Uds. _____
7. (buscar): ellos _____
8. (buscar): yo _____
9. (practicar): yo _____
10. (practicar): tú _____
11. (sacar): Ud. _____
12. (sacar): yo _____
13. (tocar): yo _____
14. (tocar): tú y yo _____

Direct object pronouns (p. 360)

- A direct object tells who or what receives the action of the verb:

    Busco una <u>cadena</u>. *I am looking for a <u>chain</u>.*

- In the sentence above, **cadena** is the direct object noun.
- You can use a direct object pronoun to replace a direct object noun.
- The direct object pronoun must match the noun it replaces in both gender and number:

    Compré <u>un suéter</u>. → **Lo** compré. (*masculine, singular*)

    Compré <u>una falda</u>. → **La** compré. (*feminine singular*)

    Compré <u>unos aretes</u>. → **Los** compré. (*masculine plural*)

    Compré <u>unas pulseras</u>. → **Las** compré. (*feminine plural*)

- The direct object comes *before* a verb in the present tense or the preterite tense.

    Lo tengo aquí. (*I have it here.*)

    Lo compré anoche. (*I bought it last night.*)

A. Underline the direct object noun in each sentence.

1. Busco unos guantes nuevos.
2. La dependienta vendió el perfume.
3. Compré dos llaveros.
4. Llevamos nuestras carteras.
5. Compramos un collar.
6. Miramos unas corbatas.
7. Buscaron una cadena.
8. Preparé el almuerzo.

B. Write each noun you circled in **part A** on the following lines. Write **M** or **F** next to the noun, depending on whether it is masculine or feminine. Then write **S** or **P** next to that, depending on whether the noun is singular or plural. Follow the model.

| Modelo | _____guantes_____ | _M, P_ |

1. _____ _____
2. _____ _____
3. _____ _____
4. _____ _____
5. _____ _____
6. _____ _____
7. _____ _____

C. Now, write the correct direct object pronoun to replace each noun you wrote in **part B**. Follow the model.

| Modelo | guantes, M, P: _____Los_____ busqué. |

1. _____ vendió.
2. _____ compré.
3. _____ llevamos.
4. _____ compramos.
5. _____ miramos.
6. _____ buscaron.
7. _____ preparé.

realidades.com
• Web Code: jcd-0715

Realidades 1

Capítulo 7B

Nombre _____

Fecha _____

Hora _____

Guided Practice Activities 7B-5

Lectura: ¡De compras! (pp. 364–365)

A. The reading in your textbook is about shopping in Hispanic communities of four different U.S. cities: New York, Miami, Los Angeles, and San Antonio. Use what you know about each area of the country and make a list of three items you would expect to find in Hispanic shopping centers in each city.

1. New York

a) _____

b) _____

c) _____

2. Miami

a) _____

b) _____

c) _____

3. Los Angeles

a) _____

b) _____

c) _____

4. San Antonio

a) _____

b) _____

c) _____

B. Now, look at the descriptions from the reading in your textbook and decide which city is being described. Write the name of the city in the space provided. Each city will be used once.

1. _____ Hay bodegas que venden productos típicos cubanos.

2. _____ En las joyerías de la calle Olvera, venden joyas de plata: aretes, collares, anillos y mucho más.

3. _____ En la calle 116, venden ropa, comida típica del Caribe, discos compactos, libros y mucho más.

4. _____ Es esta ciudad bonita, hay tiendas de artesanías mexicanas que son fabulosas.

C. The narrator from the reading in your textbook buys things in each city. Some items may have been on your list in **part A**. Look at the things below that the narrator bought. Write the name of the city for each in the spaces provided.

1. _____ una piñata

2. _____ una camiseta con la bandera de Puerto Rico

3. _____ pasta de guayaba

4. _____ un sarape

5. _____ una pulsera bonita

6. _____ una blusa bordada

Realidades 1

Capítulo 7B

Nombre _____

Fecha _____

Hora _____

Guided Practice Activities 7B-6

Presentación escrita (p. 367)

Task: Write a letter to a cousin or other relative about a gift you bought for a member of your family. Let the relative know what you bought so that he or she will not buy the same item.

❶ Prewrite. Think of a birthday gift you bought for a family member's birthday. It could be current or in the past. Answer the following questions about the gift to help organize your thoughts. Use complete sentences when you answer.

1. ¿Para quién es el regalo? _____
2. ¿Qué compraste? _____
3. ¿Dónde compraste el regalo? _____
4. ¿Por qué compraste ese regalo? _____
5. ¿Cuánto pagaste por el regalo? _____

❷ Draft. Use the form below to write a rough draft of your letter. Include all of the information you wrote in your answers in **part 1**. Look in your textbook for a model to help you.

Querido(a) _____ :
  (name of the relative you are writing to)

Compré _____ para _____ .

Lo compré en _____ .

Creo que _____ .

Pagué _____ .

Tu _____ ,
  (your relationship to the person)

_____
  (your name)

❸ Revise. Read your letter again before you give it to a partner to review. Your teacher will check:

• how easy the letter is to understand
• how much information is included about the gift
• how appropriate the greeting and closing are
• the accuracy of the use of the preterite

Realidades 1

Capítulo 8A

Nombre

Fecha

Hora

Vocabulary Flash Cards, Sheet 1

Write the Spanish vocabulary word below each picture. If there is a word or phrase, copy it in the space provided. Be sure to include the article for each noun.

la
ciudad

el
mar

el
país

_____

_____

_____

_____

_____

_____

_____

_____

_____

Realidades ①

Capítulo 8A

Nombre _____

Hora _____

Fecha _____

Vocabulary Flash Cards, Sheet 2

_____
_____

el
animal

_____

_____

_____
_____

el
árbol

_____

el
oso

_____

_____

la
atracción

_____

_____

Realidades

Capítulo 8A

Nombre _____

Hora _____

Fecha _____

Vocabulary Flash Cards, Sheet 3

aprender (a)

_____ _

_____

tomar
el sol

_____

_____

bucear

_____

montar a
caballo

_____ _

_____

visitar

_____

comprar
recuerdos

_____

_____

_____

_____

el
lugar

_____

_____

Realidades

Capítulo 8A

Nombre _____

Hora _____

Fecha _____

Vocabulary Flash Cards, Sheet 4

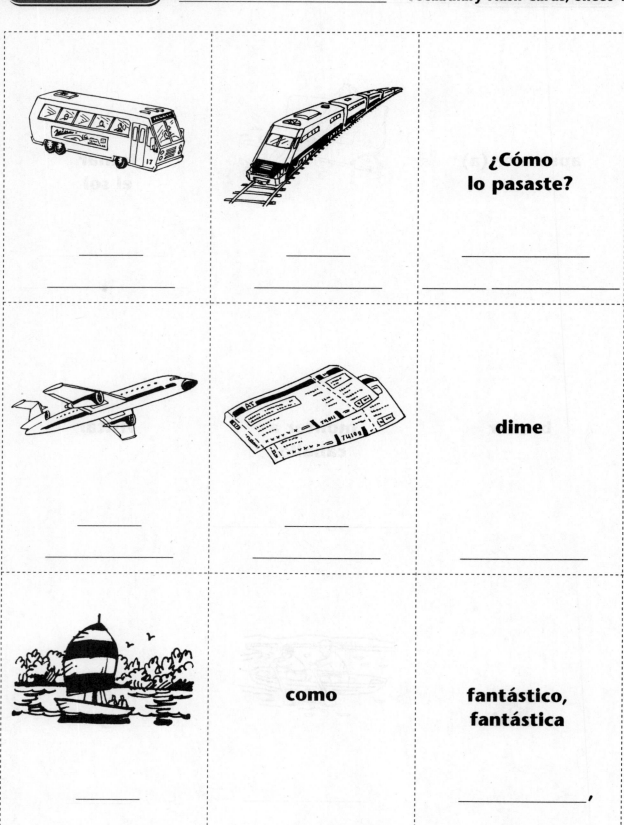

¿Cómo lo pasaste?

_____ _____

dime

_____

como

fantástico, fantástica

_____,

Realidades **1**

Capítulo 8A

Nombre _____

Hora _____

Fecha _____

Vocabulary Flash Cards, Sheet 5

Fue un desastre.

_____ _____

_____

ir de vacaciones

_____ _____

_____

¿Qué te pasó?

_____ _____

el hotel

_____

_____

Me gustó.

_____

_____

regresar

_____

impresionante

_____

¿Qué hiciste?

_____

salir

_____

Realidades 1

Capítulo 8A

Nombre

Fecha

Hora

Vocabulary Flash Cards, Sheet 6

¿Te
gusto?

_____

_____

¿Viste...?

_____

durante

_____

tremendo,
tremenda

_____,

_____

viajar

_____

tarde

_____

vi

_____

el
viaje

_____

_____

temprano

_____

Realidades 1

Capítulo 8A

Nombre _____

Hora _____

Fecha _____

Vocabulary Check, Sheet 1

Tear out this page. Write the English words on the lines. Fold the paper along the dotted line to see the correct answers so you can check your work.

la ciudad _____

el estadio _____

el lago _____

el mar _____

el monumento _____

el museo _____

el país _____

el parque de diversiones _____
_____

el parque nacional _____

la obra de teatro _____

el zoológico _____

el árbol _____

el mono _____

el oso _____

el pájaro _____

aprender (a) _____

Fold In

Nombre _____ Hora _____

Fecha _____ **Vocabulary Check, Sheet 2**

Tear out this page. Write the Spanish words on the lines. Fold the paper along the dotted line to see the correct answers so you can check your work.

city   _____

stadium   _____

lake   _____

sea   _____

monument   _____

museum   _____

country   _____

amusement
park   _____

national park   _____

                        _____

play   _____

                        _____

zoo   _____

tree   _____

monkey   _____

bear   _____

bird   _____

to learn   _____

Fold In

Tear out this page. Write the English words on the lines. Fold the paper along the dotted line to see the correct answers so you can check your work.

bucear   _____

_____

recuerdos   _____

descansar   _____

montar a
caballo   _____

_____

pasear en bote   _____

tomar el sol   _____

el autobús   _____

el avión   _____

el barco   _____

el tren   _____

ir de
vacaciones   _____

_____

regresar   _____

salir   _____

_____

viajar   _____

el viaje   _____

Fold In

Tear out this page. Write the Spanish words on the lines. Fold the paper along the dotted line to see the correct answers so you can check your work.

to scuba dive/ snorkel _____

souvenirs _____

to rest, to relax _____

to ride horseback _____
_____

to go boating _____

to sunbathe _____

bus _____

airplane _____

boat, ship _____

train _____

to go on vacation _____
_____

to return _____

to leave, to get out _____

to travel _____

trip _____

To hear a complete list of the vocabulary for this chapter, go to www.realidades.com and type in the Web Code jcd-0889. Then click on **Repaso del capítulo.**

Fold In

Realidades 1

Capítulo 8A

Nombre _____

Fecha _____

Hora _____

Guided Practice Activities 8A-1

The preterite of *-er* and *-ir* verbs (p. 383)

- Regular **-er** and **-ir** verbs have their own set of preterite (past-tense) endings, just as they do in the present tense.
- The preterite endings for regular **-er** and **-ir** verbs are exactly the same.

comer → com- + endings			
yo	**comí**	nosotros/nosotras	**comimos**
tú	**comiste**	vosotros/vosotras	**comisteis**
usted/él/ella	**comió**	ustedes/ellos/ellas	**comieron**

escribir → escrib- + endings			
yo	**escribí**	nosotros/nosotras	**escribimos**
tú	**escribiste**	vosotros/vosotras	**escribisteis**
usted/él/ella	**escribió**	ustedes/ellos/ellas	**escribieron**

- Like regular **-ar** verbs in the preterite, regular **-er** and **-ir** verbs have an accent at the end of the **yo** and **usted/él/ella** forms: **comí, escribió**.

A. Write the missing preterite forms in the chart.

	comer	escribir	aprender	salir	correr
yo	comí				
tú		escribiste			
Ud./él/ella			aprendió		
nosotros/nosotras				salimos	
Uds./ellos/ellas					corrieron

B. Circle the correct preterite form to complete each sentence.

1. Sofía (**comí** / **comió**) en un restaurante mexicano.

2. Ellos (**escribimos** / **escribieron**) una tarjeta a sus abuelos.

3. Tú (**aprendiste** / **aprendió**) a hablar español.

4. Yo (**salí** / **saliste**) para el trabajo.

5. Tú y yo (**corrieron** / **corrimos**) en el parque anoche.

6. Marta y Marcos (**comió** / **comieron**) el almuerzo en la cafetería.

7. Yo (**aprendí** / **aprendió**) a montar en monopatín.

8. Usted (**salió** / **salieron**) después de las clases.

• Web Code: jcd-0803

Realidades 1

Capítulo 8A

Nombre _____

Fecha _____

Hora _____

Guided Practice Activities 8A-2

The preterite of -er and -ir verbs (continued)

C. Complete the following sentences with the correct form of the verb in parentheses. Follow the model.

| Modelo | Tú (comer) ___*comiste*___ en la cafetería. |

1. Nosotros (escribir) _____ unas tarjetas.

2. Tú (aprender) _____ a esquiar.

3. Yo (correr) _____ en el parque.

4. Ellos (salir) _____ de la escuela a las tres.

5. Ud. (comer) _____ una hamburguesa.

6. Nosotros (ver) _____ un video anoche.

7. Ustedes (compartir) _____ una pizza.

8. Tú y yo (aprender) _____ a montar en monopatín.

9. Yo (vivir) _____ en un apartamento.

10. Ella (comprender) _____ la lección de ayer.

D. Use verbs from the list to say what you and your friends did last week.

aprender a	comer	compartir	escribir
ver	salir de	salir con	correr

1. Yo no _____ .

2. Yo no _____ .

3. Mis amigos y yo _____ .

4. Mis amigos y yo no _____ .

The preterite of *ir* (p. 385)

- **Ir** (*to go*) is an irregular verb in the present tense. It is also irregular in the preterite tense. Here are the preterite forms of **ir**.

yo	**fui**	nosotros/nosotras	**fuimos**
tú	**fuiste**	vosotros/vosotras	**fuisteis**
usted/él/ella	**fue**	ustedes/ellos/ellas	**fueron**

- The preterite forms of **ir** are the same as the preterite forms of the verb **ser** (*to be*). You can tell which verb is meant by the meaning of the sentence.

  Marcos **fue** a Nueva York.   *Marcos **went** to New York.*
  Fue un viaje fabuloso.   *It **was** a fabulous trip.*

A. Add the correct ending onto the preterite stem of **ir** to create its complete preterite form. Then rewrite the complete form. Follow the model.

Modelo   yo fu*i*___ _____*fui*_____

1. yo fu_____ _____   4. nosotros fu_____ _____
2. tú fu_____ _____   5. ellos fu_____ _____
3. ella fu_____ _____   6. ustedes fu_____ _____

B. Circle the correct form of **ir** to complete each sentence.

1. Yo (**fue** / **fui**) a la tienda de ropa.
2. Ellos (**fueron** / **fuiste**) al estadio de béisbol.
3. Tú (**fueron** / **fuiste**) a un parque nacional.
4. Nosotros (**fuimos** / **fueron**) al parque de diversiones.
5. Ud. (**fui** / **fue**) al teatro.
6. Uds. (**fuiste** / **fueron**) a la ciudad para comprar ropa.
7. Tú y yo (**fuimos** / **fuiste**) al mar para bucear.

C. Complete each sentence by writing in the correct form of **ir**.

1. Yo _____ a un lugar muy bonito.
2. Tú _____ al estadio de fútbol americano.
3. Ella _____ al lago para pasear en bote.
4. Nosotros _____ a la playa para tomar el sol.
5. Ellos _____ al teatro para ver una obra de teatro.
6. Ud. _____ al monumento en el parque nacional.

Realidades ❶

Capítulo 8A

Nombre _____

Hora _____

Fecha _____

Guided Practice Activities 8A-4

The personal *a* (p. 387)

- You have learned to identify the direct object of a sentence. The direct object tells who or what receives the action of the verb.

  Compré <u>un anillo</u>.   *I bought <u>a ring</u>.*

  Vi <u>una obra de teatro</u>. *I saw <u>a play</u>.*

- When the direct object is a person, a group of people, or a pet, you use **a** in front of the direct object. This use of the personal **a** has no equivalent in English and is not translated.

  Vi <u>un video</u>.   *I saw <u>a video</u>.*

  Vi **a** <u>mi abuela</u>.   *I saw <u>my grandmother</u>.*

  Vi **a** <u>mi perro León</u>. *I saw <u>my dog León</u>.*

A. Underline the direct object in each sentence.

1. Vi un video.

2. Escribo una carta.

3. Visitaron a su familia.

4. Comimos una pizza.

5. Compraste una corbata.

6. Buscamos a nuestro perro.

B. Now, go look at each sentence from **part A** and write **P** next to those that refer to people or pets.

1. Vi un video. _____

2. Escribo una carta. _____

3. Visitaron a su familia. _____

4. Comimos una pizza. _____

5. Compraste una corbata. _____

6. Buscamos a nuestro perro. _____

C. Look at the sentences above in **part B** that you labeled with a **P**. Circle the personal **a** in each of those sentences.

D. Look at each sentence. If it requires a personal **a**, circle the **a** in parentheses. If it does not require a personal **a**, cross out the **a** in parentheses.

1. Compramos (a) un traje de baño y unos anteojos de sol.

2. Yo vi (a) un monumento grande en el parque nacional.

3. Escribimos muchas tarjetas (a) nuestros primos.

4. Visité (a) mi familia durante las vacaciones.

5. Lavaron (a) su perro Fifí.

6. Buscamos (a) una tienda de ropa buena.

7. Compré (a) un boleto de avión ayer.

8. Busqué (a) mi hermano menor en el parque de atracciones.

Lectura: Álbum de mi viaje a Perú (pp. 390–391)

A. Sometimes you can use clues from the context of what you are reading to help discover the meaning of the word. Try to find the meaning of the five words listed below by using context clues from the reading in your textbook. Write in the English equivalent of each word in the space provided.

1. antigua _____

2. impresionantes _____

3. altura _____

4. construyeron _____

5. nivel _____

B. The reading in your textbook is a journal entry from a trip to Perú by the author Sofía Porrúa. Each day that she writes in the journal, she is in a different location. Choose the location from the word bank and write it next to the day to which it corresponds.

Cuzco	Machu Picchu	sobre las líneas de Nazca	en el lago Titicaca	Lima

1. domingo, 25 de julio _____

2. miércoles, 28 de julio _____

3. jueves, 29 de julio _____

4. sábado, 31 de julio _____

5. miércoles, 4 de agosto _____

C. In the first log entry, Sofía mentions her two companions, Beto and Carmen. Read the passage below about these two friends and answer the questions that follow.

|| *Beto está sacando muchas fotos con su cámara digital. Carmen está dibujando todo lo que ve. Las montañas son fantásticas.* ||

1. Sofía is capturing the trip by keeping a journal. How is Beto capturing the trip? _____ And Carmen? _____

2. What is Beto using to capture the trip? _____

   What do you think Carmen is using? _____

Realidades 1

Capítulo 8A

Nombre _____

Fecha _____

Hora _____

Guided Practice Activities 8A-6

Presentación oral (p. 393)

Task: You will talk about a trip you took. It can be a real or an imaginary trip. Use photographs or drawings to make your talk more interesting.

A. Think about the specifics of your trip. Answer the questions below in Spanish with as much detail as you can think of. Use complete sentences.

1. ¿Cuándo fuiste de viaje? _____
   _____

2. ¿Qué hiciste en tu viaje? _____
   _____

3. ¿Qué lugares visitaste? _____
   _____

4. ¿A quiénes viste? _____
   _____

5. ¿Compraste algo? _____ ¿Qué compraste? _____
   _____

B. You will need to create a visual presentation to go along with your talk. You can bring in actual photos or you can create drawings of a trip. Organize and attach your drawings or photos to a piece of posterboard. A good way to do this would be to put them in order of when they happened, going from the top to the bottom of the page.

C. Read the following model before you write up the script for your talk. Notice that you should add how you felt about the trip at the end.

> *En marzo de este año, fui a Florida para visitar a mi abuelita y a mis primos. Tomamos el sol en la playa y nadamos mucho. Aprendí a bucear y vi animales muy interesantes en el mar. Me gusta mucho Florida. Es un lugar fantástico. El viaje fue muy divertido.*

D. Now, write what you are going to say about your trip on the lines below. Remember to refer back to your photos or drawings.

_____

_____

_____

Realidades ❶

Capítulo 8B

Nombre _____

Fecha _____

Hora _____

Vocabulary Flash Cards, Sheet 1

Write the Spanish vocabulary word below each picture. If there is a word or phrase, copy it in the space provided. Be sure to include the article for each noun.

Realidades **1**

Capítulo 8B

Nombre _____

Hora _____

Fecha _____

Vocabulary Flash Cards, Sheet 2

llevar	**usado, usada**	
_____	_____ ,	_____
recoger	**reciclar**	**la comunidad**
_____	_____	_____
separar	**el barrio**	
_____	_____	_____

_____

_____

**la
anciana**

_____

_____

_____

_____

_____

_____

_____

_____

**la
gente**

_____

_____

**el
anciano**

_____

_____

**los
demás**

_____

_____

_____

_____

Realidades 1

Capítulo 8B

Nombre _____

Hora _____

Fecha _____

Vocabulary Flash Cards, Sheet 4

_____

_____

**la
niña**

_____

_____

_____ _____

_____ _____

**los
niños**

_____

_____

pobre

_____

_____

**el
trabajo
voluntario**

_____

_____

_____

**el
niño**

_____

_____

**el
problema**

_____

_____

**el voluntario,
la voluntaria**

_____ _____

_____ _____

Realidades ❶

Capítulo 8B

Nombre _____

Hora _____

Fecha _____

Vocabulary Flash Cards, Sheet 5

a menudo	la experiencia	inolvidable
_____	_____	_____
_____	_____	_____
decidir	Hay que...	¿Qué más?
	_____	_____
_____	_____	_____
Es necesario.	increíble	la vez
_____	_____	_____
_____	_____	_____

Realidades ①

Capítulo 8B

Nombre _____

Hora _____

Fecha _____

Vocabulary Flash Cards, Sheet 6

otra
vez

_____

_____

_____

_____

_____

_____

decir

_____

_____

_____

_____

_____

_____

Realidades 1

Capítulo 8B

Nombre _____

Hora _____

Fecha _____

Vocabulary Check, Sheet 1

Tear out this page. Write the English words on the lines. Fold the paper along the dotted line to see the correct answers so you can check your work.

la bolsa _____

la botella _____

la caja _____

el cartón _____

el centro de reciclaje _____
_____

la lata _____

llevar _____
_____

el periódico _____

el plástico _____

reciclar _____

recoger _____
_____

separar _____

usado, usada _____

el vidrio _____

el barrio _____

la calle _____

la comunidad _____

Fold In

Realidades ①

Capítulo 8B

Nombre _____

Hora _____

Fecha _____

Vocabulary Check, Sheet 2

Tear out this page. Write the Spanish words on the lines. Fold the paper along the dotted line to see the correct answers so you can check your work.

bag, sack _____

bottle _____

box _____

cardboard _____

recycling center _____

_____

can _____

to take; to carry _____

newspaper _____

plastic _____

to recycle _____

to collect; to gather _____

to separate _____

used _____

glass _____

neighborhood _____

street, road _____

community _____

Fold In

Realidades 1

Capítulo 8B

Nombre _____

Hora _____

Fecha _____

Vocabulary Check, Sheet 3

Tear out this page. Write the English words on the lines. Fold the paper along the dotted line to see the correct answers so you can check your work.

el jardín   _____

el río   _____

los ancianos   _____

el campamento   _____

los demás   _____

la escuela primaria   _____

la gente   _____

el juguete   _____

los niños   _____

pobre   _____

el proyecto de
construcción   _____
                                 _____

el trabajo
voluntario   _____

Fold In

Tear out this page. Write the Spanish words on the lines. Fold the paper along the dotted line to see the correct answers so you can check your work.

garden, yard   _____

river   _____

older people   _____

camp   _____

others   _____

primary school   _____

people   _____

toy   _____

children   _____

poor   _____

construction project   _____

_____

volunteer work   _____

_____

Fold In

To hear a complete list of the vocabulary for this chapter, go to www.realidades.com and type in the Web Code jcd-0899. Then click on **Repaso del capítulo.**

The present tense of *decir* (p. 408)

- **Decir** (*to say, to tell*) is irregular in the present tense. Here are its forms:

yo	**digo**	nosotros/nosotras	**decimos**
tú	**dices**	vosotros/vosotras	**decís**
usted/él/ella	**dice**	ustedes/ellos/ellas	**dicen**

- Notice that all the forms have an **i** in the stem except for the **nosotros/nosotras** and **vosotros/vosotras** forms (**decimos, decís**).

A. Write the correct forms of **decir** in the chart.

yo		nosotros/nosotras	
tú		vosotros/vosotras	decís
Ud./él/ella		Uds./ellos/ellas	

B. Circle the correct forms of **decir** to complete each sentence.

1. Mis abuelos (**dicen / dice**) que el parque es bonito.

2. Yo (**dices / digo**) que es un video interesante.

3. Tú (**dices / dicen**) que el restaurante es bueno.

4. Ellos (**dice / dicen**) que la profesora es inteligente.

5. Nosotros (**dicen / decimos**) que el parque de diversiones es fantástico.

6. Ustedes (**digo / dicen**) que es divertido bucear.

7. Tú y yo (**dices / decimos**) que nos gusta pasear en bote.

C. Write complete sentences to find out what the people indicated say about a museum. Follow the model.

Modelo   Inés / decir que es fantástico

   Inés dice que es fantástico.

1. tú / decir que es aburrido _____

2. yo / decir que es interesante _____

3. ellos / decir que es divertido _____

4. nosotros / decir que es grande _____

5. Ud. / decir que es impresionante _____

- Web Code: jcd-0813

Indirect object pronouns (p. 410)

- An indirect object tells to whom or for whom an action is performed. In order to identify an indirect object, take the verb in the sentence and ask "For whom?" or "To whom?"

    Te traigo un recuerdo.   *I bring **you** a souvenir.*
    "To whom do I bring a souvenir?"   *"To **you**."*

- Indirect object pronouns must agree with the person they refer to.

	Singular		Plural
(yo)	**me** (to/for) me	**(nosotros)**	**nos** (to/for) us
(tú)	**te** (to/for) you (familiar)	**(vosotros)**	**os** (to/for) you
(Ud./él/ella)	**le** (to/for) you (formal), him, her	**(Uds./ellos/ellas)**	**les** (to/for) you (formal), them

- Like direct object pronouns, indirect object pronouns go before a conjugated verb.

    Te compré una tarjeta.   *I bought **you** a card.*

- When there is an infinitive with a conjugated verb, the indirect object pronoun can attach to the end of the infinitive or go before the conjugated verb.

    Me van a comprar una camiseta.   *They are going to buy **me** a T-shirt.*
    Van a comprar**me** una camiseta.   *They are going to buy **me** a T-shirt.*

A. Underline the indirect object pronoun in each sentence.

1. Te escribí una tarjeta.   4. Nos dan regalos.

2. Me trae un vaso de agua.   5. Les compramos una camiseta.

3. Le ayudo con la tarea.   6. Le llevamos unos libros.

B. Circle the correct indirect object pronoun. Follow the model.

Modelo   tú: (**Te** / Le) damos un boleto de avión.

1. yo: (**Me** / **Nos**) ayudan con la tarea.

2. tú: (**Te** / **Les**) llevo un regalo.

3. ella: (**Le** / **Les**) escribo una tarjeta.

4. nosotros: (**Nos** / **Les**) compraron unos zapatos.

5. ellos: (**Le** / **Les**) trae un vaso de agua.

6. él: (**Le** / **Me**) lavo el coche.

7. tú: (**Me** / **Te**) damos unas flores.

8. tú y yo: (**Me** / **Nos**) traen un recuerdo de las vacaciones.

Realidades 1

Capítulo 8B

Nombre _____

Fecha _____

Hora _____

Guided Practice Activities 8B-3

Indirect object pronouns *(continued)*

C. Write the correct indirect object pronoun in each sentence. Follow the model.

Modelo yo: _____*Me*_____ traen el periódico.

1. yo: _____ ayudan a limpiar el baño.

2. tú: _____ compran una sudadera.

3. él: _____ dan una bicicleta nueva.

4. nosotros: _____ traen unas cajas de cartón.

5. Ud.: _____ escriben una tarjeta.

6. ellos: _____ compro unos platos.

7. tú y yo: _____ traen una pizza grande.

8. Uds.: _____ compro un boleto de avión.

9. yo: _____ traen un vaso de jugo.

10. tú: _____ dan unos juguetes.

D. Write sentences to say to whom Susana is telling the truth. Follow the model.

Modelo yo _____*Susana me dice la verdad.*_____

1. tú _____

2. él _____

3. nosotros _____

4. ellos _____

5. ella _____

6. tú y yo _____

7. ustedes _____

Realidades ①

Capítulo 8B

Nombre _____

Fecha _____

Hora _____

Guided Practice Activities 8B-4

The preterite of *hacer* and *dar* (p. 412)

- The verbs **hacer** (*to make, to do*) and **dar** (*to give*) are irregular in the preterite.

hacer

yo	hice	nosotros/nosotras	hicimos
tú	hiciste	vosotros/vosotras	hicisteis
usted/él/ella	hizo	ustedes/ellos/ellas	hicieron

yo	di	nosotros/nosotras	dimos
tú	diste	vosotros/vosotras	disteis
usted/él/ella	dio	ustedes/ellos/ellas	dieron

- These verbs have no accent marks in the preterite forms.
- Notice the change from **c** to **z** in the **usted/él/ella** form of **hacer: hizo**.

A. Write the missing forms of **hacer** and **dar** in the chart.

	hacer	dar
yo	hice	
tú		diste
Ud./él/ella		dio
nosotros/nosotras	hicimos	
Uds./ellos/ellas		dieron

B. Circle the correct forms of **hacer** and **dar** for each subject pronoun.

1. tú (diste / dio), (hizo / hiciste)

2. yo (dio / di), (hice / hicimos)

3. tú y yo (dimos / diste), (hizo / hicimos)

4. ellas (di / dieron), (hice / hicieron)

5. él (diste / dio), (hizo / hice)

6. Ud. (di / dio), (hizo / hiciste)

C. Complete each sentence with the correct form of the verb indicated. Follow the model. The boldfaced word is the subject of the sentence.

Modelo   **Ella** me (dar) ____*dio*____ un libro.

1. **Tú** me (dar) _____ un regalo bonito.

2. **Ellos** me (hacer) _____ un suéter fantástico.

3. **Nosotros** te (dar) _____ unos discos compactos.

4. **Ud.** me (hacer) _____ un pastel sabroso.

realidades.com ✔

- Web Code: jcd-0814

Lectura: Hábitat para la Humanidad Internacional (pp. 416–417)

A. Recognizing cognates has helped you understand many of the readings in your textbook. The reading on Habitat for Humanity is no exception. Look at the words below and write their English equivalents in the spaces provided.

1. organización _____
2. internacional _____
3. comunidades _____

4. donaciones _____
5. privadas _____
6. miembros _____

B. Answer the following questions in Spanish in order to understand the main idea of the reading in your textbook.

1. ¿Qué es Hábitat y qué hace? Hábitat es una _____

_____ .

2. ¿Cuál es el objetivo de Hábitat? Su objetivo es _____

_____ .

3. ¿Cuántos proyectos en total tiene Hábitat en el mundo? Hábitat tiene _____

_____ .

C. Now, read the following passage to get more specific information about a typical Habitat project. Answer the questions that follow.

> *Según Hábitat, las personas pobres tienen que ayudar a construir sus casas. Es una manera positiva de ayudar a los demás. Hábitat les da los materiales de construcción y los trabajadores voluntarios.*

1. According to Habitat, who has to help build the houses? _____

_____

2. Who gives these people materials? _____

_____

3. Who else helps build the houses? _____

_____

4. Why do you think Habitat has such success? _____

_____

Realidades ❶

Nombre _____

Hora _____

Capítulo 8B

Fecha _____

Guided Practice Activities 8B-6

Presentación escrita (p. 419)

Task: Imagine that you have to organize a clean-up campaign for a park, recreation center, school playground, or other place in your community. Make a poster announcing the project and inviting students to participate.

❶ **Prewrite.** Answer the following questions about your project:

a)   ¿Qué van a limpiar ustedes?

_____

b)   ¿Dónde está el lugar?

_____

c)   ¿Qué tienen que hacer para preparar a limpiar?

_____

d)   ¿Qué día van a trabajar?

_____

e)   ¿Cuántas horas van a trabajar?

_____

f)   ¿Quién(es) puede(n) participar?

_____

❷ **Draft.** Your answers to the questions above will determine what you say in your rough draft. Write your answers on a separate sheet of paper and organize them so that they will be easy to read and understand. You should also include any drawings, photos, or useful magazine cutouts you can find as part of your poster.

❸ **Revise.** Check your rough draft to make sure it is what you want. Your partner will check your work. Look on page 419 of your textbook to see what he or she will check.

❹ **Publish.** Take your partner's suggestions and do the changes necessary to make your poster as complete and effective as you can. Since you are now working on your final draft, your writing should be neat and your presentation should be on a clean poster. Your work may be presented in the classroom or even on the walls elsewhere in school, so make it look attractive!

Realidades **1**

Nombre _____

Hora _____

Capítulo 9A

Fecha _____

Vocabulary Flash Cards, Sheet 1

Write the Spanish vocabulary word below each picture. If there is a word or phrase, copy it in the space provided. Be sure to include the article for each noun.

el canal

_____

_____

_____

_____

_____

_____

_____

_____

_____

_____

_____

_____

_____

_____

_____

_____

_____

Realidades

Capítulo 9A

Nombre _____

Fecha _____

Hora _____

Vocabulary Flash Cards, Sheet 2

_____ _____

_____

_____

_____

_____

_____

_____

_____

_____

_____

_____

_____

_____

_____

**la
actriz**

_____

_____

Realidades 1

Capítulo 9A

Nombre _____

Hora _____

Fecha _____

Vocabulary Flash Cards, Sheet 3

cómico, cómica

_____,

_____

infantil

_____

violento, violenta

_____,

_____

emocionante

_____

realista

_____

me aburre(n)

_____

_____

fascinante

_____

tonto, tonta

_____,

_____

me interesa(n)

_____

_____

dar _____	**terminar** _____	**medio, media** _____ , _____
durar _____	**más de** _____	**¿Qué clase de...?** _____ _____
empezar _____	**menos de** _____	**acabar de** _____

Realidades ❶

Capítulo 9A

Nombre

Hora

Fecha

Vocabulary Flash Cards, Sheet 5

aburrir	**faltar**	**antes de**
_____	_____	_____
doler	**interesar**	**casi**
_____	_____	_____
encantar	**quedar**	**¿De veras?**
_____	_____	_____

especialmente	**ya**	
		_____
_____	_____	_____
por eso		
_____	_____	_____
_____	_____	_____
sobre		
	_____	_____
_____	_____	_____

Realidades 1

Capítulo 9A

Nombre _____

Fecha _____

Hora _____

Vocabulary Check, Sheet 1

Tear out this page. Write the English words on the lines. Fold the paper along the dotted line to see the correct answers so you can check your work.

el canal _____

el programa
de concursos _____

el programa de
dibujos animados _____

el programa
deportivo _____

el programa de
entrevistas _____

el programa de
la vida real _____

el programa de
noticias _____

el programa
educativo _____
_____

el programa
musical _____
_____

la telenovela _____

la comedia _____

el drama _____

la película de
ciencia ficción _____
_____

Fold In

Tear out this page. Write the English words on the lines. Fold the paper along
the dotted line to see the correct answers so you can check your work.

channel   _____

game show   _____

                           _____

cartoon show   _____

                           _____

sports show   _____

                           _____

interview show   _____

                           _____

reality program   _____

                           _____

news program   _____

                           _____

educational
program   _____

                           _____

musical
program   _____

                           _____

soap opera   _____

comedy   _____

drama   _____

science fiction
movie   _____

                           _____

Fold In

Tear out this page. Write the English words on the lines. Fold the paper along the dotted line to see the correct answers so you can check your work.

la película de
horror   _____

la película
policíaca   _____
                              _____

la película
romántica   _____
                              _____

emocionante   _____

fascinante   _____

infantil   _____
                              _____

tonto, tonta   _____

violento, violenta   _____

el actor   _____

la actriz   _____

dar   _____

durar   _____

empezar   _____

terminar   _____

Fold In

Tear out this page. Write the English words on the lines. Fold the paper along the dotted line to see the correct answers so you can check your work.

horror movie   _____

_____

crime movie, mystery   _____

_____

romantic movie   _____

_____

touching   _____

fascinating   _____

for children; childish   _____

silly, stupid   _____

violent   _____

actor   _____

actress   _____

to show   _____

to last   _____

to begin   _____

to end   _____

Fold In

To hear a complete list of the vocabulary for this chapter, go to www.realidades.com and type in the Web Code jcd-0989. Then click on **Repaso del capítulo.**

Realidades ❶

Capítulo 9A

Nombre _____

Fecha _____

Hora _____

Guided Practice Activities 9A-1

Acabar de + infinitive (p. 434)

- Use present-tense forms of **acabar** with an infinitive to say that you and others have just finished doing something.

  Acabo de tomar una siesta.   *I just took a nap.*

  Acabamos de patinar.   *We just went skating.*

- Here are the present-tense forms of **acabar**, which is a regular **-ar** verb.

yo	**acabo**	nosotros/nosotras	**acabamos**
tú	**acabas**	vosotros/vosotras	**acabáis**
usted/él/ella	**acaba**	ustedes/ellos/ellas	**acaban**

A. Write the correct forms of **acabar** in the chart.

yo		nosotros/nosotras	
tú		vosotros/vosotras	acabáis
Ud./él/ella		Uds./ellos/ellas	

B. Circle the correct form of **acabar** to complete each sentence.

1. Yo (**acaba** / **acabo**) de ver un programa de la vida real.

2. Tú (**acabas** / **acabamos**) de ir al cine.

3. Ellos (**acaban** / **acaba**) de ver un video.

4. Tú y yo (**acabas** / **acabamos**) de cambiar el canal.

5. Usted (**acabo** / **acaba**) de ver una película policíaca.

6. Nosotros (**acabas** / **acabamos**) de hablar de las comedias.

7. Ustedes (**acabamos** / **acaban**) de comprar un lector DVD.

C. Complete each sentence with an activity you recently finished. Use the activities from **part B** above for ideas.

1. Yo acabo de _____.

2. Mis amigos y yo acabamos de _____.

3. Mi profesor (profesora) acaba de _____.

4. Los estudiantes de la escuela acaban de _____.

Acabar de + infinitive (continued)

D. Complete the following conversations with the correct forms of **acabar**.

ADELA: Mis amigos y yo _____ de ver una película de horror.

ANA: ¿Sí? ¡Qué casualidad! Yo también _____ de ver una película
de horror.

LUIS: ¿Tú _____ de ver las noticias?

MARCOS: Sí. ¿Y ustedes?

LUIS: Nosotros _____ de ver un programa de concursos.

E. Create complete sentences. Follow the model.

Modelo   Alejandra / acabar de / sacar la basura

_Alejandra acaba de sacar la basura._____

1. Natalia / acabar de / dar de comer al gato

_____

2. yo / acabar de / lavar los platos

_____

3. ellos / acabar de / quitar la mesa

_____

4. tú y yo / acabar de / cortar el césped

_____

5. tú / acabar de / limpiar el baño

_____

6. Ud. / acabar de / pasar la aspiradora

_____

F. Complete each sentence with forms of **acabar de** to say what you and other people
you know recently did.

1. Yo _____.

2. Mi familia _____.

3. Mis amigos y yo _____.

4. Los estudiantes de la escuela _____.

• Web Code: jcd-0903

Gustar and similar verbs (p. 436)

- **Gustar** (*to please*) is different from other verbs you've learned. It is only used in its *third person forms*: **gusta** and **gustan**.
- **Gustar** is used with *indirect object pronouns* (**me, te, le, nos,** and **les**).
- **Gustar** agrees with the *subject* of the sentence, which is the object or objects that are pleasing to someone.

> indirect object pronoun + <u>**gusta**</u> + <u>singular</u> subject:
>
> Me **gusta** esa **comedia**. *I like that comedy. (That comedy pleases me.)*
>
> indirect object pronoun + <u>**gustan**</u> + <u>plural</u> subject:
>
> Nos **gusta<u>n</u>** los **drama<u>s</u>**. *We like dramas. (Dramas please us.)*

- Some other verbs are similar to **gustar**:

aburrir (aburre/aburren) *(to bore)*:	Me **aburre** ese **programa**.
	Me **aburren** las **telenovelas**.
doler (duele/duelen) *(to hurt)*:	Te **duele** la **mano**.
	Te **duelen** los **pies**.
encantar (encanta/encantan) *(to like a lot)*:	Nos **encanta** el **teatro**.
	Nos **encantan** los **museos**.
faltar (falta/faltan) *(to lack, to be missing)*:	Les **falta** un **vaso**.
	Les **faltan** los **anteojos**.
interesar (interesa/interesan) *(to interest)*:	Me **interesa** la **literatura**.
	Me **interesan** las **ciencias**.
quedar (queda/quedan) *(to fit)*:	Te **queda** bien el **vestido**.
	Te **quedan** bien los **zapatos**.

A. Look at each sentence. Circle the subject and underline the form of **gustar**. Follow the model.

> **Modelo**   Te <u>gustan</u> los programas de noticias.   <u>*P*</u>

1. Me gustan los programas de entrevista. _____
2. Nos gusta la telenovela nueva. _____
3. ¿Te gusta el canal de deportes? _____
4. Les gustan los programas de dibujos animados. _____
5. Le gustan los programas de la vida real. _____
6. Nos gusta el programa musical en el canal 27. _____

B. Now, go back to the sentences in **part A** and write an **S** if they are singular (**gusta** + singular subject) or a **P** if they are plural (**gustan** + plural subject).

realidades.com ✔
- Web Code: jcd-0904

Gustar and similar verbs *(continued)*

C. Circle the correct form of **gustar** to complete each sentence.

1. Nos (**gusta** / **gustan**) las ciudades grandes.

2. Te (**gusta** / **gustan**) los parques nacionales.

3. Les (**gusta** / **gustan**) el teatro.

4. Me (**gusta** / **gustan**) el parque de diversiones.

5. Le (**gusta** / **gustan**) los animales.

D. Write the correct form of **gustar** to complete each sentence.

1. Nos _____ los jeans.

2. Les _____ los zapatos.

3. Le _____ la gorra.

4. Me _____ el traje.

5. Te _____ las botas.

6. Les _____ el suéter.

E. These sentences use verbs that are similar to **gustar**. Circle the correct form for each verb.

1. Nos (**encanta** / **encantan**) las tiendas de ropa.

2. Me (**aburre** / **aburren**) los programas de la vida real.

3. Te (**duele** / **duelen**) los pies.

4. Les (**interesa** / **interesan**) los programas de noticias.

5. Le (**falta** / **faltan**) un cuchillo.

6. Me (**queda** / **quedan**) bien la falda.

F. Now write **a** or **an** to complete each of the following verbs.

1. Me encant_____ los programas de concursos.

2. Te interes_____ la nueva telenovela.

3. Nos falt_____ un vaso.

4. Me qued_____ bien la sudadera.

G. Write **e** or **en** to complete each of the following verbs.

1. Le aburr_____ los programas educativos.

2. Me duel_____ la cabeza.

3. Nos aburr_____ ese libro.

4. Te duel_____ el estómago.

• Web Code: jcd-0904

Realidades 1

Capítulo 9A

Nombre _____

Hora _____

Fecha _____

Guided Practice Activities 9A-5

Lectura: Una semana sin televisión (pp. 440–441)

A. Read through the reading in your textbook without stopping to look up words in a dictionary. On a separate sheet of paper, make a list of any words you don't know. Then, answer the following questions about the reading in Spanish. If you have trouble with any of the words, look them up while you answer the questions.

1. ¿Qué dos cosas hacen los niños estadounidenses más que cualquier otra cosa?

   _____ y _____

2. Según los estudios, ¿cuáles son tres resultados malos del ver demasiado la televisión?

   _____ , _____ y

   _____

3. ¿Qué hacen millones de personas durante el mes de abril?

   _____ .

B. Read through the reading in your textbook once more. If there are words or phrases you still do not understand, look them up in a dictionary. Now, answer the questions below circling **C** for **cierto** (*true*) and **F** for **falso** (*false*).

1. **C F** Según la lectura, los niños comen más que cualquier otra cosa, a excepción de dormir.

2. **C F** Ver demasiado la televisión puede resultar en un exceso de peso.

3. **C F** En cuatro horas de dibujos animados el sábado por la mañana, los niños pueden ver más de 200 anuncios sobre los deportes.

4. **C F** Hay estudios que dicen que los niños que ven demasiado la tele pueden tener más probabilidad de ser violentos y agresivos de adultos.

5. **C F** Para muchas familias en varios países una semana sin televisión les da la oportunidad de hacer cosas interesantes en vez de ver la tele.

C. You may have a discussion about the benefits and drawbacks of watching TV. Think of which argument you want to support. Then write three reasons in Spanish for why you feel this way. You can use information from the reading in your textbook or from personal experience.

Razón 1: _____

Razón 2: _____

Razón 3: _____

Realidades 1

Capítulo 9A

Nombre _____

Fecha _____

Hora _____

Guided Practice Activities 9A-6

Presentación oral (p. 443)

Task: You are going to write a review of a movie or television show that was on your school's closed-circuit TV system. Prepare a summary of the movie or show.

A. Choose a movie or show to talk about. Fill in the chart with the information about your show or movie.

Nombre	
Clase de película o programa	
Actor/Actores	
Actriz/Actrices	
Cómo es	
Cuánto tiempo dura	
Para quiénes es	

B. Collect visuals to go along with your presentation. They could be ads or photos from a newspaper or magazine, such as a TV guide, or you could download pictures from the Internet. Make a poster with all of the items you collect.

C. Use the notes you took in **part A** to prepare your presentation. Write out complete sentences for each topic in the spaces below.

1. _____.
2. _____.
3. _____.
4. _____.
5. _____.
6. _____.
7. _____.

D. Now, put together your finished poster and your sentences and practice your presentation. Remember to:

_____ speak clearly

_____ use complete sentences

_____ provide all key information about the movie or show

Realidades ①

Capítulo 9B

Nombre _____

Hora _____

Fecha _____

Vocabulary Flash Cards, Sheet 1

Write the Spanish vocabulary word below each picture. If there is a word or phrase, copy it in the space provided. Be sure to include the article for each noun.

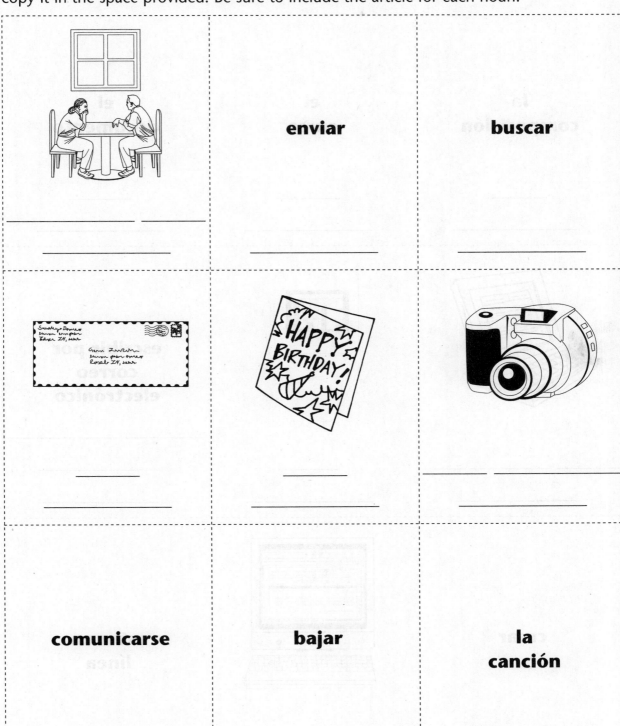

enviar

buscar

_____

_____

comunicarse

bajar

la canción

_____

_____

_____

Realidades 1

Capítulo 9B

Nombre _____

Fecha _____

Hora _____

Vocabulary Flash Cards, Sheet 2

la
composición

_____

_____

el
curso

_____

_____

el
documento

_____

_____

_____

_____

_____

_____

escribir por
correo
electrónico

_____

_____

crear

_____

_____

_____

_____

estar en
línea

_____

_____

Realidades ❶

Capítulo 9B

Nombre _____

Hora _____

Fecha _____

Vocabulary Flash Cards, Sheet 3

_____

_____

el informe

_____

_____

_____

_____

los gráficos

_____

_____

el laboratorio

_____

_____

la presentación

_____

_____

la información

_____

_____

_____

_____

_____

_____

visitar
salones
de chat

_____

_____

¿Qué te
parece?

_____ ____

_____

tener
miedo (de)

_____

_____ ____

complicado,
complicada

_____,

_____

rápidamente

_____

conocer

_____

¿Para qué
sirve?

_____

_____

Sirve
para...

_____

saber

_____

Tear out this page. Write the English words on the lines. Fold the paper along the dotted line to see the correct answers so you can check your work.

cara a cara   _____

la carta   _____

comunicarse   _____

     _____

enviar   _____

la tarjeta   _____

bajar   _____

buscar   _____

la cámara digital   _____

     _____

la canción   _____

la composición   _____

la computadora portátil   _____

     _____

crear   _____

el curso   _____

la diapositiva   _____

la dirección electrónica   _____

el documento   _____

Fold In

Realidades **1**

Capítulo 9B

Nombre _____

Fecha _____

Hora _____

Vocabulary Check, Sheet 2

Tear out this page. Write the Spanish words on the lines. Fold the paper along
the dotted line to see the correct answers so you can check your work.

face-to-face   _____

letter   _____

to communicate   _____
(with)

to send   _____

card   _____

to download   _____

to search (for)   _____

digital camera   _____

                      _____

song   _____

composition   _____

laptop   _____
computer

to create   _____

course   _____

slide   _____

e-mail address   _____

                      _____

document   _____

Fold In ←

Realidades 1

Capítulo 9B

Nombre _____

Fecha _____

Hora _____

Guided Practice Activities 9B-1

The present tense of *pedir* and *servir* (p. 458)

- You have learned other verbs with stem changes in the present tense (**pensar**, **querer**, **preferir**), where the stem changes from **e** to **ie**.
- **Pedir** (to *ask for*) and **servir** (to *serve, or to be useful for*) are also stem-changing verbs in the present tense, but their stem changes from **e** to **i**.
- Here are the present tense forms of **pedir** and **servir**. Notice that the **nosotros/nosotras** and **vosotros/vosotras** forms do not change their stem.

yo	**pido**	nosotros/nosotras	**pedimos**
tú	**pides**	vosotros/vosotras	**pedís**
usted/él/ella	**pide**	ustedes/ellos/ellas	**piden**

yo	**sirvo**	nosotros/nosotras	**servimos**
tú	**sirves**	vosotros/vosotras	**servís**
usted/él/ella	**sirve**	ustedes/ellos/ellas	**sirven**

A. Complete the chart with the correct forms of **pedir** and **servir**.

	pedir	servir
yo	pido	
tú		sirves
Ud./él/ella		
nosotros/nosotras		
Uds./ellos/ellas		

B. Write **e** or **i** in the blank to complete each verb form.

1. yo p_____do

2. tú s_____rves

3. nosotros s_____rvimos

4. ellos p_____den

5. Ud. s_____rve

6. ellos s_____rven

7. nosotros p_____dimos

8. ella s_____rve

9. yo s_____rvo

10. tú p_____des

The present tense of *pedir* and *servir* (continued)

C. Circle the correct form of **pedir** or **servir** to complete each sentence.

1. Tú (**sirve** / **sirves**) café con leche y unas galletas.

2. Yo (**pido** / **pedimos**) una hamburguesa con papas fritas para el almuerzo.

3. Nosotros (**pido** / **pedimos**) un jugo de naranja.

4. Este libro (**sirves** / **sirve**) para aprender química.

5. Ellos (**pedimos** / **piden**) un tenedor limpio.

6. Todos los domingos mi madre (**sirve** / **sirven**) pescado para la cena.

7. Tú y yo (**pido** / **pedimos**) ayuda con la computadora.

8. Las computadoras (**sirven** / **servimos**) para conectar los sitios Web.

D. Write the correct form of the verb in the blank. Follow the model.

| Modelo | Yo siempre (**pedir**)_____ *pido* _____ yogur para el desayuno. |

1. Mis amigos (**servir**) _____ café con el postre.

2. Nosotros siempre (**pedir**) _____ café con leche.

3. Las computadoras (**servir**) _____ para navegar la Red.

4. Tú y yo (**servir**) _____ jugo de naranja con una ensalada de frutas.

5. Tú siempre (**pedir**) _____ pizza para la cena.

6. Mis hermanos siempre (**pedir**) _____ huevos para el desayuno.

E. Complete the following sentences in a logical manner. Follow the models for ideas.

| Modelos | Los bolígrafos (**servir**)_____ *sirven para escribir* _____. |
| | En el restaurante mexicano, yo siempre (**pedir**)_____ *pido enchiladas* _____. |

1. Mi computadora (**servir**) _____

_____.

2. Para el desayuno, yo siempre (**pedir**) _____

_____.

3. Para el almuerzo, la cafetería siempre (**servir**) _____

_____.

4. Cuando vamos a un restaurante, mis amigos y yo (**pedir**) _____

_____.

Nombre

Hora

Fecha

Vocabulary Flash Cards

Nombre _____ Hora _____

Fecha _____ **Vocabulary Flash Cards**

Fecha _____ **Vocabulary Flash Cards,**

Presentación escrita (p. 467)

Task: Pretend that your parents think you spend too much time at the computer. Write an e-mail to a friend in Mexico defending your computer use.

❶ Prewrite. Fill in the chart below. In the first column, write in Spanish three ways you use the computer. In the second column, write the benefit (**ventaja**) to you. Use the first example as a guide.

Cómo uso la computadora	La ventaja
Busco información para mis clases, en Internet.	*Aprendo mucho y es muy interesante.*

❷ Draft. Use the information from the chart to write your e-mail.

❸ Revise. Before you have a partner review your work, check for spelling, accent marks, correct vocabulary use, and verb forms. Your partner will review the following:

_____ Is the paragraph easy to read and understand?

_____ Does the paragraph provide good reasons and support your position?

_____ Is there anything that you could add to give more information?

_____ Is there anything that you could change to make it clearer?

_____ Are there any errors that you missed?

❹ Publish. Rewrite the e-mail making any change suggested by your partner or by changing anything you didn't like.

❺ Evaluation. Your teacher will grade you on the following:

- the amount of information provided
- how well you presented each reason and its benefit
- your use of vocabulary and accuracy of spelling and grammar

Realidades 1

Capítulo 9B

Nombre _____

Fecha _____

Hora _____

Guided Practice Activities 9B-5

Lectura: La invasión del ciberspanglish (pp. 464–465)

A. The article in your textbook talks about the influence of computers on language. What computer terms can you think of in English? Write ten words or phrases that are commonly used when talking about the computer or the Internet. The first two have been done for you.

1. _surf the Web_
2. _to download_
3. _____
4. _____
5. _____

6. _____
7. _____
8. _____
9. _____
10. _____

B. Did you find words in the reading similar to those on your list? You may have found the *ciberspanglish* words as well as the more correct Spanish terms for each word. Look on the chart in your reading and find the *ciberspanglish* and Spanish words for each.

	Ciberspanglish	**Español**
1. to chat	_____	_____
2. to reboot	_____	_____
3. to program	_____	_____
4. clip art	_____	_____
5. to print	_____	_____

C. Which list has the longer words in **part B**? Read the excerpts from the reading in your textbook. Then, write in English why some people want to use *ciberspanglish* terms and why some people prefer to use Spanish terms for computer-related words.

> *A algunas personas no les gusta nada este nuevo "idioma". Piensan que el español es suficientemente rico para poder traducir los términos del inglés.*
> *Hay otros que dicen que no hay problemas con mezclar los idiomas para comunicarse mejor. Piensan que el "ciberspanglish" es más fácil y lógico porque los términos técnicos vienen del inglés y expresarlos en español es bastante complicado.*

1. It is better to use Spanish because _____

_____.

2. It is better to use *ciberspanglish* because _____

realidades.com
• Web Code: jcd-0915

Saber and *conocer (continued)*

C. Circle the correct verb form of **conocer** in each sentence.

1. Yo (**conoce** / **conozco**) una tienda muy buena para comprar ropa.

2. Ellos (**conoces** / **conocen**) muy bien la ciudad de Nueva York.

3. Ella (**conoce** / **conozco**) a todos los estudiantes de la clase.

4. Tú y yo (**conocemos** / **conozco**) la música de Carlos Santana.

D. Circle the correct form of **saber** in each sentence.

1. Nosotros (**saben** / **sabemos**) hablar español.

2. Yo (**sabe** / **sé**) la respuesta correcta.

3. Tú (**sabes** / **sabe**) dónde está la clase de matemáticas.

4. Ud. (**sabes** / **sabe**) esquiar y nadar.

E. Complete each sentence with a form of **saber** or **conocer**. Circle the correct verb form according to the context.

1. Tú y yo (**sabemos** / **conocemos**) tocar el piano.

2. Ellas (**saben** / **conocen**) dónde están las llaves.

3. Yo (**sé** / **conozco**) al presidente de los Estados Unidos.

4. Tú (**sabes** / **conoces**) bien la ciudad de Chicago.

5. Ud. (**sabe** / **conoce**) usar la computadora nueva.

6. Nosotros (**sabemos** / **conocemos**) el nombre de una canción en español.

7. Tú (**sabes** / **conoces**) a todos los estudiantes de la clase.

8. Uds. (**saben** / **conocen**) a la estudiante nueva.

F. Complete the following sentences. Use ideas from the activities above or other words you know. Follow the model.

Modelo   Yo (saber) _____*sé montar en bicicleta*_____ .

1. Yo (saber) _____ .

2. Yo no (saber) _____ .

3. Yo (conocer) _____ .

4. Yo no (conocer) _____ .

realidades.com ✔
• Web Code: jcd-0914

Realidades ❶

Capítulo 9B

Nombre _____

Fecha _____

Hora _____

Guided Practice Activities 9B-3

Saber and *conocer* (p. 460)

- Both these verbs are irregular in the **yo** form only. Here are their present-tense forms.

yo	**sé**	nosotros/nosotras	**sabemos**
tú	**sabes**	vosotros/vosotras	**sabéis**
usted/él/ella	**sabe**	ustedes/ellos/ellas	**saben**

yo	**conozco**	nosotros/nosotras	**conocemos**
tú	**conoces**	vosotros/vosotras	**conocéis**
usted/él/ella	**conoce**	ustedes/ellos/ellas	**conocen**

A. Write the missing forms of **saber** and **conocer** in the chart.

	saber	**conocer**
yo	sé	
tú		
Ud./él/ella		
nosotros/nosotras		conocemos
Uds./ellos/ellas		

- Both **saber** and **conocer** mean *to know*.
- **Saber** means *to know how to do something* or *to know a fact*:

  Ella **sabe patinar**.   *She **knows how to skate**.*

  Él **sabe la respuesta**.   *He **knows the answer**.*

- **Conocer** means *to know a person* or *to be familiar with a place or thing*. Remember to use the personal **a** with **conocer** when it is used with a person.

  Ella **conoce Madrid**.   *She **knows (is familiar with) Madrid**.*

  Él **conoce a Miguel**.   *He **knows Miguel**.*

B. Look at each person, place, or thing. Write **S** if you would use **saber** or **C** if you would use **conocer**. Follow the model.

Modelo ___S___ las matemáticas

1. _____ la profesora de español
2. _____ nadar
3. _____ tocar la guitarra
4. _____ Tokyo
5. _____ Britney Spears
6. _____ la respuesta correcta

- Web Code: jcd-0914